teach yourself®

tracing your
family history
stella colwell

D1627884

For over 60 years, more than 40 million people have learnt over 750 subjects the **teach yourself** way, with impressive results.

be where you want to be
with **teach yourself**

For UK order enquiries: please contact Bookpoint Ltd, 130 Milton Park, Abingdon, Oxon OX14 4SB. Telephone: +44 (0) 1235 827720, Fax: +44 (0) 1235 400454. Lines are open 9.00–18.00, Monday to Saturday, with a 24-hour message answering service. Details about our titles and how to order are available at www.teachyourself.co.uk

For USA order enquiries: please contact McGraw-Hill Customer Services, P.O. Box 545, Blacklick, OH 43004-0545, USA. Telephone: 1-800-722-4726. Fax: 1-614-755-5645.

For Canada order enquiries: please contact McGraw-Hill Ryerson Ltd, 300 Water St, Whitby, Ontario L1N 9B6, Canada. Telephone: 905 430 5000. Fax: 905 430 5020.

Long renowned as the authoritative source for self-guided learning – with more than 30 million copies sold worldwide – the *Teach Yourself* series includes over 300 titles in the fields of languages, crafts, hobbies, business, computing and education.

British Library Cataloguing in Publication Data
A catalogue entry for this title is available from The British Library.

Library of Congress Catalog Card Number: On file

First published in UK 1997 by Hodder Headline Plc., 338 Euston Road, London, NW1 3BH.

First published in US 1997 by Contemporary Books, a Division of The McGraw-Hill Companies, 1 Prudential Plaza, 130 East Randolph Street, Chicago, Illinois 60601 USA.

The 'Teach Yourself' name is a registered trade mark of Hodder & Stoughton Ltd.

Copyright © 1997, 2003 Stella Colwell

Typeset by Transet Limited, Coventry, England.
Printed in Great Britain for Hodder & Stoughton Educational, a division of Hodder Headline Ltd, 338 Euston Road, London NW1 3BH by Cox & Wyman Ltd, Reading, Berkshire.

Impression number	10 9 8 7 6 5 4 3 2 1
Year	2008 2007 2006 2005 2004 2003

iii

contents

acknowledgements

I want to thank Shirley Hughes for all the practical research and loose ends she tidied up for me in London, especially at the Society of Genealogists, a task she undertook with much humour and promptness. Besides thanking her I also want to express appreciation to Bill Cubin of The Laurel and Hardy Museum, Ulverston, Cumbria, for generously lending me his copy of *Laurel before Hardy*, Joyce Brown, Area Librarian at Grantham Library for her help in locating the obituary of Arthur Jefferson and other local items about him, Rev G. Shrimpton and parishioners of Barkston, in Lincolnshire, for searching out his gravestone, Malcolm Pinhorn for information about the licensee Chaplins, Neville Taylor for finding the biography of Fred Karno, Cecelia Doidge Ripper for helping with theatrical sources about him, the staff of the Office for National Statistics, the General Register Offices of Jersey, Scotland, Northern Ireland and the Republic of Ireland, Dorothy Hammond at the Office for National Statistics, staff of London Metropolitan Archives, the Public Record Offices in London and Belfast, the Scottish Record Office, the National Archives of Ireland, and National Library in Dublin, the National Archives in Washington, DC, The British Library and the Priaulx Library, Guernsey, for supplying me with up-to-date information.

I would like to thank Sue Gibbons, Else Churchill, Nicholas Fogg, Marie Hickey and Sue Spurgeon at the Society of Genealogists for help with specific queries, Eric Franckom and Jeremy Gibson for invaluable guidance on recent publications of the Federation of Family History Societies, Elizabeth Simpson for her generosity with *Genealogical Research Directory*, staff of the Guildhall Library for advice on their new books, staff of the National Register of Archives, London

Metropolitan Archives, the Suffolk Record Offices, the Friends' Library in London and Colchester Library, for their assistance, staff in the library of the United States of America Embassy in London, for information from the Internet, local volunteers of the family history centre of the Church of Jesus Christ of Latter-day Saints at Chelmsford for their pack of information about *FamilySearch* and the *International Genealogical Index*, and the following friends and associates who kept me going through a particularly difficult time in a variety of ways: Sieglinde Alexander, Celia and Ted Auld, Michael Armstrong, Janice Bloomfield (for feeding my cats and keeping them happy), John Brooke-Little, Pat and Douglas Brown, Patrick Canavan, Bobby Collins, Sue and Tony Dawkins, Tony Heybourn, Jonathan Huggins, Peter Kennedy-Scott, Alyn Marriott, Mary Neads and the dog, Daisy, Stan Newens and his daughter Sarah, Vanessa Thompson-Royds, Margaret Thomson, Roy Varley, Stanley West, David Williamson, all my other friends who know who they are, and my special cousins John, Dorothy, Gary and Marie Thexton. Thanks to Polstead Community Shop for keeping me stocked up with the usual doughnuts, treacle and liquorice toffees. Last, but not least, grateful thanks to my erstwhile editor, Helen Coward, for her patience, which is definitely worth a medal, and especially to Sarah Mitchell and Rosie Clay for seeing the project through.

I should very much like to add the name of Andrew Gough, who generously drew my attention to his discovery of a sister for Arthur Jefferon while he was researching his own ancestry. I gathered much up-to-date information from the Internet (what would we do without it?), from the General Register Office for Scotland, and from Connie Potter of the National Archives, in Washington, DC.

For some unforgivable reason I omittted to Roger Powell in the 1997 acknowledgement. It was he who pushed this book in my direction, so I now very belatedly and apologetically say *mea culpa* for this regrettable oversight. Thanks too to Catherine Coe, my long-suffering editor. Any errors are mine, changing, new and vanishing websites notwithstanding.

Stella Colwell, 1997

preface

Since the last edition of this book, which appeared in 1997, the family history scene has taken another giant leap forward, into the land of the Internet. Many people have come to the subject having found one or two websites that have stirred their curiosity to learn more about their past, or have heard other people wax lyrical about what they have learned from contacts with new-found relatives overseas using e-mail lists and message boards provided by some of the largest online specialists like **www.rootsweb.com**. **www.ancestry.com** and **www.genealogy.com**. You can receive instant replies to e-mails and posted enquiries, and meet up with relatives and fellow-enthusiasts you would not otherwise have known about.

But a word of warning to you Internet buffs: there is no substitute for searching original documents. Although increasingly important genealogical sources are being made available on the Internet as indexed digital images which you pay to view, indexes are not perfect, you might be tempted into thinking either the person or family isn't there, or into giving up in despair if an index search is negative.

You can search any website, any time, but this can develop into a scattergun exercise, for it is so easy to get diverted into website after website link, until you have soon forgotten why you first logged on, and who and what you were looking for.

Websites and online databases have no existence outside the computer. They are the creations of the people who designed them. This means they are telling you only what they want you to know, which may not always be the whole story. You need to read the home page to find out what the website is trying to achieve, and what it will and will not do to assist you with your research. Have a look and see how often it has been updated. If this is not recently, then is the information still current? Many websites are short-lived, and you will find some recommended sites have disappeared by the time you have tried to visit them, although usually if the address has changed, there will be a link to the new site.

Database compilations may not accurately reflect what was in the original record, which might have been difficult to read, contain too much information for the fields the programmer had available, or be outside the scope of the project. An example is the claims made for certain indexes to ships' passenger lists, which turn out to be only for one or two years instead of the boasted period, and are full of queried spellings of names, rendering them a frustrating taste of what lurks in the original record. An instance of an excellent and much-used website containing databases of millions of personal names drawn from a wide range of sources is **www.familysearch.org** which is hosted by the Church of Jesus Christ of Latter-day Saints. This site includes an online catalogue of the contents of its library in Salt Lake City, which you can trawl and then use to hire in any item to search in one of the LDS family history centres scattered throughout the world. Online registration indexes save you huge amounts of time wading through book after book, especially when you are not exactly certain of when a particular event occurred. But if the original indexes were defective, such databases multiply the error, and new innocent users may accept them at face value and without question.

You may want to rely on a portal or gateway site which acts as a central clearing-house to direct you to websites arranged according to subject, place, personal name or type of record or repository. These involve a massive amount of work by the host to make sure the links are up to date and new ones added, but it takes a lot out of the uncertainty in knowing where to look for genealogical information. Examples of three really good portal sites are **www.genuki.org.uk** which has links to websites of national and county record offices in England, Wales, Scotland, the Channel Islands, Isle of Man and all of Ireland, to the website of the Federation of Family History Societies and thus to all its member societies, to the website of the Guild of One-Name Studies, and to a list of family history events for the year; **www.familyrecords.gov.uk** is the central link to the websites of the National Archives, Kew, the National Library of Wales, the National Archives of Scotland and its associated online projects, the Public Record Office of Northern Ireland,

The Family Records Centre, the General Register Offices for England and Wales, Scotland, and Northern Ireland, the Oriental and India Office Collections in The British Library, and the Commonwealth War Graves Commission; the third, **www.cyndislist.com** is hosted by Cyndi Howells, based in the United States of America and although particularly strong on online sources and information on sources within the Continent of North America, it also has extensive links to websites worldwide.

To be really sure you have not missed anything, try a search engine and request a search for your chosen keywords. Each search engine will produce different responses to your search commands. Try a web crawler like **www.ixquick.com**, which drills down other search engines to retrieve results. If you use a search engine such as **www.google.com** you can change the address to **www.google.co.uk** to confine the results to information relating to the United Kingdom. This is helpful if you are looking for certain place-names, for instance. I find a search engine useful for updates on online birth, marriage and death registration indexes. The search engine will display its results in order of proximity to the search term requested, and tells you the total number of entries it has found. Scan down the numbered list and click on the title of the most likely one, whose website address will be written underneath. When you visit the website you can quickly see if this is the one you want, and if not simply return to the list and try another one.

You can download, e-mail to friends, and print out information on the websites. Usually each site will have an e-mail contact address if you want to know more. Some websites offer both on-screen and printable versions of text.

Many sites are enhanced by pictures, which take much longer to load up onto the computer screen. Where there are digital images of original documents, you can print these out to read at leisure or insert into an online folder to build up a family scrapbook. If you live on the other side of the world from the actual documents, the Internet can be a godsend in this respect, and for people with British roots, the appearance of the 1901 census returns digitally, soon to be amplified by similar images of earlier censuses, has meant you can trace several generations of a family's life through almost a century.

Accept that the answer to everything is not on the Internet. You cannot rely on the Internet alone to trace your family's history, but it can be a powerful tool when handled properly. A computer is brainless so has no intuition and cannot evaluate or analyse what is loaded into its memory. This is up to you, and many new family historians come unstuck simply because they do not know how to set about their research in a constructive and structured way.

New websites are appearing daily, so by the time you read this book, some of the ones I mention may already be obsolete and vital fresh ones will have arrived to transform our researches even more. Genealogy is allegedly the second most popular search subject on the Internet, and there are millions and millions of genealogy sites to choose from, with no signs of a slow down.

Tread carefully, and remember that official websites are far more likely to be reliable and regularly updated than some of the smaller efforts. Use the Internet as a finding aid, not an end in itself, and use it in conjunction with original records or the traditional microform copies of them. Merged together, these electronic and paper sources will give you hours of fascination and a family story all your own.

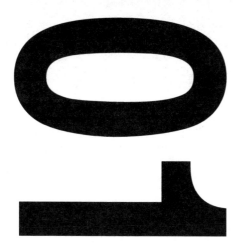

01

getting started

In this chapter you will learn:
- what this book is all about
- why it is so much fun doing original research
- what prime sources are available

I set out to be an archaeologist. That is, until the summer I went on one dig too many and ended up staying with a friend in London. Ticking off our list of things to do we made our way to the General Register Office, then in Somerset House, in the Strand, to look up our indexed birth registrations. For years I had been convinced I was adopted because I didn't resemble either of my parents. Now I found out the truth. For 5s 3d (1s 6d for the search and 3s 9d for the certified copy of my registration) they were shown to have been my parents from the outset. I was smitten. My initial brush with those vital records made such a deep impression on me that we have had a very close working relationship ever since. I have been excavating the past in a rather different way than I had planned.

When I first became interested in family history research as a career, there was only a small clutch of books to tell me how it was done. I had to learn the hard way, picking up practical tips from the occasional willing professional searcher, backed up by my university academic training in history, and relying on books and articles written about some of the sources I would be using, but directed at a totally different audience. This was long before the age of microfilm or microfiche copies of original material, or the plethora of personal name indexes and databases, CD-ROMs and Internet access we take for granted today. It was a struggle battling my way through the heavy volumes of centralized indexes of births, marriages and deaths, to the largely unindexed census enumerators' books in pursuit of my quarry. I simply could not understand that I would not always find the person where expected, and spent hours scouring through census book after census book until I was successful. Then came the big leap into the unknown, from centralized sources to local, from births and deaths to baptisms and burials, and a bewildering choice of documentation scattered in record offices, libraries and private collections.

I can sympathize with the beginner, for there is nothing more daunting and frustrating than not knowing what you are doing. However, this journey into the unknown is part of the challenge, for you will gradually build up your working knowledge of a vast range of the raw materials of family history, cast over a long period and broad geographic spread. You may discover that your family travelled around the country, and some members might have come from or gone overseas. How on earth did they link up? From studying old records you can learn about the communities in which your ancestors lived, which surnames were dominant and continuous, which families were most prolific, when and how frequently they intermarried, disappeared or died out. You will learn about changing population size and occupations over time, and how national and local events impacted on their lives. This information brings an added dimension to the chain of milestones in people's lives, their births, marriages and deaths, and sets them in their wider context of kinsfolk, friends, neighbours and associates. It is your own personal stake in our shared history. Family history tells us who made us what and who we are.

What you can learn

You will definitely be in for surprises. You may even be reunited with missing relatives you have never met before, but who are descended like you from the same root stock, however far back. Family history is a global hobby, and the advent of the Internet has made worldwide communication fast, easy and an effective means of advertising who and where you are, and of sharing your discoveries with others. There is no substitute for pursuing your own research. The sense of achievement when searches succeed is what drives millions of researchers on to ever-new goals.

If you adopt a step by step approach, once you have decided who and what you want to find, you will avoid ending up in a muddle, and have a much clearer idea of what you are doing. To do this, you will need to draw up a search plan. You will have to identify those sources most likely to provide the answer, and their whereabouts. You will need to know their original purpose and scope. Do they cover the period and region you are interested in? Will you be able to read the old handwriting, translate it from another language, or decipher any abbreviations, and understand archaic words and dating schemes? A logical line of thought, resoluteness, persistence, patience and accuracy are important ingredients, as well as a resistance to accepting what you read at face value simply because a statement or assertion seems to be the missing piece of the jigsaw. You will need to assess the relevance and value of your sources. Do not believe everything is on the Internet. What appears in print, in an index or transcribed copy of an original document is not necessarily complete, let alone accurate. Always check the original source wherever possible, and experience the unique excitement of handling a piece of history. Work methodically and tidily, so you can easily find and understand the information you have collected. At all costs avoid stacking up piles of paper and scraps of unsourced notes with the intention of sorting them out on a rainy day. Family history research is fun, filing is not. Develop good habits at the outset, by adopting a simple filing system and sticking to it as you go along, so you can quickly retrieve information, and share your findings with others.

How to begin

This book's purpose is to help you teach yourself, step by step, where to look for key facts linking the various generations of your family and pinpointing its members in time and place. It will explain why four pivotal sources were created (vital records of birth, marriage and death, census returns, church and chapel registers, and wills), as well as their genealogical content and limitations, for none was ever intended for the future family historian. It will direct you to other sources which might help where these are deficient or unclear. There is a select bibliography and lists of useful addresses and websites, whilst the case studies illustrate some of the problems you may encounter. I have chosen Fred Karno and two members of his army, Charlie Chaplin and Stan Laurel, but they could have been examples from your own family.

It is never too soon to start, and the best place to begin is with living relatives, not forgetting yourself, for who is better qualified than you to write an authoritative account of your life and times?

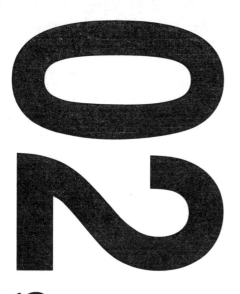

02
getting help

In this chapter you will learn:

- how to get started
- how to enlist help from relatives
- what to do if you have no living relatives

Your family's history starts with you, the golden rule being to work back from the known to the unknown, seeking names, family relationships, dates, places and occupations. None is much use without the other, a name without a date or place attached to it is next to useless, and likewise the absence of any connection between a name and a specific individual or a family group.

Your first step is to draw up a sketch family tree of your known relatives. Write down their names, dates and places of birth, marriage and death, their known places of residence, and occupations, together with those of their spouses, children, parents, grandparents, brothers, sisters, uncles and aunts. Your family tree may not extend very far vertically, but it may stretch out horizontally, so be sure to include everyone of the same generation on the same line, whether brothers and sisters or cousins, because they are related to you equally, sharing the same common ancestor. Now you can see the gaps.

Your second step is to decide which side of the family you want to research. The paternal line is usually preferred by family historians, because of the continuity of the surname, but there is nothing to prevent you from tackling your mother's ancestry. It is, however, best to search one branch of your family at a time, to avoid confusion, but if you get stuck with one, you can turn to another, because each generation you push back doubles the pool of surnames to choose from: those of your parents (two), your grandparents (four), great-grandparents (eight), great-great-grandparents (16) and so on. Sometimes families intermarried or married unrelated people of the same surname, so the actual number of surnames may not always be so great.

Choosing your relatives

Next, you need to find out if anyone in the family has already researched its history or can add to what you know. So, identify living relatives on your family tree, their precise connection to you, and their present whereabouts. It is obviously wisest to choose older kinsfolk first, but do not ignore younger members who may have cared for elderly parents or who may have memories of their grandparents. Spoken history has the advantage of immediacy, a source which can be questioned or elaborated on by others. Remember though that we tend to edit our recollections and may embellish or prune them to suit our audience.

Setting up a visit

If you are regularly in touch with certain relatives, provide reasonable advance warning (say a fortnight) of what you are up to and an idea of the information you hope they can supply. This will allow them time to rack their brains, consult with other relations, and perhaps unearth some family mementos to help build up the picture. However, there may be people in the family with whom you have had no personal direct dealings, but who remain in touch with known relatives and whose whereabouts they may be willing to disclose. Write to them, stating your place in their family, your interest in learning more about its history and seeking their help with specific information. If practicable, suggest one or two dates for a meeting, at least three weeks ahead, and await the response. This may be negative, for not everyone is interested in reliving or reviving the past, so you will have to respect this. You may find some will actively try to suppress it. A measured approach is preferable to springing a surprise call, which catches a person off-guard and unprepared. Panic may set in and key information overlooked.

My parents first met because my father served at sea with my maternal uncle, George Thexton. This uncle later became a captain in the merchant navy and frequently sailed to Australia where he delivered messages and news from Grasmere village folk to their emigrant relatives and friends. We knew that a branch of the Thexton family had gone to Australia in the nineteenth century, but as all links had long been severed, my uncle never attempted to try and renew them. My uncle's only son moved out of the village when I was a teenager away at boarding school. We lost touch after his father died in 1981, and while he was working abroad. He discovered my whereabouts in the early 1990s from the publisher of a book I had written and we began to correspond. We reminisced about our parents and village characters, and because he is older, he could remember things that happened before I was born, and I could tell him about events after he had departed. Eventually he retired back to England and the ties began to loosen again. One day he rang to say he had been contacted by a Gary Thexton from Australia, who thought we might be related. Gary had found him and other Thextons listed in the UK online phone directory, and had been approaching each in turn. My cousin gave him my address and before the day was out, Gary and his wife were on my doorstep and the family reunion was complete.

A quick glance at his sketch family tree revealed that we share a direct ancestor and are third cousins (see the pedigree chart, Figure 1, opposite). His great-great-great-grandfather, John Thexton, born in 1804, in Whittington, Lancashire, was our great-great-grandfather. John's eldest son, William, had sailed to Australia in 1851, settled in what is now the State of Victoria, married and started a Thexton dynasty. Meeting Gary in this way was like an echo from the family's past, but I was unable to make the most of his whirlwind visit, because I had had insufficient time to collect my thoughts and family papers together to show him.

If you begin with relatives you see frequently, you will feel more relaxed. As a place for conducting an interview about your family's history, your relative's own home is best, surrounded by his or her own possessions, and with family archives within easy reach. This also ensures privacy, since some of what is disclosed may be intensely personal and sensitive. Try not to have anyone else present who might inhibit the conversation or interrupt its flow. A checklist of questions to steer you through the conversation and ensure you find out the essentials appears in Appendix 1, p.278. However, you may not want to ask about everything on the list, certainly not in one sitting, so arrange to visit again another time to avoid your informant becoming mentally and physically exhausted and perhaps even hostile to your efforts. An hour is quite enough for anyone to try and recall stuff that may have remained dormant and unaired for decades.

Questions to ask

A list of questions tracking a person's life story chronologically is the simplest strategy to adopt, rather than jumping from one era to another and thus risking the loss of some of it. If dates are imprecisely remembered, anecdotes recalled chronologically will fit more easily into the timeframe. A list gives the discussion a structure, but need be not rigidly adhered to so that it degenerates into something of a market research exercise. Try breaking up the session by looking at some old family photographs, which will serve as excellent memory prompts.

Your main objective is to draw out genealogical facts, so good listening skills and empathy are paramount. Avoid making any interruptions and corrections, or value judgments. Resist imposing your own life history unless called for, because you are

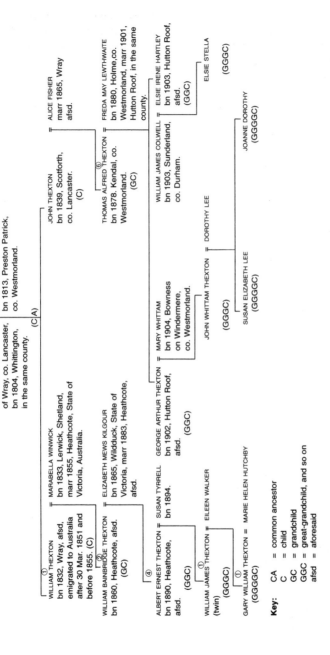

figure 1 the Thexton family tree

Key:
CA = common ancestor
C = child
GC = grandchild
GGC = great-grandchild, and so on
afsd = aforesaid

trying to fill in gaps in your knowledge. Refer to people's relatives in the way they were described in the conversation, as their father, grandfather, or brother, not their relationships to you, to avoid later misinterpretation. The two grandfathers should be identified as mother's father, or father's father, especially when it is unlikely that their forenames and surnames will be mentioned more than once.

What to be wary of

Memories play tricks, as editing commences very soon after an experience – one person's selective processes operate differently from another's, which can lead to several versions of the same incident. Memory is, after all, a mixture of fact and opinion, full of inconsistencies and excisions, and operates from each person's unique standpoint. Events may be re-interpreted over time, relate to insignificant occurrences in one person's life which had a far greater impact on someone else'. Several may be telescoped together or relayed out of order, whilst a person's role in them may be enlarged by wishful thinking, or concealed through guilt or embarrassment. Some may remember events as participants, others as impressionable bystanders, especially if something dramatic happened when the person was a child. Other stories may be based merely on hearsay, perhaps to protect the listener. Each time an anecdote is repeated it stands a chance of further embellishment.

Personal descriptions can be misleading, such as 'aunts' and 'uncles' who were actually friends of the family. Occasionally you may need to track down these friends or their descendants to discover more about your family. Pet family names, some bearing no resemblance to those registered at birth or baptism can also put you off the scent.

Family souvenirs

Set aside some time to pore over family ephemera such as old family photographs, franked letters and postcards, journals and diaries, medals, uniform buttons, samplers, rent books, ration books, house deeds, newspaper cuttings, certificates, school reports and prizes. Some may not have seen the light of day for many years. Some of the things you see are likely to date from beyond living memory, such as paintings and letters which have been carefully preserved because of their family associations. Make sure you find out the stories behind them.

A family Bible is a special treasure, often given as a wedding present, the first entry recording the recipients' marriage, followed by the names and birthdays of their children. Details might be entered of infant deaths and births of offspring before the introduction of civil registration and as such the family Bible may be the only surviving record of their existence. However, some events were written up many years after they occurred, and perhaps incorrectly, especially if a birth was uncomfortably close to or preceded the date of the parents' marriage. Always look at the publication date of the volume to check it predates the earliest entry. Birthplaces may be omitted too, so you may be left with a chronicle of family events whose whereabouts are unknown. Always ask living family if they can fill in these gaps or solve special mysteries. For instance, I inherited my maternal grandmother's Book of Common Prayer, and a hymn book inscribed 'To Freda May Bush' in 1897. My mother was adamant that her mother's birth surname was Lewthwaite, the name she used when she married my grandfather. As an orphan she was brought up by a Mrs Bush, and was obviously identified locally by that name. Conversely, I possess the family Bible of the Wilsons, who are totally unrelated, but whose personal property came into my parents' hands when they bought the family home from the widow of the last male descendant.

Ask if you can list the various items you have examined and make copies of any documents and old photographs. Note the names, addresses and relationship to you of their owners. It is worthwhile taking copies of unattributed photographs around with you on your family travels because others may recognize who the people were or have similar copies. Don't forget to photograph the relations you have spoken to, to construct a lasting visual archive for future generations to enjoy.

Dealing with different types of relative

One person's fascination may be viewed by someone else as an obsession, so do not outstay your welcome. People's concentration wavers after about an hour, older people's perhaps in less time if they are unused to much conversation, particularly when it is all focused on them and half-remembered individuals and events of long ago. The interview should not be rushed, but treat it as an opportunity for quiet reminiscence, not an interrogation. Reliving the past leaves people vulnerable and exposed, so respect their trust and confidence, and once the chat is over, do not hurry away but make sure the revelations have not caused emotional distress. Having your sole attention for even a short time may be enjoyable, allowing memories to flood back in which no-one else has recently or ever expressed much interest, and he or she may have eagerly looked forward to your visit. A gift, such as a box of good chocolates or biscuits or a home-made cake is also welcome and makes the person feel that you have thought of them.

Before you leave, ask for names, relationships and addresses of anyone else in the family in the area you might contact (especially married daughters, because their surnames will have changed), as you may be able to combine a second trip with a visit to them.

By interviewing as many family members as possible, you may be able to piece together the essential ingredients of its more recent history. Sharing what you know with relatives you have never met before will bring them up to date and make them feel that the exchange is two-way.

You are almost certain to come across relatives who do not want to talk to you, or may clam up when you are certain they have crucial information. This reticence has to be respected however much you long to quiz them; memories might be too painful to resurrect, or there might be an embargo on discussion of certain subjects, so you will need sensitivity and tact. Others may be only too happy to reveal everything and will become valued allies, but be discreet about their revelations, as what they divulge might have been suppressed by others or have cast them in an unfavourable light. At all costs, avoid stirring up a family feud or resurrecting buried resentments.

What to do if there is a language problem

If your informants are first-generation immigrants there may be a language barrier to overcome, so what they say may not always accurately represent what they actually intend, or it may be ambiguous. Talking to others of the same ethnic origin, especially if they originated from the same region, might help relax them and recreate a picture of their former life and community. If they can converse together in their native language, such people may be able to translate for you. Be sure first that your relative consents if you adopt this approach or decide to hire a professional interpreter. You may find a local member of an Anglo-ethnic family history society who is able to act as interpreter. Be sensitive to the possibility that the family may have left their homeland under tragic or politically dislocative circumstances, so do not probe into parts of their lives which are likely to hurt or disturb them.

Seeing it from your relatives' point of view

Do not expect all your questions to be answered fully or unequivocally on a single visit. Be prepared to interview your relatives at least twice, but not so often that it becomes an ordeal. It is important that they do not feel 'used' by a single visit without any follow-up by way of thanks or a share in the results of their efforts. Your relatives will probably also much appreciate being kept in touch with your progress summarized clearly and simply, but avoid bombarding them with minutiae. Christmas is a good time to send an updated family tree which is easy to understand and pass round, and recent additions to the family can be included on it. It may even provide an impetus for yet more anecdotes.

The second interview gives you the chance of providing a short progress report, filling in gaps or resolving conflicting assertions or misunderstandings. Your relative may appreciate having a short list of these points to mull over beforehand. An interval of a week or so between visits lets them think about your conversation and jog the memory, and your informant will know what to expect next time. A trip to your informant's childhood haunts, if it can be arranged, may trigger more memories and give them something to savour. Hopefully, the first visit will provide you with some ideas of places to visit.

Write or record?

You will need to decide how to permanently record your family interviews. If you intend to keep a written account, an A4 pad with a narrow feint and margin for notes is recommended, for easy filing, headed by the name and relationship to you of the relative, the date and place of the interview. Do not attempt to commit the conversation to paper verbatim, unless you are a shorthand expert, as you will slow down the proceedings and distract the speaker. All you need do is jot down dates, places, names, relationships and other key facts, with headings for anecdotes which can then be written up as soon as you reach home. Make sure you have plenty of writing implements and do not mark any documents or items shown to you. Pencils are less likely to leak or run dry, but be sure they are sharpened beforehand to avoid interrupting the flow of conversation.

Tape-recorded interviews

If you elect to tape-record, you can build up an oral archive, preserving individual nuances of pronunciation, and local dialect words. Because I no longer have any family ties with Grasmere, I have forgotten my mother's everyday stock expressions and turns of phrase. I can still hear my father's voice echoing in my head, with his mixture of Durham, Scots and Lake District vocabulary which he picked up during the course of his travels, but I deeply regret not having recorded his stories about his past, particularly as he was the one who gave me my first tape-recorder. Be wary of this equipment, though, because the speaker may be inhibited by it if he or she fears what purposes it may be put to.

Copyright

The copyright of the tape content belongs to the speaker. If you wish to use it for later publication or to lodge a copy in a local oral history collection you must ask for copyright to be assigned to you. Always secure the written consent of your interviewee in advance, to avoid any later misunderstanding by you or anyone else who comes by the tape. A pro-forma which can be signed by each recorded relative is best, and this provides a safeguard in the event of your informant's death.

You may already own a tape-recorder or decide to borrow or invest in one. A recommended model is a portable cassette-player with two sockets for external microphones, one each for the speaker and the interviewer. A battery-operated type is more versatile than a plug-in recorder, as you can do the interviewing anywhere without the need of an adaptor, but always carry new or recharged spare batteries with you. The best microphones are tie-clip or lapel type, worn about 20 cm away from the mouth, the lead tucked under the person's arm. This allows the speaker to concentrate on the interview without affecting the quality of recording by head movements. Ferric tape, running for 30 minutes each side (C60), and sold by a brand-leader, is the most reliable and stable medium.

The room selected for tape-recording should have no extraneous background noises such as a ticking clock, creaking chair, pets, children or boiling kettle, and if possible all phones should be temporarily immobilized. The microphone is very sensitive and will pick up every sound; a bad recording will forever remain a bad and irritating reminder. Try and place the recorder out of the speaker's line of vision, and sit facing each other, at a slight angle. If you have to share a microphone, sit close together, and if it is free-standing, place it at a different level to the recorder, on a soft, absorbent surface. The tape should run for at least five seconds before you begin. Start by giving your name, the date, place and name of the interviewee, and have your questions ready, preferably written down to stop you 'freezing'. It is helpful to agree the questions beforehand, so your interviewee knows what to expect and has mentally prepared responses.

Allow the person to develop responses to your questions at his or her own pace, and do not be tempted to interrupt a train of thought. Silence can often be meaningful. A nod of the head as encouragement, and open questions which require more than a 'yes' or 'no' will produce a more fluent exchange, but expect the first few minutes to be slightly stilted until the speaker relaxes. Then let the interview run its course, and be prepared for it to go off at a tangent occasionally. When it does, gently steer it back to what you want to know, or pursue a promising line of conversation. This is where your structured list of questions will come in handy. Do not have more than 20 questions ready and do not insist on asking all of them!

It is tiring listening attentively and picking up on extra topics, so practise with a friend first, until you feel comfortable in charge of the recorder, and know what to do should anything mechanical go wrong. Ask to be interviewed yourself, so that you know how it feels. Training in oral history and interviewing skills under expert tuition will help too. Details about local courses and oral history society activities should be available in your local library.

Each recording is unique and irreplaceable, so once it is completed you should break the safety tab at the top of the cassette (one for each side of the tape) to prevent accidental erasure or over-recording, and label it with the date of the interview, the name of the speaker and his or her date of birth, plus your own name, and to whom the copyright belongs. Give each tape a sequential number for listing and easy retrieval once stored away. A copy should be made of each tape and kept apart from the original (marked 'Master'). They should be filed upright in their boxes, in a shady, cool, dry and dust-free place away from the television set or any other electrical equipment which might interfere with their magnetic fields.

Next, write a summary of the taped conversation. A complete transcript is not necessary, just a short precis of the salient points, as you listen to the replay, and then arrange it under headings.

Writing to relations

If your relatives live too far away for a visit, then you may have to rely on e-mail exchanges or letters. With e-mails you can be certain of your intended recipient, but they may forward your message on to others without your knowledge, so be very careful what you say. You can of course send it as a confidential communication, but even then there is no guarantee this request will be honoured. Letters sent by the traditional 'snail mail' are individual, and take more time for a response. Remember though that some people have an aversion to committing to writing anything intimate about themselves or their family. Your communication should be succinct, stating your place in the family and listing those questions you want answered. If the list is kept short, you can always ask more questions later: if it is long, then you may receive no answers at all. A list is easy to follow and gives the request for information some kind of framework. Always retain a copy of your letter, since the reply may simply refer to your questions by number. It may take a long time to respond, or your request might be mislaid. A second, friendly, letter, with your address on the outside of the envelope will offer another opportunity, and if the person has moved away the letter can be returned to you. Remember that you are asking a favour and a reply is not obligatory. Always enclose a stamped self-addressed envelope or International Reply Coupons.

Those moved away and the dead

If a relative was last known at a specific address the new occupiers may have forwarding details or know the town or place they moved to. Neighbours may also have kept in touch and can supply you with details. If you only know the name of the town they moved to, try the phone book, the online directory at **www.bt.com/index.jsp** (United Kingdom) or **www.infobel.com/teldir** (worldwide) or the electoral register. The 2001 edition of the UK electoral register, phone directory and street atlas is available on UK-Info Disk, a CD-ROM. If you are looking for missing living relatives in England and Wales, then you could approach Traceline. This service is run by the Office for National Statistics, and for a fee the National Health Service Central Register will be searched and you will be notified if the person is still alive. For an extra fee you will be invited to send a letter which will be forwarded to the missing relative with their consent. No information as to their whereabouts is ever disclosed to the enquirer; it is left to the missing relative to respond. Traceline cannot assist with cases involving adoption, where the enquirer or person sought is under the age of 18, or where renewed contact may be disruptive, for instance with current or former partners. You can find out more about Traceline at **www.statistics.gov.uk/ registration/traceline**.

Sometimes you may find your relative has recently died. Nursing home staff, neighbours and friends in the same street may know more about the person than their own family, for people often confide more in associates than in their relations, fearing disapproval of their actions or wanting discretion. A trip to the nursing home or street can pay dividends, because you may be referred to the person's solicitor and funeral director. The solicitor may have handled the deceased person's estate and know the names and whereabouts of the next of kin, and what became of any family papers, but this approach requires tact. The funeral director may be able to give similar information, and certainly about where the person was buried or cremated. A local newspaper obituary or death notice, the parish magazine, priest or churchwarden may reveal more about the chief mourners and friends who you can contact.

If you have no known living relatives, but remember where your parents came from, then a search of the phone book of that area may reveal people of the same surname. You can do this in your local reference library, or visit **www.bt.com/index.jsp** for United Kingdom and Ireland subscribers, and **www.infobel.com/teldir** for addresses and phone numbers throughout the world. Sometimes a visit to the street or area where they once lived can elicit information from former friends and neighbours about what became of other members of the family who have now left or died; **http://www.phonenumbers.net** includes maps showing the exact location of individual addresses. Headstone inscriptions in the local cemetery may help you fill in gaps too. The cemetery owner may be willing to search the burial registers for details of plot number to help you locate a particular grave. You can find out the contact number and address from the phone book or local district council office. Look also in R. Blatchford, *The Family and Local History Handbook* for lists of local cemeteries.

Making use of the Internet

You can also employ a search engine such as **www.ixquick.com**, **www.google.com** or a web directory like **www.yahoo.com** to search for the names of specific people, surnames and places in the millions of databases and websites on the Internet. Try several of these, as none is fully comprehensive and each responds to your commands in different ways, so the number of hits will vary. However, the first of the above search engines should do most of this job for you. For people on e-mailing lists in the United Kingdom and Ireland, visit **www.genuki.org.uk/indexes/ MailingLists.html** and for worldwide listings try **http://lists. rootsweb.com** You may want to register your own e-mail address, but once registered remember to check incoming mail regularly and be prepared to receive some junk mail.

You may like to post a message on a website such as **http://boards.ancestry.com** or **http://boards.rootsweb.com** and also check if someone is looking for you. The messages are listed by locality and by surname so are easy to search. These reach a global audience. You can contribute information without having to subscribe to a mailing list, but you must regularly check for any responses, so that you can make direct contact and advertise the questions you want answered.

Advertising in the press

A short letter to the editor of the local newspaper, setting out your interest in the family and its history, seeking information about present-day relatives and their whereabouts will often result in its publication and wide circulation. A local magazine, published less often, but subscribed to by people further afield with local connections, is also worth considering. *Willing's Press Guide*, available in your local reference library, contains a place-name index and alphabetical listing of all national and provincial newspapers and periodicals published in Great Britain, Ireland and overseas, together with editorial addresses and publication dates.

03

sorting out the facts

In this chapter you will learn:
- how to set out your family findings on a family tree chart
- what to add on your pedigree
- how to discover if anyone else has researched your family

When you have gathered all the information you can from your family, arrange it in a ring binder or on cards for easy filing and retrieval. Use separate sheets or cards for each person. Put the details about yourself at the top or at the front, followed by your father and mother, brothers and sisters (oldest first), their spouses and their children, in family groups, then your grandparents, and their other children (oldest first), spouses and children, and so on, going back a generation at a time. Any compiled sheets of paper or cards relating to your mother's family should be separately and similarly organized. You can now extract details from these to draw up a pictorial summary of your ancestral line.

The sooner you begin to sort out your information into a pictorial summary, the less formidable the task; you will be able to see at once exactly what stage you have reached in your research if you add newly discovered facts as you go along. The family tree should clearly and tidily show every generation link, and should be capable of being understood by anyone without need of further explanation.

You may prefer to use one of the many available genealogical software packages to feed your details directly into a pre-set database, and save it. Read up and ask friends who have used these for advice and recommendations on what to buy.

Some simple guidelines

There are several ways of recording your ancestry, but the one you will find simplest to follow is the drop-line pedigree chart, which starts with yourself at the bottom (leaving sufficient space underneath for your own descendants), and shows each previous generation in a series of steps up the page, with your earliest known forebear at the top, and leaving enough room above for new names to be added. There are no hard rules for setting out the information, but you may find the following advice helpful. A large sheet of ruled paper (or several sheets of ruled A4 glued together), a sharpened pencil, rubber and ruler are all that are required.

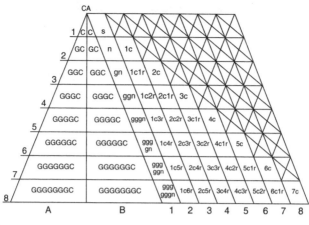

- Find the common ancestor of the two relatives.
- To work out a family relationship, identify the person of the earlier generation in column A. Note the number to the left.
- Then find the relative you want to link with the person in column B. Note the number to the left.

Look at the THEXTON pedigree on page 9; for example, JOHN WHITTAM THEXTON is the great-great-grandson of JOHN THEXTON and MARY WILCOCK. The number next to this is 4.

GARY WILLIAM THEXTON is the great-great-great-grandson of this couple, the common ancestors. The number next to this is 5.

- With your finger on the line at the higher diagonal number (5) move it across to find the box over the lower horizontal number (4). This shows that they are 3rd cousins once removed. JOHN THEXTON is the 3rd cousin of GARY's father, one generation earlier.

In canon law they are related in the 5th degree, the maximum number of steps away from their common ancestor; in civil law it is the 9th degree, the total number of steps back and forwards separating them both.

Key:

CA	= common ancestor	s	= sibling (brother/sister)
C	= child	n	= nephew or niece
GC	= grandchild	gn	= great or grand nephew (or niece)
GGC	= great-grandchild		
		ggn	= great-great nephew (or niece) and so on
GGGC	= great-great-grandchild and so on	1c	= 1st cousin
		1c1r	= 1st cousin once removed and so on

figure 2 working out family relationships

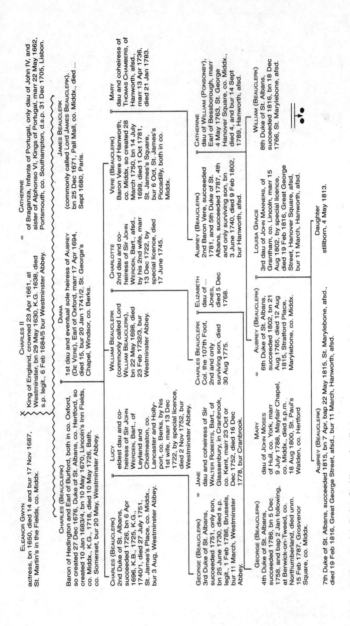

figure 3a finding the 8th Duke: St Albans family tree

this illustrates most of the guidelines in drafting a pedigree, and the often tortuous route taken to find the next heir to a title

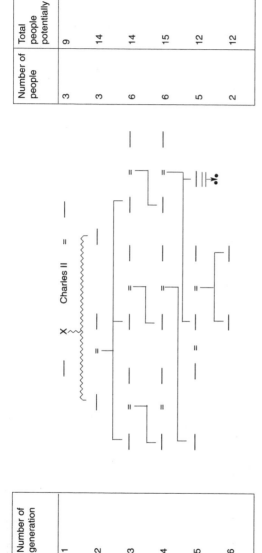

Number of generation		Number of people	Total people potentially
1		3	9
2		3	14
3		6	14
4		6	15
5		5	12
6		2	12

Key:
Generation
1 Charles II had 7 known mistresses.
2 He had 14 known bastards.
3 The 1st Duke had 5 other sons and 3 daughters.
4 The 3rd Duke had a sister; Charles Beauclerk an elder brother and 2 sisters; the 5th Duke had 3 older brothers who died young and 2 sisters.
5,6 and so on ...

figure 3b sketch plan of the tree: counting up the generations and the people in them

Here are some rules to follow when drafting a pedigree:

- Record everyone of the same generation on the same line, so you can see their precise place in the family tree.
- Place children of the same parents in birth order, the oldest on the left. Sometimes you may have to alter the order to slot in interfamily marriages, so indicate their birth seniority by numbers above each name.
- Write people's names in capital letters; record surnames for males, females their forenames only.
- Write a wife's name to the right of her husband's. When he has married more than once place the name of the first wife to the left of his name, and the second to the right. The same applies when it is the woman who has married twice.
- Use a vertical descent line from the marriage symbol (=) to connect parents to their children, and a horizontal line the children to each other.
- Indicate illegitimate chldren by a wavy vertical descent line from the parents down to their names.
- Record adopted children's names after the names of other children of a couple, but without a descent line, because there is no blood relationship.
- Where it is uncertain but likely that there is a parental or sibling link, use a dotted line.

What to include

Here is a checklist of items to include, although you will not manage all of them, and the further back you go in time the more scanty the information will be.

1 Full name.
2 Residence now, and previous ones, with dates if possible (earliest first), including county.
3 Occupation now and earlier occupations, with dates if possible (earliest first), any service rank or title, any awards and decorations, public appointments such as Justice of the Peace, degree and university.
4 Date of birth, and place, with the county (and date of adoption if appropriate).
5 Date and place of baptism, with the county, and religious denomination if not Anglican.
6 Where educated, starting with the first school, plus dates; date of any apprenticeship, and details of any wartime service.

7 For females only: date and place of marriage, and the county.

8 Ownership of land, and its whereabouts, including the county.

9 If included in a census return, which years (earliest first), and at what age.

10 Whether named in someone else's will, giving its date, and the probate date if he or she was the executor.

11 Date and place of death, and the county. The given age might also be recorded here.

12 Date and place of burial, with the county, and if there is a gravestone inscription. The given age might be recorded here.

13 If a will was made, its date and when and where proved, or the date a grant of letters of administration was made and where.

14 For people marrying into the family, the full name, address, occupation, rank, title and degree of the father are recorded immediately after the name of the man or woman concerned, and whether that parent was deceased at the time of the marriage. Then include the same information as above.

A list of abbreviations frequently used in compiling pedigrees is given in Appendix 2, p.280. All dates should give the day first, then write in the month to avoid misinterpretation, and preferably with 'Jan' for January and 'Jne' for June, as handwriting legibility varies. Remember to identify places by their county, to avoid ambiguity. This family tree will serve as your working document and summarize all you know so far, so it must include only proven facts. You may want to square-bracket or question-mark doubtful information for checking if you wish to add this.

Alternative types of family tree

Another type of pedigree chart is the birth brief, recording horizontally from left to right your own name and vital events, the names, births, baptisms, marriages, deaths and burials of parents, grandparents and great-great-grandparents. This rarely leaves space for any siblings. The room for personal details shrinks as the number of names grows, but the chart illustrates the different families from which you are directly descended. This sort of family tree is used at **www.familysearch.org**, the website of the Church of Jesus Christ of Latter-day Saints, where you can see only three generations of a family displayed on the screen. This is deliberate, so that you concentrate on a limited number of names at a time before moving on to view more generations.

You may prefer to feed your information into a computer package, such as Family Tree Maker, where you insert names, dates and other details in a pre-set format. You can download this, print as many copies as you like, and make corrections, amendments and additions. Such packages may offer both the above and other types of pedigree layout. Don't forget that these packages are less flexible and leave less space for information than if you are writing up a pedigree from scratch, but they do save you time and give the end product a professional look.

If you have lots of relatives to include, you may find it easier to have a master chart showing your own direct descent, cross-referenced to other numbered charts on which the progeny of individually numbered uncles and aunts and other collateral branches are recorded. If you have to resort to this remember to space out each generation in the same way as on the master chart, so that you can slot them together and see where each person fits into your family's story. Above all, don't create extra work for yourself, and generate more paper than you need to, otherwise you may lose control. Keep it simple and keep it factual.

A family tree written up as an indented narrative, moving in a couple of character spaces for each generation, where each person is allotted a number according to his or her place in the parents' family, can often be difficult to follow, whereas a pictorial chart can be quickly interpreted. Examples of narrative pedigrees are to be found in published peerages and volumes about the landed gentry.

Once you are happy that your family tree is as complete as you can get it, send a copy to each of your informants in case they can add anything extra, rectify mistakes or omissions.

Is anyone else researching your family?

Having established what you know and don't know about your family's history, you then need to discover if someone else has already made some investigations. If a relative has done some hunting this will prevent you wasting valuable time, money and energy duplicating their efforts and provide an opportunity for collaboration or sharing resources.

Since 1981, a completely new edition of K. A. Johnson and M. R. Sainty's *Genealogical Research Directory, National and International* has been published annually, listing contributors' surname research interests, relevant places and dates, with contact details. There is a consolidated list covering entries from 1990 to 1999 on CD-ROM. Be very careful if you find one which you think applies to your family, since not every contributor may be as generous as you in exchanging information. The Directory includes a section on One-Name Study Groups, which concentrate on extracting every entry from specific records and indexes to construct a picture of regional surname distribution over time, rather than the reconstruction of family trees.

The Guild of One-Name Studies, founded in 1979, and based in London, publishes a list of registered one-name projects at its website (**www.one-name.org**). To join, prospective members of the Guild have to copy down all references to their chosen surname and its variants in vital records indexes of births, marriages and deaths registered in England, Wales and Scotland, current phone books, all published will indexes to the present day, relevant parish registers of baptism, marriage and burial, the *International Genealogical Index* (made up of births, baptisms and marriages of deceased individuals extracted from vital and parish records), county histories and serial publications of local historical and antiquarian societies. Whilst name-collecting does not necessarily yield filial links, nonetheless it can be a pointer to geographic clusters, and may present clues to where you should be looking. For Scotland, *Whitaker's Almanack* publishes an annual list of addresses of Chiefs of Clans and Names, and for Ireland, the Clans of Ireland Office, in Dublin, maintains a list of associations of family surnames.

The *British Isles Genealogical Register* (BIG-R) is a microfiche index of researched family names in this country, setting out the places, counties and periods currently under investigation. This is produced by the Federation of Family History Societies, an umbrella body serving well over 200 county, one-name and other societies as well as a number of overseas organizations. The numbered entries are linked to the names and contact details of contributors, enabling you to get in touch and discover if you might be related and to exchange information.

Over 200,000 entries are included in each edition (1994, 1997 and 2000), the last of which is also available on CD-ROM.

The Federation of Family History Societies, founded in 1974, hosts its own website, **www.ffhs.org.uk**, with links to the websites of member societies, including the Guild of One-Name Studies. You can e-mail relevant local societies to see if anyone is registered as researching your family name and to express your own interest. Many of the one-name societies have their own websites, so it is worth trawling these too. For lists of family history societies worldwide, look in R. Blatchford, *The Family and Local History Handbook*.

The oldest family history society in the British Isles is the Society of Genealogists, founded in 1911. Its library holds thousands of copies of published family histories, manuscript pedigrees, research notes and indexed birth briefs deposited by members stretching back four generations to 16 great-great-grandparents. The library is open to non-members for a fee, and details of its opening hours, charges and limited search services can be found at its website, **www.sog.org.uk** Again, none of this material will have been independently authenticated, so you will need to evaluate it for yourself and double-check its contents against cited original sources.

For researched family histories visit **www.familysearch.org**, the website of the Church of Jesus Christ of Latter-day Saints. This contains Ancestral File, made up of millions of pedigree charts and family group sheets submitted by members of the Church seeking Temple Ordinances. Source references and notes are lacking, so you will need to verify the information for yourself. The family group sheets forming Pedigree Resource File, a similar database, are however annotated with source citations. The subscribers' given addresses for both of these may no longer be current, and they may be unwilling to supply more information to you. Consult the Family History Library catalog too, at the same website, for lists of any books, microfilms or microfiche relating to your surname and family home. If you find any, note their call numbers, which can be quoted when hiring them for a small fee to read in a family history centre near you. You can find the whereabouts and contact details of family history centres throughout the world from the same website. Because family history centres are run by volunteers, their facilities and opening hours vary, so you will need to phone prior to your visit.

Another excellent resource for finding out about researched family histories is **www.cyndislist.com**. This contains links to worldwide family history resources on the Internet, and includes a 'Finding people' section.

You may also like to try a powerful search engine such as **www.ixquick.com** to scour the Internet for your family name, adding 'family tree' or 'family history' to see how many entries are displayed. As before, if you make contact with any of the contributors do not give too much away, but treat it as an information exchange, once you have established that you are interested in the same family. You may even find a relative in a different part of the world anxious to trace their British roots with whom you can share your interest and ideas on how to solve research problems.

Manuscript pedigrees

For verified pedigrees you will be fortunate if your family paid to register its ancestry at the College of Arms, in London, particularly if it was granted a coat of arms. In the sixteenth and seventeenth centuries, the heralds travelled officially into each county approximately once a generation to inspect family muniments and evidences supporting the local gentry's right to bear heraldic arms. One of the by-products was the registration of their family trees, some extending back to the Middle Ages. You cannot inspect these volumes yourself, but for a fee a search will be undertaken for you. Unofficial copies of many of the heraldic visitation pedigrees have been published by the Harleian Society. The website address of the College is **www.college-of-arms.gov.uk**. The Court of the Lord Lyon, in Edinburgh, preserves Scottish heraldic and genealogical archives, and The Genealogical Office, Dublin, holds similar Irish records. Like the College of Arms, neither is open to the public, though both offer a paid research service to enquirers.

Collections of catalogued manuscript pedigrees and notes, many compiled by antiquarians, heralds, herald painters or their assistants in the sixteenth and seventeenth centuries and extending back well into the Middle Ages, may be inspected in The British Library, London, and in the Bodleian Library, Oxford. You will need a reader's ticket to use these. Many of the pedigrees were constructed from private family documents and monuments which no longer exist, and were compiled before most historical central government and legal records were made accessible to the public. You can search the catalogues to these at **www.bl.uk** and at **www.bodley.ox.ac.uk/guides/wmss** respectively.

Even though the pedigrees officially registered in the College of Arms or kept in The British Library and Bodleian Library may seem to relate only to the higher reaches of society, because of the inheritance system of primogeniture, and social mobility upwards and downwards, they do contain references to family members who were relatively humble. The pedigrees can also be used to trace English and Welsh family connections of overseas emigrants, as well as tracking migrants from county to county, into and out of London. This information can then be checked and elaborated on using original documentary sources of the period.

The National Archives, at Kew (**www.nationalarchives.gov.uk**), the National Archives of Scotland, Edinburgh (**www.nas. gov.uk**), and National Archives of Ireland, in Dublin (**www.nationalarchives.ie**), harbour thousands of pedigrees which were produced as evidence for legal purposes in courts of law. The websites of the first two can also be accessed at **www.familyrecords.gov.uk**. You can search for lodged pedigrees in your surname by using the online catalogue of the National Archives at Kew at **www.nationalarchives.gov.uk**.

The principal series of manuscript Welsh pedigrees are held by the National Library of Wales, in Aberystwyth (**www.llgc. org.uk**), and the College of Arms. Many of them were written in the native language, and include fifteenth- and sixteenth-century copies of ninth- and tenth-century genealogies which were transmitted orally from generation to generation. There are published catalogues to both collections, and a number of the pedigrees have been printed. You will need a reader's ticket to use the National Library of Wales, and you can also access its website via **www.familyrecords.gov.uk**.

Welsh genealogies are remarkable for the common ancestry claimed by a lot of families from a small number of 'patriarchs', and for the substitution of patronymics for surnames. A genealogical string of personal names identified at least an individual's father and grandfather, which changed with each new generation. Settlement, place-names, occupations and associated nicknames therefore assume great importance in identifying who and where Welsh ancestors belonged to, because the pool of personal names was small.

County record offices and family history societies may include manuscript and printed pedigrees of local families in their collections. You can access the websites of most record offices via **www.genuki.org.uk** and family history societies via **www.ffhs.org.uk**.

Published pedigrees

Published pedigrees and their whereabouts are listed in S. A. Raymond's series of county genealogical bibliographies, which enshrine and bring up to date G. W. Marshall's *The Genealogist's Guide*, first issued in 1903, and updated in 1953 by J. B.Whitmore in *A Genealogical Guide*, and then by G B Barrow in 1975 in *The Genealogist's Guide*.

If the family's history has been written up and printed, then it too should be listed by Raymond and by T. R. Thomson's *Catalogue of British Family Histories* if published before 1980. For printed Scottish pedigrees you will need to consult M. Stuart and J. Balfour Paul's *Scottish Family History*, updated by J. P. S. Ferguson in *Scottish Family Histories*; printed Irish pedigrees may be listed in B. de Breffny's *Bibliography of Irish Family History and Genealogy*, and E. MacLysaght's *Bibliography of Irish Family History*. Copies of many of these publications are in the libraries of the Society of Genealogists, in London, and can be hired from the Family History Library of the Church of Jesus Christ of Latter-day Saints, in Salt Lake City. Consult the online catalogues of both of these institutions at **www.sog.org.uk** and **www.familysearch.org** respectively.

The Library of Congress, in Washington, DC, has in its care thousands of manuscript pedigrees, listed alphabetically in *National Union Catalog of Manuscript Collections*, to which there is a consolidated index. You should also trawl *Genealogies in the Library of Congress: A Bibliography*, edited by M. J. Kaminkow, and the three *Supplements*, which record the Family Name Index entries of printed and manuscript pedigrees, together with their call numbers. *A Complement to Genealogies in the Library of Congress* covers other library holdings in the United States, including foreign and unpublished family trees. Search the catalogues at **www.loc.gov/catalog**. The New York Genealogical and Biographical Society (**http://nygbs.org/**), New England Historic Genealogical Society, based in Boston (**www.newenglandamcestors.org**), and the Newberry Library in Chicago (**www.newberry.org**), all boast notable collections of compiled pedigrees. Visit their websites to search their online catalogues and databases.

The *American Genealogical–Biographical Index*, Series 1 and 2, edited by F. Rider, aims at listing alphabetically all printed family histories in books, articles and brief biographies before 1950. Each entry sets out the name, birth year and state of the person, abbreviated biography and book and page reference. This is avi[a]lable online at **www.ancestralfindings.com/agbi.htm**.

Some words of warning

As with manuscript pedigrees, printed, Internet compilations and family histories should not be accepted uncritically, especially if references to sources are lacking, because you need to know why each assertion was made. Always read any accompanying introductory notes to find out about the editor's intentions and scope of research. If given dates are scanty or look dubious, then this should make you suspicious, particularly if a lifespan seems extraordinarily short or long. Unexplained migrations may indicate a set of facts about one family being conveniently tacked onto those of a quite distinct unit of the same surname. Newly accessible sources, databases and finding aids are surfacing all the time. By utilizing these, you may be able to elaborate, disprove or modify statements made before they were available. High standards of evaluation of evidence have never been universally adopted, but that is not to decry the many scholarly and carefully researched works.

If you are lucky, the information revealed by other people's publicized work may link in with what you already know about your direct forebears or may provide leads on where to look, because the researched family stems from the same part of the country as yours, or perhaps because forename patterns seem similar to those of your own line.

Regard the above resources as signposts, not as an end in themselves. As you work back from the known to the unknown, they may bring you into contact with others sharing a common interest. You may eventually want to share your own researches by advertising them on the Internet, so make sure what you find is accurate and can be verified against the sources you have tapped.

04
starting your research: births, marriages and deaths

In this chapter you will learn:
- what centralized records of births, marriages and deaths there are
- how you can find specific entries
- how to solve some common problems

What to do next

By now you will have established what you already know from contacts with relatives and studying others' research. Have you been able to add anything new? Is it reliable?

The next step is to decide who and what you want to find. Look at your family tree tracing your direct ancestry. What is the earliest date on it? Most probably it will fall in the mid- or late nineteenth century. What does the date relate to? If it was a birth, do you know the names of the parents, including the mother's surname before marriage? Do you know the person's exact place in the family, as the eldest or other child? If it was a marriage, where was this information taken from? Was the ceremony in a church, chapel or register office? If a chapel, do you know its denomination? Do you know the full names, ages and paternity of the couple? If it was a death, do you know the person's purported age, and where he or she died? Did it happen in England, Wales, Scotland, Ireland or elsewhere? If in Scotland, Ireland or elsewhere, look at the next two chapters.

This is where your original research begins. It is also where you start to spend money. It is a good idea to keep a check on your spending by drawing up a checklist of necessary searches to establish your direct ancestry, and then if you are feeling generous, widen the scope to include other branches of the family. You may need to do this anyway if you cannot locate your own forebears. The important thing is to stay focused on who and what you are looking for and not become distracted.

The first of the four basic sources cited on p.4 to capture details about the vital events of people's lives is civil registration.

In England and Wales civil registration of birth, marriage and death started on 1 July 1837, under the control of the Registrar General, in London. The country was divided up into superintendent registration districts, based on the newly created civil Poor Law Union boundaries of 1834. These were sub-divided into smaller units called registration districts, each consisting of about seven civil parishes. The district registrars, appointed by the superintendents, recorded births and deaths in their area in special books. Clergymen of the Established Church of England kept two sets of marriage registers in their churches for completion. Until 1898, superintendent district registrars presided over marriages in dissenters' chapels, after which other authorized persons could do so. Quakers and Jews maintained their own registrations of marriages. The superintendent district registrars also performed civil weddings in their offices. Civil marriages since 1970 have been allowed in exceptional circumstances by Registrar General's licence in other premises such as hospitals, where people are housebound or detained, and from April 1995 in hotels, country clubs and other licensed venues outside the residential area of either party.

Once every three months, the superintendents send to the Registrar General certified copies of the district registrars' returns of births and deaths notified during the quarter of the year up to the end of March, June, September and December. Copies of marriage registers are furnished quarterly to the Registrar General by the clergy, the superintendent, chapels and officers of the Quakers and Jews. When the original birth and death register books are full they are passed to the superintendent for safekeeping, and from these, district indexes are compiled. One of the duplicate marriage registers is similarly deposited when full, but it might be many years before this happens if a parish is thinly populated.

The indexes

Members of the public can freely inspect the centralized quarterly indexes of registered births, marriages and deaths in England and Wales to 1983, and the subsequent yearly indexes, in the General Register Office search area in the Family Records Centre (FRC), London. If you arrive early in the day, you will avoid the crush, when it tends to get congested. You may prefer to search the database of indexes relating to births, marriages and deaths from 1837 to 1983 which are being loaded onto the Internet at **http://freebmd.rootsweb.com** or to pay to search scanned images of the index pages from 1837 to the present at **www.1837online.com/trace2web/.** In either case there are direct links to the online application form for a certified copy of the registration itself, which you can then complete and forward to the General Register Office with your credit card details.

The indexes for births, marriages and deaths are kept separately, each arranged alphabetically by surname, then forename, giving the registration district, volume and page number of every entry in the register, to which are added from 1984 the registration district number, and from 1993 the month and year. At the FRC, you will need to transfer all this information onto one of the relevant coloured application forms and pay for a certified copy of the registration. Microfilm and microfiche copies of these indexes are widely available, including at the National Library of Wales, many county record offices and family history centres.

By visiting **www.familia.org.uk** you can discover which libraries in this network hold copies. To order a copy locally of the relevant certificate you can then complete the online application form at **www.statistics.gov.uk** providing your credit card details and e-mail it to the given address.

If you do not have access to the Internet, then post the full index details to General Register Office, PO Box 2, Southport, Merseyside PR8 2JD, enclosing a cheque or postal order for the correct amount and made payable to 'ONS', or quoting your credit or debit card details. Payments from overseas are required in £ sterling, either by cheque or international draft and bearing the name and address of a London clearing bank. You can also order a certificate by phone or by fax (see the list of addresses at the back of this book for full details). Certificates are despatched within five working days. In the event of a wrong reference, you will be charged for each reference checked on the same application.

If you do not have access to the GRO indexes, you can request a search of any three-year period for a fee, which covers the cost of any resulting certificate, but this service takes 20 working days to complete.

If you know when and where your antecedent was born or died, it may be easier and cheaper to make an appointment to have the superintendent registrar's indexes checked for a fee. For district office addresses, look under 'Registrations of births, deaths and marriages' in the phone book, or in the latest edition of *The Family and Local History Handbook*, edited by R. Blatchford, or visit **www.statistics.gov.uk/registration/localservices.asp**. You can find out which present-day registrar's office holds registers for defunct districts (1837–1930) at **www.fhsc.org.uk/genuki/reg/district.htm** which includes a complete alphabetical list of towns, villages and hamlets belonging to each district.

If you are doubtful as to which superintendent's district a place belonged, you can also look it up in *Poor Law Union Records, Part 4: Gazetteer of England and Wales*, by J. Gibson and F. A. Youngs, Jr, which should be available in your local reference library. Otherwise a contemporary county trade directory will identify the relevant Union. The Guildhall Library, in London, has an excellent collection of regional directories, a number of which are being made available on CD-ROM. Try also **www.familia.org.uk** for listings of directories in local libraries, and at **www.historicaldirectories.org** for online editors.

If your ancestors came from Cheshire you will be able to search the indexes to local registrations between 1837 and 1950, which are gradually being loaded onto **www.cheshirebmd.org.uk**, together with an online application form to send to the relevant local register office. Other counties are following suit. Check which these are by visiting **www.genuki.org.uk.big/eng/ RegOffice/**. Remember, though, that local index references are not the same as those of the Registrar General. There is no consolidated index to marriages within a superintendent registrar's district, so the registers are more easily (and freely) examined if deposited in a county record office. You can find their addresses and phone numbers from J. Gibson and P. Peskett, *Record Offices, How to find them* and from **www.genuki.org.uk**. If the marriage registers are still in the church or chapel then you are likely to incur a search fee, but of course you can inspect the signatures of the bridal couple and their witnesses. Consult the current edition of *Crockford's Clerical Directory* for addresses of Anglican clergy, and similar directories should be available in your local library for other denominations. Find out first how much any search is going to cost, and always fix a mutually convenient day to visit.

Tips

- When browsing birth, marriage and death indexes, be careful to look under all likely surname spellings, including the first letter, for instance Aughton as well as Haughton, changing vowels such as Bermingham, Birmingham, Burmingham, varying consonants, such as Burningham, and dialect spellings such as Tuddenham, Tudman, Studman, Birkett and Birkhead.

- Check out misread letters, like L and S, T and F.

- Because of the Welsh patronymic naming system, and relatively few surnames and forenames in circulation, you may find it difficult sorting out who was who in the indexes, even if you know the district where an event occurred. Children of the same father might be registered under different surnames. In some cases hyphenated surnames developed, perhaps giving a clue to the mother's surname before marriage.

- Search the indexes consecutively, as it is easy to miss one out. Note down every likely entry you locate, thus saving yourself needless repetition if you do not find exactly what you are looking for.

- Names might be misspelled, written phonetically, or misread by the Registrar General's clerks compiling the central indexes.
- Two entries might be mistakenly combined to make one, or even omitted altogether. If you know when and where the event happened, it is worth approaching the local registrar's office.
- There is no alternative to purchasing a birth or death certificate if you want all the registration details.

Looking for a birth

Until 1874, the district registrars were responsible for collecting information about births in their area, thereafter registration became the responsibility of the parents. Births are supposed to be registered within 42 days, extended with a financial penalty to six months. You should therefore always search at least the two subsequent quarterly indexes after that covering the three-month period in which the birth took place, as not everyone registered their children's births promptly, if at all. Indeed, there is evidence that in the early years of civil registration some parents opted either to have their children baptized or to register their births, but not both, in the misguided belief that they had a choice. So if you cannot locate a birth, look at the baptism registers serving the parish where your family lived.

Starting in the September quarter of 1911, the mother's given maiden name has been recorded in the indexes, making it easier to find the correct registration of people with common names and to locate brothers and sisters.

Illegitimacy

Late registration of a birth to parents who later married may give a false date to conceal illegitimacy. A child born out of wedlock was usually registered under its mother's surname, though before 1875 there was nothing to prevent an informant naming or inventing a putative father for an illegitimate infant. Later, only if the father agreed and was either present to register the birth, or his written or sworn acknowledgement of paternity was produced, could his name be inserted. After the Legitimacy Act of 1926, if this child's parents subsequently married the child became legitimate and the birth was frequently registered a second time, under the married name. Sometimes children born to couples in an illicit relationship might have had a concocted father's name to protect a man who was already married to someone else, or both parents passed themselves off as married to each other when they were nothing of the kind.

Some reasons why you may not find a birth registration

Parents sometimes altered their children's names at baptism. The officiating minister was obliged to inform the Registrar General, and although the registration itself was then amended, the index was not. First names might later be dropped or reversed, names shortened into nicknames, or further names adopted, so always ask your relatives about this. Occasionally, informal childhood names might stick with someone throughout later life and the true registered name be lost, for instance 'Joan' seems to have been popular in the 1930s, but the registered name was totally different. Where parents had not decided on a name at the time of registration, the child would be recorded as 'male' or 'female', and names added later, but again left out of the index.

Births were registered in the district where they took place, which might not be local to the parents' usual residence, so faced with several entries of the same surname, forename and quarter of the year, the correct registration district may be inadvertently ruled out. If you discover several possible entries, take the most likely one first, list them all in order of probability and then request a reference check, to stop at the first entry which tallies with your certain facts about the parents' names, date of birth or birthplace, for instance. You will then be refunded any balance of the search fees for the remaining unchecked index entries. Sometimes you can solve problems of identification by searching the *International Genealogical Index*, which is readily available on microfiche and CD-ROM, as well as at **www.familysearch.org**, or the *British Isles Vital Records Index*, on CD-ROM, both of which contain extracted details of baptisms, and which may eliminate one or two of the possible registrations. Neither database includes people alive today.

If you fail to locate a likely entry, and you have tried the various permutations outlined above, including unamed 'male' or 'female' registrations, consider the possibility that you may have been looking in the wrong year, or that your information is incorrect. Examine the indexes for the previous and following years, extending this if necessary to two years either side of the expected birth, then three years, and so on. This may pick up other siblings' births, or children of the same surname in the relevant district; note down the index details, because if you still cannot find your direct ancestor, such a birth certificate of a brother, sister or parent can be an invaluable substitute.

Make sure you order a 'full' birth certificate, because a 'short' one will omit the parents' names and personal details, and so is of little genealogical value other than confirming the child's name, sex, date and place of birth and the district where the birth was registered. If the birth registration you want occurred within the last 50 years you will need to supply details of the child's parents anyway, or produce some kind of personal identification for yourself.

The birth certificate

A full birth certificate sets out the date and place of birth, registered forenames, surname and sex of the infant, both parents' names including the mother's former or maiden name, the father's occupation, name, address and relationship to the child of the informant, whether he or she signed or marked the register, and the date of registration. Since 1 April 1969, the parents' birthplaces and usual address have been recorded too. There is space left on the certificate for any names given to the infant after registration.

When the informant was one of the parents, his or her address might be different to that of the birth. It is always worth looking at the informant column, because if the child was illegitimate it might be another relative, whose name, relationship to the child and address will be recorded.

Adoption

Indexes of adoption by court order in England and Wales since 1 January 1927 are accessible to the public only at the Family Records Centre in London, but you can request an index search and adoption certificate by post, by sending your application to Adoptions Section, General Register Office, Smedley Hydro, Southport, Merseyside PR8 2HH, making your cheque, postal order, international money order or draft payable to 'ONS'. If no trace is found you will receive a partial refund. The indexes cannot be used as a cross-reference to the indexes of birth registrations, because they are arranged under the adoptive names only. To 31 March 1959, a full adoption certificate contained the child's date of birth, adoptive name, the names and address of the adopting parents, the adoptive father's occupation, the date of the adoption order and the court making it, plus the date of entry in the Adopted Children's Register. From 1950 to 31 March 1959, merely the child's country of birth is recorded, but later certificates disclose the English or Welsh registration or sub-registration district or country of birth if elsewhere. A short adoption certificate contains the adoptive name and date of birth, and registration or sub-registration district (before 1 April 1959 the country of birth), if embedded in the adoption order.

Only the adopted person is given sufficient information to order a birth certificate. You can make a link with the actual birth registration in one of two ways. If you were adopted before 12 November 1975, you are obliged under the Adoption Act 1976 to see a counsellor before you receive enough facts to enable you to obtain a copy of your birth certificate, and thus discover the names of your natural parents. The aim of the counselling is to help you understand the possible consequences of trying to establish contact with your true parents. You can ask for an interview with an adoption counsellor at the Family Records Centre, or if it is more convenient, ask your local Social Services Department. The Registrar General will notify the counsellor of your original name, that of your birth mother and possibly that of your birth father, and the details of the adoption order, which is then passed on to you. However, if you were adopted on or after 12 November 1975, and you have reached the age of 18, you do not have to see a counsellor unless you elect to, and you can apply direct to the Registrar General for your birth details. The National Organisation for Counselling Adoptees and their Parents (NORCAP), 112 Church Road, Wheatley, Oxfordshire OX33 1LU (**www.norcap.org.uk**) can lend support.

You might want to insert your name and address in the Adoption Contact Register. Part 1 is for adopted persons, and Part 2 contains names and addresses supplied by birth parents or other relatives of adopted people who would like to renew contact. If a match is found, the Registrar General will send the adopted person the registered details of the relatives to enable them to get in touch, and the relatives will be advised that this has been done, but not be given the adopted person's address. You can obtain an application form from the Adoptions Section, and there is a fee for registration. It usually takes about two to three weeks to process applications. Don't forget that if you change your mind, or move, you will need to let the Adoptions Section know.

Adoptions before 1927 were often effected privately, or via parish officers, the Board of Guardians of the local Poor Law Union, or channelled through charities, to which there are no central indexes open to the public. Most parish records are now in county record offices. *Poor Law Union Records,* by J. Gibson, C. Rogers and C. Webb, contains references to the known whereabouts of material relating to Union adoptions and boardings out (fostering). You will need to approach the charities direct, using *Whitaker's Almanack, Charities Digest* or the phone book as your guide.

Abandoned children

Foundlings are indexed under 'Unknown' following births of children registered with surnames beginning with 'Z'. A special indexed Abandoned Children Register has been kept since 1 January 1977 by the Family Records Centre, giving the date and place of birth, name, surname and sex.

Stillbirths

Certified copies of registrations of stillbirths from 1 July 1927 can be issued only with the Registrar General's permission to the parents, or if they are both dead, to the siblings of a stillborn child. There are no indexes available to the public, so you will need to apply in writing to the Registrar General in Southport.

Looking for a marriage

As a full birth certificate should tell you the names of both parents, and the mother's former name, you can then start looking for their marriage. It may be that the earliest date on your family tree is that of a marriage anyway. If you know exactly where it took place it might be easier and cheaper to search the original registers which would have been signed by them, at least two witnesses, and the officiating priest. Many thousands of church registers have now been deposited in county record offices, but some remain in the church or chapel itself. Check their present whereabouts with the county record office, remembering to give the year or approximate years in which you are interested. The website **www.genuki.org.uk** has links to record offices with websites; otherwise look in R. Blatchford, *The Family and Local History Handbook* for addresses and contact phone numbers.

Many registers are available on microfilm or microfiche, and may have been indexed. To find out if you can hire a copy at a family history centre near you, search the Family History Library catalogue at **www.familysearch.org**. A number of registers are now being loaded onto the Internet, in addition to the entries in the *International Genealogical Index*. Search the county by county listing of *Births, Marriages and Deaths on the Web*, 2 Parts, compiled by S. A. Raymond, and **www.genuki.org.uk** for your county of interest for updates and access to many of these databases. *The British Isles Vital Records Index*, on CD-ROM, includes marriages up to about 1906, but not all the information you would find on the actual certificates themselves. Look at J. Gibson and E. Hampson, *Marriage and Census Indexes for Family Historians,* for details about indexed marriage registers. Such indexes can save you a lot of time, but will not reveal all the information in the original record, because they are much shortened versions and should be treated as a finding aid only.

The centralized marriage indexes from 1 July 1837 contain two entries for each marriage, one for the groom and one for the bride. The given registration district, volume and page references will exactly tally. From the March quarter of 1912 the spouse's surname appears as a cross-reference against each index entry. You can search scanned images of these indexes online at **www.1837online/com/Trace2web** for a fee and an ongoing database of entries up to 1983 at **www.freembmd. rootsweb.com**. With this last option, if you are uncertain of the name of the other spouse, you can click on the given page reference for the person you are looking for and the screen will display the names of everyone else whose marriages were registered on the same page. You can then see if any of the details look familiar with known facts in your family, or try your luck with an application for a paid reference check.

Begin searching the same quarter of the year of the eldest known child's birth and work backwards (you may have to search several years afterwards as well!). If you are unsure who was the eldest child then the search may be protracted, so look for the person with the more unusual surname or forename, as there will be fewer volumes to cross-check for an identical match with the spouse. Sometimes you may not find the bride's name in the index if her former name given on her child's birth certificate was that of a previous marriage, and she reverted to her birth surname on marrying the child's father, or vice versa. If you see an entry that otherwise looks correct, have it checked in case there has been an indexing error, especially if the other known facts agree. Occasionally the parents were not married at all, but cohabited in a common law arrangement, perhaps because one of them was already married. Sometimes they may have married out of the country, so try the indexes to Scottish, Irish or overseas marriages, particularly if the husband was in the armed forces.

The marriage certificate

Having found the correct entry, you can then apply for a copy of the certificate. This will indicate the date and place of the religious or civil ceremony, the denomination if a church or chapel, and whether the wedding was after the reading of banns, by licence or registrar's certificate. The full name, age, current marital status, rank, profession or occupation, and residence of each party at the time of marriage, is followed by the father's name and occupation, plus the names of at least two witnesses and that of the officiating minister.

Tips
- Asserted ages can be misleading. Until raised to 16 in 1929, 12 was the minimum age at which a girl could marry, and 14 for a boy. Up to 1969, parental consent was necessary until the minor attained 21 and his or her majority. Thereafter it has been 18. A certificate may therefore describe a party as 'of full age' or a 'minor'. An under-age couple marrying against their parents' wishes might add on a few years, conversely where there was a significant different in their ages, one party might add on or deduct some.
- Given occupations were frequently exaggerated to suggest a higher social or employment status, whilst the precise nature of others might now seem obscure or obsolete. You may need to consult the *Oxford English Dictionary*, or C. Waters, *A Dictionary of Old Trades, Titles and Occupations* for explanations.
- Addresses were often only temporary lodgings, to comply with the legal residential requirement of three weeks for banns to be read, or 15 days for a licence, in order to wed in the chosen church.

- Be wary of the father's given name, since this might have been invented to conceal illegitimacy, or have been given in good faith when the person had been brought up by grandparents or as part of another family. If the father had died some time before, his forename might have been forgotten, or never known by his offspring, so a guess might have been made from his initials. A certificate may not always disclose that a father was already dead, and similarly if he had disappeared out of his child's life and was thought no longer living, he might be described as deceased. If the father's surname is different to that of the child, then this may indicate adoption or fostering just as much as natural parentage. Where the birth certificate has a gap for the father's name, illegitimacy may be assumed, but not guaranteed.

- Don't ignore the names of the witnesses, who might be relatives of the couple. If your searches grind to a halt you may be able to pick up the trail again by pursuing their family background, which may soon merge with your own.

- If one of the parties was widowed this points to an earlier marriage, and the possible existence of half- or step-brothers and sisters for your ancestor. When it was the bride, you should find her birth surname from that given for her father on the certificate.

- In 1907 it became legal for a man to marry his deceased wife's sister, and after 1960 the sister of his divorced wife. Since 1968 a step-parent has been able to marry a step-child aged 18 or over, provided that person has not been treated as a child of the prospective partner's family while under age.

Divorce

Divorced partners are described as such on marriage certificates. From 11 January 1858, petitions for divorce dissolving a marriage by decree absolute have been filed in the Principal Registry of the Court for Divorce and Matrimonial Causes (from 1873 part of the Probate, Family and Admiralty Division of the High Court of Justice, and since 1970 called the Family Division), in London, and in regional district registries since 1927. Originally, cases could only be heard in London, but from 1922 a number of assize towns were able to hear undefended divorce petitions, and since 1967 county courts have granted divorces. Microfilmed copies of the indexes to divorce petitions filed in London between 1858 and 1958 (including unsuccessful ones) and applications for legitimation of children, judicial separation, protection of earnings and property of wives, and for restitution of conjugal rights of co-habitation, can be searched at the Family Records Centre, and in the National Archives, Kew. The indexes are arranged in tranches of years, with some overlap, so you may need to search several sets of these covering the years you want. Each case is given a unique number and is filed under the year the petition was lodged, which might be a few years before any divorce was granted. From 1938 onwards the indexes list the cases by name.

All the numbered petitions between 1858 and 1927, and other relevant papers can be inspected in the National Archives. These include affidavits, responses of defendants, cited co-respondents and amended petitions, copies of marriage certificates, children's birth certificates, and summaries of the evidence produced to the court. There is rarely an indication of the final outcome, or a copy of the decree nisi granted to the petitioner six weeks (originally six months) before the final decree absolute or of the decree absolute itself. From 1927 to 1937 the paperwork relating only to those cases heard in London has been preserved in the National Archives, and from 1938 to 1954 only a selection of those London cases deemed to be of especial interest have been kept. For locally heard causes, only the decrees have been saved, so you will need to apply to the Decree Absolute Search Section, Principal Registry of the Family Division, First Avenue House, 42–9 High Holborn, London WC1V 6NP for an index search and a copy of the decree itself. There is a charge for every ten-year period or part of a ten-year period searched, including a copy of the decree. You can also apply to this address for a copy of any decree granted in London, quoting the National Archives index reference number and year, and the fee should be less. However, the Principal Registry indexes relate only to successful petitions and are arranged by the year of the decree. If the divorce was granted in a county court within the last five years, you are advised to contact it direct, since the search charge is a lot less.

Until 1923, wives could only sue for divorce if they could prove their husbands had not only committed adultery, but had shown them life-threatening cruelty. This meant that divorce was often denied, and they might have to settle for a judicial separation which did not free either party to remarry. A deserting husband could resurface at any time to claim his wife's property, earnings or inheritance, until the passing of the Married Womens

Property Acts in the 1880s, so she might be forced to apply for a protection order over them.

Before 1858, marriages ended in a variety of ways other than death. Divorce permitting remarriage could only be granted by a private act of Parliament or if the marriage had been declared null and void by a church court. An act of Parliament was expensive and involved two preliminary stages: a judicial separation granted by a church court was the precursor to a common law writ of trespass filed by the husband in the Court of King's Bench or Court of Common Pleas, alleging criminal conversation (crim.con.) against the wife's lover, and seeking damages. Armed with a favourable judgment the husband could then promote a private bill for divorce. A marriage declared by a church court rendered it void only on certain grounds (an error in the banns or licence, incest, incapacity of mind or body, a pre-exisiting marriage, pre-contract to marry, and after 1753 minors without the written consent of parents). The practical effect of this was as if the marriage had never taken place. An annulment made a marriage voidable if it had taken place by force or with the wrong person, or when underage. The marriage remained valid and the children legitimate. It could later be declared null and void by a church court.

A divorce '*a mensa et thoro*' granted by a church court merely led to a lifetime suspension of the union, as with an annulment, neither party being released to remarry. Some marital disputes were pursued in the Consistory Court of London in preference to local church courts. Appeals against court decisions went to the Court of Arches and finally to the High Court of Delegates to 1833 and thereafter to the Judicial Committee of the Privy Council. The records of the London Consistory Court are held by London Metropolitan Archives. Look at J. Houston, *Index of Cases in the Records of the Court of Arches in Lambeth Palace Library, 1660-1913,* for names of appellants. The Process Books have been filmed. High Court of Delegates records and those of the Privy Council are among the National Archives, Kew.

Private separation deeds were mutual agreements to maintain the status quo, the husband promising to pay the wife alimony and the wife indemnifying him against any future liability for her debts in cases brought by her creditors. They were not enforceable in a court of law, but usually had the advantage of both parties agreeing not to sue the other in relation to the marital breakdown and any future 'marriage'. Desertion was a more popular resort, the absconder sometimes, but not invariably, assuming a new identity, maybe even entering into a bigamous marriage or common law union. Wife-selling involved her being led by the halter to a public place and exchanged for a nominal sum like a chattel. None of these solutions legally freed either party for remarriage, so any issue by later partners was strictly illegitimate.

Looking for a death

Family historians tend to overlook death certificates as a genealogical source, yet they reveal addresses both for the deceased and the informant, plus any family relationship between them. This can be invaluable if death occurred close to a census year, as you can then search this address for other occupants as well as the named person. A death certificate marks a date beyond which you are unlikely to discover anything more about the deceased, unless from the will, obituary notice in a newspaper, or gravestone inscription, and it tells you where the informant was then living, so you can track his or her later movements. Deaths were required to be notified within eight days to the local district registrar (reduced to five days in 1953), by a witness, someone in attendance during the last illness, the occupier of the premises, or by the person causing disposal of the body, such as a coroner. Since 1874 a doctor's medical certificate has been mandatory, setting out the time and cause of demise, supplemented since 1 January 1927 with details of any secondary causes. From 1902 onwards, two doctors' signatures have been necessary for cremation. The doctor's medical certificate is presented by the informant to the registrar, and the resulting death certificate is the undertaker's authority for burial or cremation.

The indexes from 1837 contain the surname, forenames, registration district, volume and page number of each person. Between the first quarter of 1866 and the first quarter of 1969, they include given ages as well. Because so many people died young it can sometimes be difficult to identify the person you want if they died before this. The indexes from the June quarter 1969 record instead the date of birth, if known. Indexes of unknown persons' deaths appear after surnames beginning with Z. If you are applying for the death certificate of someone aged 16 or younger, you will be asked to give the names of the parents.

The death certificate will tell you the date and place of demise, the person's name, sex, age, occupation, cause of death and duration of the last illness, plus the signature, description and residence of the informant, and the date of registration. In the case of a married woman, you will find the name and occupation of her husband and whether she was widowed. Certificates for deaths from 1 April 1969 onwards give the date and place of birth, and usual address of the deceased, if known, and the maiden name if a married woman. This will enable you to look for the wedding, and if she was a widow, for the death of her husband.

> **Tips**
> - A person may have died under a different identity to that of his or her birth registration. Formal name changes are not obligatory. People can easily disappear, only to resurface and commence a new life.
> - A person may have died outside his or her usual area, so positive identification may be difficult if the name was a common one.
> - Given ages at death may be wildly inaccurate. Until 1866, when applying for a death certificate, specify the minimum age you would expect the deceased to have been, to avoid being supplied with that of an infant, as ages are not included in the indexes.
> - Cause of death may indicate inherited diseases or family proneness to certain illnesses.

Possible substitutes for finding out about deaths

To save time, try the online database of deaths to 1983 at **www.freebmd.rootsweb.com**. You can also search images of all the death indexes using the charged service at **www.1837online.com/Trace2web**. Details of date and place of death from 1858 onwards can be obtained from the annual published National Probate Indexes of wills and administration grants of people leaving property in England and Wales. You can search these in the public search room of the Principal Probate Registry in London, and in each of the local district probate registries. Consult **www.courtservice.gov.uk/using_courts/wills_probate/probate/probate_famhist.htm** for their addresses and contact details, or look at R. Blatchford, *The Family and Local History Handbook*. Microfiche copies of the indexes are widely available, though the end dates vary, for instance, in the Family Records Centre and National Archives, Kew, the indexes run up to 1943 only. *Probate Jurisdictions: Where to Look for Wills*, edited by J. Gibson, lists cut-off dates of local holdings. The indexed death duty registers, 1796–1903, on microfilm to 1857 in the Family Records Centre and the National Archives, and available as original documents in the National Archives from 1858 to 1903, also note dates of death of most of the people whose estates attracted this tax. The filmed indexes for the entire period are available at both sites, and from 1889 include dates of death. However, not everyone made a will, neither were letters of administration always applied for when someone died intestate, and not every estate was liable.

Churchyard, cemetery and cremation registers, and memorials, should reveal at least the person's date of death and age. Cemetery burial registers and headstone inscriptions often refer to other family members interred in the same plot. There is a complete list of cemeteries and crematoria, with contact details in R. Blatchford, *The Family and Local History Handbook*. For London, try P. W. Wolfston, *Greater London Cemeteries and Crematoria,* revised by C. Webb. To locate a particular grave, most cemeteries will have a plan marking out each plot number. These can be inspected, together with the burial registers, in a county record office, at the local authority or private cemetery company office by appointment, or on your behalf. You may have to pay a fee for this. You may be lucky and find a transcript of gravestone inscriptions for the place in question. The county record office, local history library, Society of Genealogists and the National Library of Wales, in Aberystwyth, will be able to advise on their holdings.

The Federation of Family History Societies is in the process of compiling a national database of burial entries extracted from church, chapel and cemetery records throughout England and Wales. You can search the first edition of this *National Burial Index*, containing 5.4 million names from more than 4,000 records, on CD-ROM, but it is far from complete, and some counties have not been covered at all. You can find out which places and dates are covered from the database itself, or by visiting the Federation website at **www.ffhs.org.uk**. The date ranges vary widely between 1538 and 2000, but it is especially good for the years between 1813 and 1837. Updated editions are planned.

Hospital records

When a death occurred in a hospital or infirmary, surviving admission and discharge registers may provide more information. You will not be able to search these books yourself, since they are closed for 100 years, but the custodian may search them for you. You can find the whereabouts of such documentation by searching a database called HOSPREC, at **www.pro.gov.uk.**

Coroners' inquests

When registration was by coroner's order, look for a local newspaper account of the inquest. Coroners are obliged to retain their records for 15 years, after which they can exercise their discretion about their disposal (usually to the county record office) or destruction. Generally, coroners' records remain closed to the public for 75 years, and not all are transferred to county record offices; access to them is granted by the coroner's prior written consent. Many reports before 1875 survive, and *Coroners' Records in England and Wales*, edited by J. Gibson and C. Rogers, gives a county by county listing of most known local holdings. Try also the online catalogue to some county reports at **www.a2a.pro.gov.uk.** In the case of post mortems, the examination reports are kept by coroners, but again there should be a local press item. If the coroner's inquest ruled that a person died as the result of foul play and the assailant could be identified, the report served as an indictment and would be filed among the records of the relevant assize session for that county, in the National Archives.

Coming up against a brick wall

If the centralized indexes of births, marriages and deaths have yielded nothing, you may wonder what to try next to locate a particular ancestor. If you have some idea of the year and vicinity, then the following sources may help, assuming you have already trawled the *International Genealogical Index* and *British Isles Vital Records Index*, and explored the possibility of local registrations which were missed out of the central indexes:

- Baptism registers may contain entries of children whose births were not registered. Bear in mind that in the nineteenth century fewer parents took their offspring for baptism. You will also need to consider that a large number of new churches and chapels were erected during the nineteenth century and others were deconsecrated as congregations shrank.

- From 1862, statutory admission and discharge registers began to be kept by schools receiving government funding. However, you will discover that many only start in 1880, because education was not made compulsory countrywide for children between five and ten until then, though local districts could do so from 1870. The books may still be stored in the school, or may have been deposited in the local county record office. The entries generally give each new pupil's name, date of birth, father's name, place of residence and occupation, date of admission, progression through each stage of schooling from infant class to senior, or until the date of departure, giving the reason and place moved to if changing schools. The books are often indexed making it possible to trace the attendance of several generations of a family.

- School attendance registers, kept by local education authorities from 1875, disclose similar information, as well as placements of youngsters in schools throughout the county. The 'particulars registered ... concerning the deaths and births of children' submitted to local education authorities by district registrars ensured that their books were an up-to-date summary of local educational need, provision and satisfactory completion. The returns of deaths and births record the date and place of the event, the name and sex of each child, the father's name, and the description and abode of the informant. Like the school attendance registers, surviving returns are most likely to be found in county record offices.

- Often unknown and untouched by family historians are the compulsory smallpox vaccination registers, dating from a series of enactments after 1853, and recording up to 1948 under sub-district the date and place of each registered birth in England and Wales, the child's name, sex, father's name (or that of the mother if illegitimate), his or her occupation, and the date when notice of the birth was provided by the district registrar to the local vaccination officer. The registers also record the date of the medical certificate reporting successful vac-cination, cases of insusceptibility in spite of three failed vaccination attempts, or of children having already had smallpox, or the date of death if it happened before vaccination could take place. *Poor Law Union Records*, by J. Gibson, C. Rogers and C. Webb, in three parts, indicates the whereabouts of surviving registers, which are mostly in county record offices.

Parents were put on three months' notice by the district registrar to take their baby for vaccination by the public vaccinator or medical practitioner where they lived. Since parents may have registered a birth away from their usual place of residence, this could prove difficult to enforce, and similarly newcomers with children whose births had been registered in another district might not have taken them to be vaccinated.

Six-monthly parish lists of names of children lacking certificates were presented by the registrar to the Poor Law Union Board of Guardians, and to the governing vestry meeting or council so that parish officials could make further enquiries, and extant collections of these are mentioned in the above books.

The vaccination registers are augmented by weekly vaccination returns made by the vaccinators to the registrars, giving the places of residence of the parents at the time of vaccination, but not their names, nor the child's date and place of birth. This should prove sufficient for you to track the birth registration or to search the census returns of that address if it was close to one of the decadal census years (1861, 1871, 1881, 1891 or 1901). Infant deaths were annotated against each entry too.

Monthly returns of registered deaths of infants under a year old, as well as births, were produced by district registrars to vaccination officers, recording the date and place, name, age, father's name and occupation, cross-referenced to the returns of birth if both occurred in the same district. The father's home address was supplied in cases where death took place elsewhere, such as in hospital.

A major drawback of the above records is that if a birth went unregistered then the child slipped through the net, but they may be of assistance if you have missed crucial entries in the centralized indexes, or if names were omitted from them.

• Registers of the British Lying-In Hospital, Holborn, London, contain details of admissions between 1749 and 1868 by personal recommendation of servicemen's wives and poor married women for their confinements. These are available on microfilm in the Family Records Centre, the National Archives at Kew, and in family history centres. The father's occupation, current whereabouts or last place of legal settlement are noted, as well as the mother's name and date of admission, discharge or death, and the child's date of birth.

From 1849 onwards, the parents' place of marriage is included too. The birth and baptism details have been extracted for inclusion in the *International Genealogical Index*, but you will need to search the original microfilmed registers for the full entry.

- Notices of intended chapel or civil marriages after 1 July 1837, made to superintendent district registrars and minuted by Poor Law Union Boards of Guardians, indicate where they were to take place. They were often signed by the informant. However, notification of intent does not necessarily mean that the ceremony actually took place. Surviving records and their whereabouts are listed in *Poor Law Union Records*.

- Burial Boards were set up after 1850 in London and from 1852 in the provinces to administer public cemeteries when churchyards were closed for reasons of public hygiene. The registers are now held at the cemetery offices or in county record offices. They contain the name of the deceased, abode (which may have been elsewhere), occupation, age, date and place of death, date of interment and plot number in consecrated ground (or unconsecrated if the person was not a member of the Established Church of England). You may find references to stillbirths, and some entries show the relationship of the defunct to the head of the family or to the person paying for the burial, the cost of the plot and who paid for it. Remember that not everyone was buried where he or she died, neither could everyone afford to purchase grave space. Some people continued to be interred in the churchyard or from 1902 opted to be cremated. Some of the Burial Board registers have been included in the *National Burial Index*.

- Local press announcements of births, marriages and deaths provide another source of information. However, you will need to know the approximate date of the event, since such newspapers were generally published weekly, and few have been extensively indexed. You can find out which newspapers served your area from *Willing's Press Guide*. You may find more death announcements, obituaries and funeral notices than those for births and marriages.

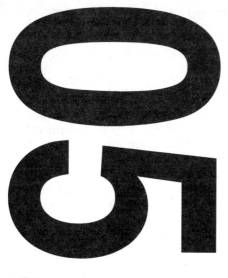

05

births, marriages and deaths in the Channel Islands, Isle of Man, Scotland and Ireland

In this chapter you will learn:
- what sources are indexed and online
- how to apply for copies or registrations
- how some provide direct links to an earlier era

The Channel Islands

Civil registration of births, deaths and marriages began on Jersey in August 1842. The records are kept by the Superintendent Registrar, in St Helier. A five-year prepaid search can be undertaken only by staff. Copies of the indexes to 1900 are available in the Société Jersiaise and the Channel Islands Family History Society research room. The certificates are similar in content to those of England and Wales, though marriage certificates include the couple's birthplaces. There is also an Adoption Register, commencing in 1948.

Statutory registrations of births, non-Anglican marriages and deaths on Guernsey date from 1840, on Alderney from 1925 and of deaths on Sark from 1915. Since 1919 all marriages on these islands have been registered in Guernsey, plus births and deaths from 1925. Registers of births and deaths on Aldemay from 1850, and of marriages since 1886 are held by the Greffier, on Aldernay. The records and indexes are held by the Greffier, in St Peter Port. The indexes are open to the public by appointment, on payment of an admission fee, and there is a postal specific search service available for a five-year period, including the cost of a certificate. Deaths occurring before 1963 are indexed under parish, and married women dying before 1949 are listed by their maiden names. Anglican weddings prior to 1919 are registered by parish. You can inspect microfilm copies of the birth indexes and registers, 1840–1966, death indexes and registers, 1840–1963, marriage indexes, 1841–1966, and registers, 1841–1901, at family history centres, where you may have to pay a small fee to hire them in. The civil registration indexes from 1842 to 1969 are also available on microfilm in the Society of Generalogists in London. Some indexed births, marriages and deaths between 1831 and 1958 in the Channel Islands are included in the indexed Miscellaneous Non-statutory Foreign Returns of the Registrar General, available on microfilm in the Family Records Centre, the National Archives, and in family history centres. The *International Genealogical Index* is also worth consulting, at **www.familysearch.org**, on CD-ROM, or on microfiche.

Isle of Man

Registers of births and deaths on the Isle of Man after 1878, marriages since 1883, and an Adopted Children Register starting in 1928, are in the care of the Civil Registry, Douglas.

Voluntary civil registration of births and marriages had, however, been possible since 1849. An appointment is not necessary, but recommended, to search the indexes. There is an additional charge for a certificate, and you may make postal applications. The staff undertake index searches based on a fee per year requested, plus the cost of any certificate. Also at the Registry are stored records of people married outside the Established Church from 1849 onwards, with a few birth registrations after 1821. You can pay a small fee to hire in at a family history centre microfilm copies of the above births, baptisms, marriages and burials recorded between 1821 and 1964. Extracts of births, baptisms and marriages up to 1906 are also included in the *British Isles Vital Records Index*, available on CD-ROM, and microfilm copies of the civil registration indexes are held in the Manx National Heritage Library, in Douglas.

Scotland

Civil registration of births, marriages and deaths in Scotland commenced on 1 January 1855. The computerized indexes (including adoptions from 1930, and divorces from 1984) and the registers are held at the General Register Office (GROS), in Edinburgh, which is open to searchers aged 16 or over. A search pass is issued before or on the day by postal or personal application, based on a daily or weekly fee. There are also monthly, quarterly and yearly rates. A limited number of cheaper 'Apex' bookings may be available from time to time, and can be done by phone. These schemes guarantee a seat for you in the search room up to 10 a.m., unless you advise otherwise. All other seats are offered on a first-come first-served basis. A part-day search fee is available after 1 p.m. Access to the digital copies of the registers is self-service. Once you have found an entry in one of the indexes, you can also help yourself to the relevant microfilm and copy down the full registration details. You can buy official extracts of any entry, if you choose.

Looking at the indexes

You do not need to go to Edinburgh, however. The indexes to registered births to 1901, marriages to 1926, and to deaths up to 1951, can be searched at **www.scotlandspeople.gov.uk** with an extra year being added annually. The service is pay-per-view. Images of the actual birth records (excluding 1855), death registrations (also excluding 1855) and marriages (except for

1889, 1897, 1899–1901, and 1921) are online too. Alternatively you can order transcriptions of registered births, marriages and deaths from 1855 to 1990 using the charged service operated by www.scotsorigins.com. Copies of births registered in 1855 are available to hire on microfilm in family history centres. You can also search the annual Scottish indexes between 1855 and 1956 on microfilm at family history centres, plus the filmed registers from 1855 to 1875, for 1881, and for 1891. Consult the Family History Library catalogue at www.familysearch.org for their call numbers. Another option is to visit the Family Records Centre, in London, and book yourself a slot at one of the two computer terminals with links to the Scottish GRO indexes to births, baptisms and marriages in the Old Parochial Registers of the Church of Scotland since 1553, centralized civil registrations of births, marriages and deaths from 1855 to date, and to the 1881, 1891 and 1901 census returns. You pay per half hour, up to a maximum of two hours per session. There are application forms available for you to complete to send to the General Register Office in Edinburgh with your fee for a certified copy of any entry. You can also access similar computerized links at some local Scottish registration offices, which may also have facilities for you to consult microfilm copies of the statutory registers for their area. A list of all the Scottish registration district offices is published in R. Blatchford, *The Family and Local History Handbook*.

The indexes list males and females separately under surname, forename, parish or registration district and entry number. From 1966, the district or parish registration number is cited too. The mother's maiden name is written alongside her child's name in the birth indexes after 1929. Be careful to look under surnames with the prefix Mc- and Mac-. Married women may well be registered twice or more under their married and maiden names.

Scottish birth registration

Scottish birth, marriage and death certificates are far more informative than their English and Welsh counterparts. Exceptionally, the birth registrations in 1855 reveal the exact time of birth, ages and birthplaces of both parents, their date and place of marriage, and the number and sex of older siblings (but not their names), whether they are still alive, and the parents' usual address. Thus you can discover where the parents came from and their approximate birth years, where they were married and how many earlier offspring you should be looking for. As these events took place before civil registration began, you can pursue them in the indexes to the Old Parochial Registers, which are available online at **www.scotlandspeople.gov.uk**, on CD-ROM, and on microfilm. A certificate from 1855 may guide you to the whereabouts of the parents in the 1851 and 1861 census returns, and stretch the family's history back to the start of the century. Between 1856 and 1860, Scottish birth registrations were modified to follow the English model, except that the hour of birth was retained. In 1861, the date and place of the parents' marriage were restored.

Adoptions and stillbirths

An Adopted Children Register was started in Scotland in 1930, and information about birth parents can be released to adopted persons aged 17 and over. Indexes to adoptions in Scotland are embedded in the computerized birth indexes, but the resulting certificates will not reveal the names of birth parents or the original registered name. Birth Link, Family Care, 21 Castle Street, Edinburgh EH2 3DN, operates a voluntary contact service for adopted people and their natural relatives.

The Registrar General's consent is necessary for disclosures about stillbirths in Scotland after 1939.

Looking for a marriage in Scotland

From the outset, Scottish marriage indexes show the married name of the wife in brackets next to her maiden name, but only from 1929 is there a cross-reference to her surname beside that of her husband. In 1855 only, the marriage registers contain the following additional details to those appearing on English certificates: dates and places of birth of the couple, any blood relationship between them, whether this was a second, third or later union, the number of living and deceased children by each previous marriage, and the forenames and maiden names of their mothers and if now dead. Between 1856 and 1921 information about birthplaces and previous marriages was omitted, but birthplaces were restored in 1922. Any known blood relationship between the bridal pair ceased to be recorded in the same year.

Up to 1939, if a marriage took the form of a declaration between the parties before witnesses, but without a clergyman being present, as was the case at Gretna Green, in Dumfries and Galloway, it was still legal, though irregular. The marriages are indexed in the usual way, and each entry will record the date of any conviction, decree of declarator or sheriff's warrant issued by the local sheriff's court in connection with these.

Divorce

From 1922, the registers note if a person was divorced. Divorce has been possible in Scotland since 1560, and until 1830 the Commissary Court of Edinburgh dealt with all matrimonial cases including legitimation of children. Since 1831, such cases have been heard by the Court of Session, though some continued to be heard by the Commissary Court to 1835. These records are held by the National Archives of Scotland, in Edinburgh. Look in *The Commissariot of Edinburgh – Consistorial Processes and Decreets, 1658–1800,* which contains a personal name index, then at an index volume for the years between 1801 and 1835, which is arranged by the first initial letter of each surname, for cases in the Commissary Court, and at the indexed printed minute books of the Court of Session for the relevant years from 1831 onwards, to find the document references you require.

From 1855 until 30 April 1984, decrees of divorce inside and outside Scotland notified to the Registrar General were annotated as 'divorce RCE' (Register of Corrected Entries) against the marriage entry itself, though not in the index. A central register of divorces in Scotland has been kept since February 1984 (when sheriff courts also began to hear cases), setting out the names of both parties, the date and place of their marriage, and of its dissolution, with details of any court order relating to children. This information does not appear in the marriage entry itself, but both the online indexes and computerized link to Edinburgh operated by the Family Records Centre in London will disclose the other spouse's name, date of the marriage, together with the divorce year, name of the court, and serial number of the decree.

Looking for a death in Scotland

Indexes to deaths in Scotland include ages from 1866, as with the English and Welsh indexes. Starting in 1974, the maiden surname of the deceased's mother is added too. The 1855 index records in brackets the maiden name of any married woman, and from 1859, the indexes consist of two entries, one under each surname.

The death registrations for 1855 will tell you when and at what age the person died and his or her usual address if not the place of death, plus the birthplace, how long a resident in the district of demise, the duration of the last illness, name of the medical attendant certifying death and when he last saw the deceased,

28938

1861–1965

Extract of an entry in a REGISTER of DEATHS
Registration of Births, Deaths and Marriages (Scotland) Act 1965

No.	1 Name and surname Rank or profession and whether single, married or widowed	2 When and where died	3 Sex	4 Age	5 Name, surname and rank or profession of father Name and maiden surname of mother	6 Cause of death, duration of disease and medical attendant by whom certified	7 Signature and qualification of informant and residence, if out of the house in which the death occurred	8 When and where registered and signature of registrar
636	Margaret Jefferson Married to Arthur Jefferson Theatrical Manager	190 8. December First 8 h. 30 m. a.m 17 Craigmillar Road Langside	F	50 years	George Metcalfe Bootmaker (Retired) Sarah Metcalfe M.S. Brierbly	General Debility as cert by Robert MacLeod Watson L.R.C.P. & S.	William Jefferson Widower (Present)	190 8. December 2 nd at Mount Florida George Burnell Acstat: Registrar J.A.

The above particulars are extracted from a Register of Deaths for the .... District .... of .... Cathcart

in the .... Burgh .... of .... Renfrew

figure 4 Margaret Jefferson's 1908 Scottish death certificate
she was the mother of Stan Laurel
the design of the death certificate is Crown copyright and is reproduced with the permission of the Controller of HMSO

the names of any spouse and offspring, father's name and occupation, mother's name and maiden name and whether the parents were dead. Potentially these certificates may span three generations of a family.

From 1856, however, the deceased's birthplace was omitted, although registrations since 1967 include the date of birth where known, enabling you to find the relevant birth registration. Between 1856 and 1860 a person's marital status was inserted in place of the spouse's name and details about offspring were excluded too, though one may be mentioned as the informant, and from 1861 the spouse's name was restored. Up to 1860, the place of burial and name of the undertaker were also included.

Ireland

Irish civil registration of births, Roman Catholic marriages, and deaths began on 1 January 1864, although marriages between non-Catholics were centrally recorded from 1 April 1845.

Indexes and microfilm copies of original registers sent by superintendent registrars for all Ireland up to 31 December 1921, and those in the Republic after 1 January 1922, are held at the General Register Office, in Dublin. You can carry out a prepaid 'particular search' of the indexes for up to five years. If you intend to cover a longer period you can undertake a general search of the indexes, by paying a daily fee. Photocopies of identified registered entries can then be purchased. Prepaid postal applications can be made too.

There are yearly indexes to births, marriages and to deaths, except for 1878–1903, and 1928–65, when they are arranged by quarter of the year. Later indexes have been computerized. Each person's index entry contains his or her registered surname, forename, registration district, volume and page number. From 1903, the birth indexes record the mother's maiden name, enabling easy identification of all her children. Microfilm copies of the indexes between 1864 and 1958 may be hired in and searched for a small fee in family history centres. Extracts of Irish births registered between 1864 and 1875, and non-Catholic marriages between 1845 and 1863 have been extracted and included in the *International Genealogical Index*, which you can search at **www.familysearch.org**, on CD-ROM, and on microfiche in many family history centres, local libraries and county record offices.

By law, births in Ireland should be registered within 21 days, with an extension up to three months, for which a financial penalty is payable. Late birth and death registrations are listed at the end of the annual index of the year in which the event occurred, late marriage registrations alphabetically by place amongst other marriages. Nonetheless there seems to have been widespread non-registration of these events.

When searching the indexes, look under surnames with and without the prefix O'-, Mc-, and Mac-. Where the pool of surname ranges was relatively small, positive identification of one of several people registered with the same names in the same period can seem daunting, so it helps to know the district or townland of birth.

Searching the indexes in Northern Ireland

Microfilmed duplicate indexes and registers of births and of deaths for the whole of Ireland up to 31 December 1921 are kept in the General Register Office, in Belfast. Thereafter, the indexes relate to births, marriages and deaths registered only in the six northern counties (Antrim, Armagh, Derry, Down, Fermanagh and Tyrone), and these are computerized. You can also examine the indexes to registered marriages in all of Ireland from 1845 to 1921 online.

You can carry out a pre-paid 'particular search' of the indexes for up to five years. If your search is likely to cover a longer period you can undertake a general search of the indexes, by paying a daily fee. Photocopies of identified registered entries can be purchased as well as certificates.

Filmed copies of the indexes and registers from 1922 to 1959 can be hired for searching in family history centres in return for a small fee. If you are able to visit the Family Records Centre in London, you can use the computerized link to the Northern Irish birth registration indexes from 1922 to date. Having identified the entry you want, post your application and fee to the GRO in Belfast for a copy of the certified registration, quoting the index details. You can download the application form at **www.groni.gov.uk/birth_certs.asp**.

The contents of an Irish certificate

Details recorded in the Irish birth, marriage and death registers match those for England and Wales, and like them, are withheld from the public, although you can pay a small fee to inspect microfilmed copies of the birth registers between 1864 and 31 March 1881, 1900 and 1913, and from 1930 to 31 March 1955 (for the Republic of Ireland only), of marriage registers from 1845 to 1870, and deaths between 1864 and 1870, in family history centres.

Pre-1922 duplicate marriage registers for all Ireland, including those between non-Catholics from 1845, are held in the GRO, in Dublin, and in district register offices for Northern Ireland. You can find their addresses in *The Family and Local History Handbook*. Use the centralized indexes to find the relevant district and religious denomination.

The death registers up to the end of 1921 are also arranged by district, and from the beginning include the purported age of the deceased. Date and place of death may be gleaned from the post-1858 annual printed calendars of wills and administrations in the care of the National Archives of Ireland, in Dublin, and for the six northern counties, in the Public Record Office of Northern Ireland, in Belfast.

Adoptions and stillbirths

Adoptions by court order in Northern Ireland commenced on 1 January 1931, the papers being filed in the GRO, in Belfast. Any enquiry should be addressed to the Registrar General. You can apply online or download the application form at **www.groni.gov.uk/adoption_certs.asp**. People over 18 adopted in Northern Ireland can request details of original name and birth mother. There is an Adoption Contact Register similar to that for England and Wales. An indexed Adoption Children Register for court orders made in the Republic since 10 July 1953 is in the GRO, Dublin.

Certified copies of registered stillbirths in Northern Ireland since 1 January 1961, and in the Republic of Ireland from 1 January 1995 can only be issued to the parents. You will need to apply in writing to the appropriate Registrar General in Belfast or Dublin.

Divorce

Records of divorces in Northern Ireland are held by the Royal Courts of Justice, in Belfast.

06

births, marriages and deaths at sea and abroad

In this chapter you will learn:
- how to locate Britons overseas in UK records
- the whereabouts of local registraion material overseas
- how to find American births, marriages and deaths at home and abroad

Britons at sea and on land

Births and deaths of Britons at sea, in the air or abroad (excluding British colonies before independence) were notified to the Registrars General of England and Wales, Scotland and Ireland as appropriate, together with marriages overseas. To 1965 there is a variety of indexes to choose from, but from 1966 onwards a series of union indexes covers all the births, marriages and deaths. You can search the index books to the English and Welsh returns in the Family Records Centre, and microfiche copies of them are available up to 1992 in the National Archives, Kew, in family history centres and other places. For Scots, the indexes and registers are held in the General Register Office, in Edinburgh; indexes and registers relating to overseas Irish citizens are in the General Register Office, Dublin, and for Northern Ireland from 1922 in the General Register Office, Belfast.

The following indexes to registers held by the Registrar General of England and Wales are available for consultation:

- Births and deaths at sea between 1 July 1837 and 1965 (Marine Returns). From 1875 these relate also to passengers on foreign-registered ships leaving and arriving in British ports as well as those registered in the United Kingdom. Unknown deceased are listed after surnames beginning with Z.
- Births and deaths on British civil aircraft from 1947 to 1965 (Air Register Book), including people missing, presumed dead from 1948 to 1980, listed at the end of the index.
- Consular returns of births, marriages and deaths of British subjects abroad from July 1849 to 1965. From 1906, cross-references are given to the surname of the spouse in the marriage indexes, and from 1901, ages are included in the death indexes.
- UK and British High Commission returns of births to 1966, marriages and deaths up to 1965, from the date of independence of the Commonwealth country.
- Returns of births and deaths at sea and abroad, and marriages overseas (marriages at sea may not always have been recognized legally), from 1966 to date. These include births and deaths on British-registered hovercraft from 1 November 1972, and deaths on off-shore installations since 30 November the same year.

You will have to buy certified copies of the registrations to obtain full details. Generally, their content is the same as if the person had been registered in their home country.

In the Family Records Centre, the National Archives and family history centres you can search the microfilmed indexes, 1627–1960, and copies of the Registrar General's Miscellaneous Non-statutory Foreign Returns of births, baptisms, marriages, deaths and burials recorded between 1627 and 1965. Some of these entries relate to foreign nationals at sea, to people in the British colonies, to Asian and African Protectorates. The indexes are incomplete, so search the registers as well. The bulk of these begin only in the early nineteenth century, but you can search them for free. A number of the entries overlap or duplicate those found in the GRO, but others are missing altogether from the official GRO returns listed above.

If you are interested in births and deaths of passengers and crew of merchant ships at sea, have a look at *Births, Marriages and Deaths at Sea*, one of the information leaflets produced by the National Archives, which you can find at **www.nationalarchives.gov.uk**, or request by phone or personal visit. The returns, made to the Board of Trade for deaths of seamen from 1852 and for births, marriages and deaths of passengers from 1854, sometimes contain entries lacking in the above returns, and relate to Scottish and Irish residents and people of other nationalities as well as English and Welsh citizens. The births run up to 1960, deaths to 1964, and there is a register of marriages from 1854–1972. Most of the volumes are indexed, as well as being microfilmed for the years up to 1890, making them easy to use. However, at present you will have to visit the National Archives at Kew to search them.

For details of other vital records concerning Britons abroad, on deposit in the National Archives, look up the country by country listing of references in A. Bevan, *Tracing your Ancestors in the Public Record Office. The British Overseas,* a Guildhall Library Handbook, lists the whereabouts in the United Kingdom of known records of birth, baptism, marriage, death and burial of Britons abroad, again listed by country. Consult T. J. Kemp's *International Vital Records Handbook* for any filmed copies of indexes and registration records of countries throughout the world, for which you might be able to pay to hire in to search in a family history centre. This book also includes start dates of civil registration, copies of application forms, and contact addresses of local registrars.

If your relatives were born, married or died in one of the British colonies, Commonwealth, dominions or territories it is likely that you will have to approach them direct unless there are listed copies of the indexes or records in the above publications. However, the *Australian Vital Records Index, 1788–1905* (which includes New South Wales, Tasmania, Victoria and Western Australia), is available on CD-ROM in the Family Records Centre and the National Archives, at Kew, and in family history centres. The indexes to vital records in New South Wales are also available online at www.bdm.nsw.gov.au/, as are those of British Columbia, in Canada at www.bcarchives.gov.bc.ca/textual/govermt/vstats/v_events.htm for a limited period. More and more vital registration indexes are being loaded onto the Internet, so for up-to-date information on how to access them use a search engine such as www.google.com, keying in 'births, marriages and deaths' and the country, State, or Province in which you are interested.

Service families

The General Register Office indexes to births, baptisms, marriages and deaths of British armed personnel and their families can be searched in the Family Records Centre, and microfiche copies are available up to 1992 in the National Archives, Kew, and in family history centres:

- Regimental registers of births and baptisms, 1761–1924, which include entries relating to events in Britain and Ireland.
- Army chaplains' returns of births and marriages, 1796–1955, and of deaths, 1796–1950, of officers, soldiers and their families recorded at overseas stations. These include Royal Air Force families from 1920 onwards.
- Military, civil and chaplains' registers of births, marriages and deaths in the Ionian Islands, 1818–64.
- Service Departments' registers of births and marriages, 1956–65, and deaths, 1951–65, of Army and RAF personnel and their families, and of Royal Navy families from 1959.
- Annual union indexes to births, to marriages, and to deaths from 1966.

You will need to write to the Overseas Section, General Register Office, PO Box 2, Southport, Merseyside PR8 2JD for a search of surviving marriage registers of a particular regiment. A list of deposited records can be searched in the Family Records Centre. This list is not available anywhere else.

Try also the filmed indexes and registers in the Family Records Centre and the National Archives, Kew, of the Registrar General's Miscellaneous Non-statutory Foreign Returns for additional or overlapping entries.

Men at war

For casualties of war there are special GRO indexes and registers, and once you have located the correct entry you will need to order a certificate in the usual way:

- Natal and South African Field Forces, 1899–1902 (Boer War deaths).
- Army officers, 1914–21 (First World War), including officers in the Royal Flying Corps, and from 1 April 1918, the Royal Air Force.
- Army other ranks, 1914–21, including airmen and airwomen.
- Royal Navy, all ranks, 1914–21, including submariners, Royal Marines, and members of the Royal Navy Air Service. Try also the indexes to Marine returns for this period.
- Indian services, all ranks, 1914–21.
- Army officers, 3 September 1939 to 30 June 1948 (Second World War).
- Army other ranks, for the same period.
- Royal Navy officers, for the same period.
- Royal Navy ratings and petty officers, for the same period.
- Royal Air Force, all ranks, for the same period.
- Indian services, all ranks, for the same period.

The indexes also relate to deaths after the war resulting from wounds.

Deaths of servicemen and women during both wars in England and Wales, such as in hospitals or air crashes, were registered with the local district registrar.

Other places where you can find Britons abroad

First World War deaths of military personnel away from the theatres of war in France and Belgium may be found in the Registrar General's Miscellaneous Non-Statutory Foreign Returns described earlier, and similarly those of victims in the Far East during the Second World War. Consult the filmed indexes for references to these.

You can also search the Debt of Honour Register of the Commonwealth War Graves Commission at **www.cwgc.org** for details of casualties during the First and Second World Wars. There are CD-ROMs relating to *Soldiers (and Officers) Died in the Great War*, in the Family Records Centre, and the National Archives, which provide details about birth, death, place of residence, regiment, rank and regimental number. There is an *Army Roll of Honour* for soldiers killed or dying in the Second World War, on CD-ROM.

If your ancestor was in the armed Services, look beyond the GRO indexes because there is a wealth of information in the National Archives, at Kew. For a detailed explanation of these sources, consult A. Bevan, *Tracing Your Ancestors in the Public Record Office*. You might like to read the relevant online leaflets at **www.nationalarchives.gov.uk**, which are also available on site. There is a brief summary below about some of the things you can discover when you visit.

You can search for service records of soldiers and officers who were discharged or died before 1920 on microfilm in the National Archives, though less than 40 per cent relating to other ranks survived a fire in 1940, and less than 86 per cent of officers' records survived. Document references to the latter can be searched by keying in the officer's surname and initials in the 'search catalogue' option at **www.nationalarchives.gov.uk**. Later service records are held by the Army Personnel Centre, to whom you should apply for information, stating your exact relationship to the individual concerned. A fee is charged for this research service.

The National Archives also holds registers of deaths of Royal Naval ratings from 1854 to 1948, as well as microfilmed indexed service records between 1853 and 1923. From 1873 these are arranged by entry number, found in the indexes. Details of dates and places of birth are mentioned too. Indexes to deaths of officers cover the years 1903 to 1933, and there are also indexed service records for them, which also record birth details. For records about executive officers whose service began after May 1917, and warrant officers after 1931, you will need to contact the Ministry of Defence.

Births and deaths of officers commissioned and men enlisting in the Royal Marines before 1925 and from 1793 and 1790 respectively, can be traced in their records of service, though obviously their careers will run much later than this. For later records contact the Royal Marines Historical Record Office.

For men in the merchant navy, their deaths at sea are recorded from 1851 onwards to 1964, and their service up to discharges as late as 1972 can be traced in various series. Many of these series are indexed, and a number are available on microfilm or microfiche. A ticketing scheme for merchant seamen was introduced in 1835, and these indexed and microfilmed records up to 1857 contain details about their births. After 1857 there was no registration of seamen until 1913, but very few records survive before 1921. A voluntary scheme of certification of competency and long service for masters and mates was introduced in 1845 and gradually made compulsory. The records run to 1921, and include their births, and deaths in service. There are similar series for engineers from 1862, and skippers and mates of fishing boats from 1883. Between 1910 and 1969 these three are merged into one series of indexed registers, which are available on microfilm.

Details of births, marriages and deaths of Royal Flying Corps officers and men before 1 April 1918 are included among the army service records described above, and the births and deaths of members of the Royal Naval Air Service for the same period among those of the Royal Navy. Service records of officers in the Royal Air Force, formed on 1 April 1918, and discharged before 1920 also supply personal information, as do the indexed service records of airmen and airwomen. Later personnel records are kept by the R.A.F. Personnel Management Agency.

Scottish travellers

Scots born, marrying or dying at sea or abroad can be tracked via the following indexes and registers in the General Register Office, in Edinburgh:

- The Marine Register includes births and deaths on board British-registered merchant ships from 1855, where at least one of the parents or the deceased was usually resident in Scotland.
- The Air Register extends to births and deaths on UK-registered civil aircraft from 1948 onwards.
- Separate indexes for each of the births of children of Scottish parentage, marriages, and deaths of Scots in foreign countries notified between 1860 and 1965, and of marriages taking place *lex loci* (according to local law) after 1947 without a British consular official being present.
- Consular Returns of births and deaths of people of Scottish birth or descent from 1914, and marriages from 1917.

- High Commissioners' Returns of births and deaths of persons of Scottish descent or birth in Commonwealth countries from 1964. There are some returns of marriages too.
- Army Returns of births, marriages and deaths of Scots at overseas military stations, 1881–1959, marriages performed by army chaplains abroad since 1892, where one party was Scottish and at least one serving in the armed forces.
- Service Department Registers dating from 1 April 1959 of births, marriages and deaths of Scots and their families serving overseas or employed by the armed forces.
- Army fatalities of Scots, 1899–1902 (Boer War).
- War deaths of other ranks in the army, 1914–18.
- War deaths of Royal Navy petty officers and ratings, 1914–18.
- Incomplete returns of Scots killed in all three forces, 1939–45.

Irish migrants

Irish people who were born, married or died outside Ireland may be found in the following indexed records held at the General Register Office, in Dublin:

- Births of children with at least one parent who was Irish, and deaths of Irish-born people at sea, 1864–85 (indexes are available on request), and 1886 onwards (listed at the end of each yearly index of births and deaths in Ireland itself). These relate exclusively to subjects of the Republic after 1 January 1922.
- Unindexed British Consular Returns of births abroad to Irish parents, and deaths of Irish-born people from 1864 to 1921.
- Registers of births, marriages and deaths of Irish subjects outside the State since 1972, and a register of Lourdes marriages from the same year onwards.
- Births, marriages and deaths of Irish servicemen and their families in the British Army stationed overseas, are indexed at the back of the yearly Irish birth indexes from 1879 to 1930, marriage indexes 1888-1930, and death indexes 1888–1931. Deaths of Irish soldiers serving during the South African War, 1899–1902, are listed in the 1902 death index.

Northern Irish records since 1922

The General Register Office in Belfast holds indexes to the following registers:

- Births at sea of children with at least one Irish parent, and deaths of Northern Irish-born people from 1 January 1922 onwards.
- Consular Returns of births and deaths abroad on similar conditions, from the same date; the returns of marriages commence in 1923. Marriages in foreign countries, according to the local law (*lex loci*) and without a British consular official being present, 1947 onwards.
- High Commissioners' Returns of births, marriages and deaths in Commonwealth countries since 1950.
- Service Department Registers of births, marriages and deaths in the British Army from 1927.
- War deaths of Northern Irish servicemen, 1939–48.

Don't forget that births, marriages and deaths at sea and abroad of Scottish and Irish nationals may also be found in deposited material in the National Archives at Kew, particularly those of ships' passengers and crew, and armed service records, all of which are freely accessible.

The British in India and Asia

Ecclesiastical returns of baptisms, marriages and burials of Britons in India (excluding Roman Catholics before 1836), and civil registrations of birth, marriage and death up to 1968, are now in the Oriental and India Office Collections of The British Library in London. The indexed ecclesiastical registers relate to the Presidencies of Madras from 1698, Bengal from 1709, and Bombay from 1713. The civil registration records are only complete as far as 1948. Former parts of India (Burma, Pakistan and Bangladesh) are included. Look also in *The British Overseas* for other records of Britons in India held in the United Kingdom.

The British Association for Cemeteries in South Asia has deposited a lot of material in this collection, including notes and photographs relating to graves and epitaphs of European residents on the sub-continent, especially those territories once administered by the Honourable East India Company. The Association publishes monograph booklets listing in full gravestone inscriptions in various cemeteries, with potted biographies and articles about the social life of residents.

The Family History Library of the Church of Jesus Christ of Latter-day Saints, in Salt Lake City, Utah, holds copies of many indexes and registers of vital events throughout the world. You can consult its online catalogue at **www.familysearch.org** or consult T. J. Kemp, *The International Vital Records Handbook* for details. By paying a small hiring-in fee you can consult these at any of the 3,700 or so family history centres worldwide. Look for the *Vital Records Indexes* which are gradually being loaded onto the website. So far these cover Mexico and Scandinavia. There is online research guidance to help you plan research among sources containing details of birth, marriage and death, available at the website. It is arranged by regions throughout the world, and then broken down into time periods. In the self-service library in Salt Lake City, you will find qualified staff able to help you decipher copies of records written in the native language, and there are word lists available.

United States of America

Kemp's *International Vital Records Handbook* lists start dates, whereabouts of indexes and registers of births, marriages, deaths and divorces, and filmed copies for individual American States. Visit **www.cyndislist.com** for detailed information on each State, listed under 'Records'. You will see that in some States civil registration began as late as the twentieth century. The indexes and registers of many can be searched in the relevant county courthouses and copies in family history centres.

There is no standardization of the content of birth, marriage and death registrations beyond the date, place and name of the people involved. Death certificates can be rewarding, as parents' names and birthplaces are frequently recorded, as well as the date and place of birth of the deceased, plus the place of interment or cremation. If the person was a first-generation settler, you can thus immediately discover a link to the country of origin. Because they are so full, death certificates also establish generational relationships within the family. You may learn more from newspaper obituaries and gravestone inscriptions. Conversely, a tombstone may be the only source you have for birth and death dates.

Most States record late birth registrations, mainly filed by applicants for Social Security benefits after 1937. Unfortunately, these are usually kept in the county in where the applicant then resided, which may not be where he or she was born. The submitted information had to be supported by documentary evidence such as affidavits, school records, a baptism certificate or family Bible, so they are worth tracking down.

Other ways of finding recent deaths and military killed in action

You can search for names of people registered for Social Security benefits who died between 1962 and 2000 at **www.family search.org**. These will reveal the dates of birth and death, last place of residence, Social Security number and the State in which he or she lived when it was issued, plus the address to which death benefit was to be sent.

The US Military Index can be searched at the same website. This contains details about American servicemen and women who perished in Korea, 1950–7, and in Vietnam, 1957–75. From this you can discover both the birth and death dates, marital status, religious affiliation, address at enlistment, country of death, rank, serial number and service branch, and date of last tour of duty.

Records about personnel and veterans of the US armed forces are kept in the National Archives in Washington DC, but you will need to write to NARA – Personnel Records Center (Military Personnel Records), 9700 Page Avenue, St Louis, MO 63132-51200 for information about men and women enlisting after the First World War.

Americans abroad

Births and marriages of American citizens overseas, registered at Foreign Service Posts, and reports of deaths up to 1974, are filed in the National Archives in Washington, DC. Details about registrations can be obtained from Civilian Records (Room 2600) of the National Archives, College Park, 8601 Adelphi Road, College Park, MD 20740-6001. For deaths since 1974 contact Passport Services, of the Department of State, Correspondence Branch, 1111 19th Street NW, Suite 510, Washington, DC 20524-1705.

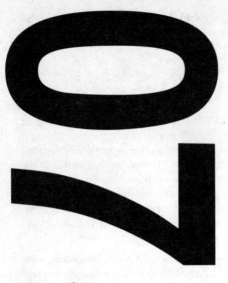

07

searching the census

You can start tracing your family's history by finding out who and where they were just over 100 years ago. So long as you know the name of one of them you should be able to pinpoint that person and the rest of his or her immediate family at an address in the 1901 census returns of Great Britain. This is available on the Internet at **www.census.pro.gov.uk** for England, Wales, the Channel Islands and the Isle of Man, and at **www.scotlandspeople.gov.uk** for Scotland. Both operate a charged service. If you have the Internet at home you can visit these sites as and when you want. Otherwise, you should be able to arrange access in your local library or record office. Unfortunately the online service does not extend to the returns for Ireland. The extent of your knowledge may already stretch beyond 1901, but you are almost certain to discover information you did not know before, and which will spur you on to finding out more about your ancestors' lives and times.

The first ten-yearly census, or complete population count, was undertaken in the United Kingdom in 1801. A specific Sunday night was always chosen, when families and workers were most likely to be at their usual addresses. Names were not systematically recorded until the census night of 6 June 1841, but because parish clergy and schoolmasters were the first census enumerators, some parish lists of name of heads of household exist for earlier years. You can find their whereabouts from J. Gibson and M. Medlycott, *Local Census Listings, 1522–1930, Holdings in the British Isles*. No enumeration was done in 1941.

How the census was organized

The civil registration districts created in 1837 formed the basis of the census districts, which were further broken down into enumeration districts, each comprising about 200 households, considered to be what each local enumerator could cover in a day. The district registrars, under the supervision of the superintendent district registrars, were responsible for appointing the enumerators and for their payment. The enumerators delivered numbered schedules to each head of household for completion on census night, and then collected them up again during the following week, helping to fill them in if necessary. A household was defined as people sharing the same roof, boarding and eating together. The schedules requested personal details about each household member. This information was duly copied into special enumerators' books which were presented with the schedules for checking by the district and superintendent registrars and for eventual transmission to the Registrar General in London. The individual household schedules were then destroyed.

The returns are made available to the public on the first working day in January once 100 years have elapsed, because the personal information contained in them was confidential. Those for 1931 no longer survive. The census returns for the whole of England, Wales, the Channel Islands and the Isle of Man from 1841 to 1891, can be searched on microfilm, and for 1901 online and on microfiche at the Family Records Centre in London. You can also search the 1901 census online and on microfiche at the National Archives, Kew. It is planned to make indexed scanned images of the earlier census returns available via a charged service in due course, beginning with those for 1891.

Filmed copies of the Welsh census returns are available in the National Library of Wales, in Aberystwyth, for Jersey, in the States Library, and Société Jersiaise, both in St Helier, for Guernsey, Alderney and Sark, in the Royal Court House, St Peter Port, and for the Isle of Man in the Manx Museum Library, in Douglas. Many local libraries and record offices have copies of returns for their own areas, and you can pay a small fee to hire in copies for consultation in family history centres. For library holdings visit **www.familia.org.uk**, for record offices use **www.genuki.org.uk** as your link, and for family history centre copies search the online catalogue at **www.familysearch.org**, which also lists details of family history centres worldwide. If you do not have access to the Internet, study *Census Returns, 1841–1891, on Microform: a directory to local holdings in Great Britain, Channel Islands, Isle of Man*, edited by J. Gibson and E. Hampson. As you will find that your ancestors did not always conveniently live in the same county as you, or crossed from one county to another over time, centralized microfilm holdings mean you can easily follow your ancestors around from place to place.

Scottish census returns are held in the General Register Office, in Edinburgh, but indexed digital images of those for 1881, 1891 and 1901 are accessible at **www.scotlandspeople.gov.uk**, which offers a charged service. It is planned to make the earlier returns available at this website.

Most of the earlier census returns for Ireland (which was surveyed every ten years from 1821) were destroyed, those for 1861–91 completely. The 1901 and 1911 returns can be searched in the National Archives of Ireland, in Dublin, and microfilm copies for the six northern counties, in the Public Record Office of Northern Ireland, in Belfast. Filmed copies of the 1901 returns can also be searched in family history centres, for a small hiring-in fee. A number of transcripts and extracts from earlier census years have been preserved, compiled by researchers or presented by pension claimants as proof of age, and are available to the public. Their whereabouts are listed by Gibson and Medlycott's *Local Census Listings, 1522–1930*.

Though never intended for use by genealogists, census returns are a prime source, not only because they form a ten-yearly dated snapshot from 1841 to 1901 of people within each household, but because they record details of their relationship to its head, their current marital status, age, employment, and birthplace. Unlike records of vital events, which concern a single individual and his or her parents, spouse or informant, the census returns capture an entire family or household unit on a particular night. You can find out who were their nearest neighbours and the occupations of other locals and thus build up a picture of the community in which they lived.

Birth, marriage and deaths registrations are indexed by personal name, whereas the census returns are organized by place, be it a hamlet, village, town or a city. You will usually need to know the whereabouts of your ancestors around a census year, even if you are searching an online database of names, unless the name was unusual or unique. The address or place of residence noted on a dated birth, marriage or death certificate can be searched in the nearest census year to see who was living there on census night. Conversely, you can trawl the census returns to elicit when and where people were alleged to have been born, calculate when to start looking for marriages of children's parents. When a person vanished between census years or changed marital status to widowed status, you have a start date to work back from for a death registration. If these events occurred before civil registration began, the census provides a specific place to turn to for local church or chapel registers of baptism and burial.

The census was taken on the following nights:

- Sunday 6 June 1841
- Sunday 30 March 1851

- Sunday 7 April 1861
- Sunday 2 April 1871
- Sunday 3 April 1881
- Sunday 5 April 1891
- Sunday 31 March 1901

Anyone born early the next morning would not be enumerated, nor someone dying during the evening of census night.

Indexes and transcripts

You can search the indexes to the 1901 census free of charge, but to view digital images of the relevant census pages, or a transcript of the entire household, you pay to view using a special voucher, or, if you prefer to use a credit or debit card you will be charged a minimum amount for every session or 48-hour period from the moment you log on to set up an account. Vouchers can be bought in £5, £10 or £50 units from the Family Records Centre, National Archives at Kew, local libraries and record offices, and are valid for six months. You can find details of these and other sales outlets at **www.census.pro.gov.uk**.

The six free index search options are Person Search, Address Search, Place Search, Institution Search, Vessel Search, or Direct Search. You will probably want to try the Person Search first. You will need to key in the surname (last name search) or forename (first name search), age and birthplace in the boxes on the screen. For a double-barrelled name, you may have to request separate searches under each of the names. You will always need to key in the first two letters of a surname, however. Forename searches are especially useful when you do not know the married or maiden names of female relatives, but know when they were born. Since surnames and forenames were occasionally recorded in reverse, if you fail to find an entry, try this as an option too. An Advanced Person Search is available to locate synonyms and abbreviated names, and you can do wild card searches using * to represent missing letters, or _ if a single letter is in doubt. Try not to be too specific about birthplaces, ages and addresses, which might be recorded differently to your expectations.

The results displayed on the screen include the person's name, place and county in which enumerated, given age, and place and county of birth. You may see a number of 'hits' (entries) corresponding to your request. Select the one which most closely matches what you already know. You now have two choices: to view the digital 'Image' of the whole original census page on which the person was recorded, or to inspect the 'Transcription' of that household only. Should a household run over to two census pages, you will need to pay to view them both if selecting the first option, whereas the transcription will include everyone in the household, but nothing else that appeared on the same census page. The images can be enlarged, and you can print them out by clicking on 'Print Request', or pay extra to order a copy from the National Archives. Don't forget to click on 'Submit' each time you place an order for a copy. This amount will be added to your basket of items to pay for at the end of the session.

Open your account only when you are ready to pay to view. At the end of the session don't forget to 'Log out' so that a summary of your expenditure will appear on the screen and be debited from your account. If you have a small balance left on your voucher this can be added to your new voucher total when you next log on.

The other five free search options enable you to look for the references to particular houses, and addresses in streets or roads in the enumerators' books; for towns, villages or hamlets; for institutions such as schools, army barracks, prisons, hospitals and workhouses; for boats and ships; and if you already have a National Archives reference to a particular census piece number, folio and page, you can go directly to a digital image of it using the 'Direct Search' option. If you want to find out who was recorded in any of these rather than looking for a specific person, or a person search has been unsuccessful and you suspect an individual was in a particular street or place, institution or on board a ship, these options can prove invaluable.

The 1881 census returns have also been fully indexed and transcribed. You can search the personal name indexes and transcriptions of the returns for England, Wales, Channel Islands and the Isle of Man at **www.familysearch.org** and on CD-ROM (which also includes Scotland). You can buy copies of the CD-ROMs directly from the Latter-Day Saints (LDS) Distribution Centre, 399 Garretts Lane, Sheldon, Birmingham B33 0UH, and the database is widely available in many local libraries and record offices, as well as in the Family Records Centre, and the National Archives, at Kew, and in family history centres. Unlike with the 1901 online index, you do not need to insert the first two letters of each surname or forename to search for these transcriptions. If you prefer, you can search the indexes on microfiche: one set is a complete national personal name index, excluding Scotland, giving full National Archives film, folio and page references for each individual, and the other set contains the same information, arranged county by county. Both are available in the Family Records Centre, in local libraries, record offices and family history centres. The local family history society will have a set at least for its own county, since its members were responsible for compiling the index, in collaboration with the Church of Jesus Christ of Latter-day Saints, and the Public Record Office (now the National Archives).

These two fully indexed series of census returns are a wonderful resource, because for 1881 and 1901 over 60 million names are just a click away. If you are not sure exactly where somebody was in either of those years the databases are a godsend. They show how family members were distributed around the country. They also record people 20 years apart, so you can detect how a household changed and what became of its members.

Indexed images of the returns for 1891 are gradually being made available at **www.ancestry.co.uk**. This is a subscription service and the returns are accessed by county. A number of other personal name indexes to census returns have been compiled by members of family history societies or by individuals, many of which have been published on CD-ROM, microfiche or in booklets. You can find out about these and their whereabouts from *Marriage, Census and Other Indexes for Family Historians*, by J. Gibson and E. Hampson. There are other online projects in hand, especially that of **http://freecem.rootsweb.com,** to make county census indexes of years prior to 1881 available on the Internet.

The most extensively indexed census returns after 1901, 1891 and 1881 are those for 1851, including a CD-ROM for Warwickshire, Devon and Norfolk residents, which is widely available, but other individual counties have been covered as well. A good collection of these is available in the Family Records Centre, listed by place in 'Surname Indexes' for each of the census years from 1841–91. When you find someone mentioned in one of the indexes, note down the National Archives film and folio references, so that you can help yourself to the relevant film immediately. Some personal name indexes are in private hands, and you will need to pay a small fee for a search of these, by writing to the address given in Gibson and Hampson's book.

If there is no personal name index for your place or locality, you will need to identify the film reference for the street or place itself. At the Family Records Centre, returns for towns with populations over 40,000 have been street-indexed. The numbered books tell you the film and folio numbers in which a particular road, street, public house, institution or named property will appear. Some of the street indexes actually cover a much wider area than the named city, town or locality, as revealed in the column headed 'Street Indexes' in the 'Place-Name Indexes'. It is planned to make these street indexes available on the Internet. Locally held street indexes are mentioned in Gibson and Hampson's book.

Sometimes you may not find your particular street in an index, so you may need to look at a contemporary or near-contemporary map of the area to identify other streets in the vicinity, and then start again. For London there is also *Names of London Streets and Places and their Localities* available in the Family Records Centre, listed alphabetically by street, giving its locality and parish. This should enable you to find the neighbouring street in the index, and thus the one you want in the returns themselves. Street directories of London and larger towns and cities published around census years indicate which other roads, streets and terraces intersected each other. A number of these are now available on CD-ROM, of which some are available online in the Family Records Centre, and others are at **www.historicaldirectories.org**. Try also **www.multimap. com** for the whereabouts of current streets, bearing in mind that some may have disappeared or been renamed since your chosen census year. You can study copies of nineteenth-century Ordnance Survey street plans of some larger towns and cities in the Family Records Centre too.

If there is no street index for the place you want, you will have to use the 'Place-Name Indexes' and linked 'Reference Books' in the Family Records Centre to find the film for the place you want, or depend on the local cataloguing system if searching copies of the census elsewhere. Unfortunately, you cannot rely on the registration district name given in the centralized birth, marriage and death indexes as being the exact place where someone lived because each one covered up to seven different parishes. In any case, the family's usual address might have been somewhere altogether different. For unlisted townships, communities or settlements try the Hamlet Index in the Family Records Centre, and for Welsh localities try *Welsh Administrative and Territorial Units*, by M. Richards or **www.gazetteer-wales.co.uk**. You can also search **www.multimap.com** for geographic areas too small to be listed.

What the censuses reveal

When you search the returns, you will see that every enumerator's book was numbered and prefaced by a short description of the hamlets, townships, roads and streets it encompassed. The pages in the 1841 books are headed by the title of the relevant township, hamlet, village, town, city ward and parish, with columns recording only limited personal details about each person. Road, street and house names are rarely identified, so you need to be careful when picking your way down the strings of names to note when one building ends and another starts (indicated by two diagonal lines drawn through the margin immediately to the left of a name). If a building was divided into apartments or was occupied by more than one household who did not eat together, then a single diagonal line will be shown. The name of the head of the household is followed by those of others in the household. Only the first forename and initials of other forenames are included for each person. People of the same surname as the individual whose name appeared immediately above were indicated by 'do' (ditto). Ages given by the head were rounded down to the nearest five for people over 15 years of age. Occupations were recorded too. Finally, 'Y' = Yes, 'N' = No, or 'NK' = Not Known showed if the person was born in the county where enumerated on census night. If the birthplace was in Scotland ('S'), Ireland ('I') or Foreign Parts ('F', relating to non-British subjects only), then this will be indicated instead.

Precise ages are lacking in the 1841 census returns, so if someone was 28 for instance, the age would have been listed as 25. The birthplace might be in the same county (Y) or anywhere else except in the same county (N) where an individual spent census night. Because idiosyncratic spelling of forenames such as 'Francis' as 'Frances' and 'Jesse' and 'Jessie' may make sex uncertain, look in the age columns, which separate males and females. Family relationships and marital status are absent, and it was not always the oldest member who headed the household. Avoid drawing false conclusions by assuming exact ages and blood connections without first searching later census returns or other sources in which they can be clarified. For instance, a man and woman of similar ages and of the same surname sharing a household might actually be brother and sister rather than husband and wife, and younger people of the same surname in the household may turn out to be the offspring of neither.

The 1851 and later census returns are much simpler to understand. Every household was assigned its own sequential number, and roads, streets and houses will be identified by name if not number. In 1891 and 1901, you can even discover how many rooms the household comprised, if less than five, so you can learn about housing conditions. From 1851, the relationship of everyone in the household to the head was entered in the schedules, plus current marital status, precise given age, occupation, birthplace and county. On the whole, as in 1841, only the first forename will be recorded, with initials for subsequent names, so if you cannot find the expected name of a person but the age tallies, this may be the explanation. Beginning in 1851, the returns show who was blind, deaf and dumb, and from 1871 anyone suffering from certain mental disabilities.

From 1871 if a household schedule had been completed in Welsh and then translated into English, this will be indicated, and in 1891 and 1901, you can see which Welsh residents were bilingual or spoke only Welsh or English.

Because relationships to the head of household were given, wives, children and other kinsfolk, servants, lodgers and apprentices can be easily picked out. Although not stated as such, some of these servants, lodgers and apprentices might be remoter kinsfolk or related by marriage, so it is always worth writing down details about them as well, and following up their immediate family histories. Bear in mind that the head of household's children might not all have been born to his current wife; they will still be described as his offspring since the given relationships are to the head. A change in marital status between census dates, or a differently named spouse, should trigger a search for the death of a husband or wife during that ten-year period. There may not always be enough information to identify the second marriage entry unless you already know the new spouse's surname, you are dealing with an uncommon name, or come up with a likely entry at **http://freebmd.rootsweb.com**. The *International Genealogical Index* and *British Isles Vital Records Index* may also be worth trawling. You may have to obtain a copy of the birth certificate of one of the children of the new family in order to discover the mother's former name. Try the above website for the death registration of the former partner and for births of children.

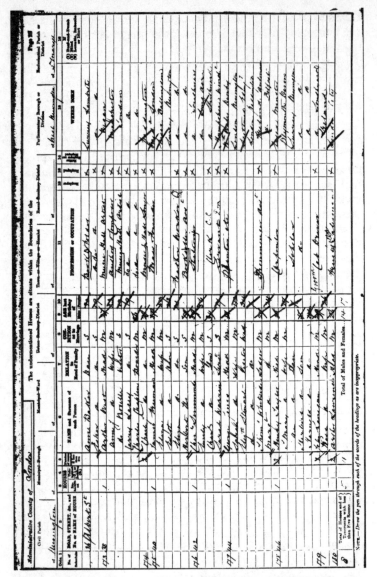

figure 5 Newington census return 1891. Charles Chaplin (Charlie's father) was enumerated twice, by his landlord and on his own schedule. Note the variation of information given. He occupied two rooms of the house. (I am grateful to Dan Harris and *Family Tree Magazine* for this information. (Reproduced by permission of London Metropolitan Archives)

Given ages were as of the last birthday before the census date. They do not invariably increase or decrease consistently every ten years, and similarly, given birthplaces may vary, because it was the head, not the relevant occupant, who filled in the census schedule for the entire household. The head may change, or memory become blurred over time. Where infants under a year old are listed, their ages will be given in months, weeks, days or even hours! You can still estimate approximately when and where a person was born from such information, which is invaluable for the period before civil registration.

Descriptions of common occupations were often abbreviated, such as agricultural labourer to 'ag lab', framework knitter to 'fwk'. If you find an occupation and do not understand what it was, have a look in *The Oxford English Dictionary, A Dictionary of Old Trades, Titles and Occupations*, by C. Waters, or *Instructions to the Clerks Employed in Classifying the Occupations and Ages of the People* (which grouped them together for statistical purposes). A copy of each of these is available in the Family Records Centre. 'Living on their own means' usually indicated a person drawing an income from rents or shares, whereas an annuitant would be described as such, and likewise someone at the other end of the social scale receiving poor relief would be listed as a pauper. A pensioner is likely to have been a former serviceman, so you might want to pursue his career through army or Royal Navy records in the National Archives at Kew.

Up to the 1861 census, people were described by their last or usual job, which can be misleading if they were out of work at the time of the census. From 1871 onwards, however, any retired or unemployed people were described as such. From 1891, the returns indicate whether a person was an employer, employee, or neither. If someone carried on several occupations, it was the one which earned the most income during the season of the year when the census was taken that would be recorded. Nightworkers were enumerated at the address to which they returned once their shift was over on the morning after census night.

Farm acreages were included in the returns from 1851 to 1881, setting out the number of labourers, men and boys, engaged by the farmer. The number of business employees and apprentices were noted as well, although many were family enterprises. The employment of wives and children in the family business, but not receiving wages, was not acknowledged in the census until

1891. Children were frequently described as scholars, regardless of how many hours' weekly formal teaching they received compared with the time spent at work. It was only in 1891 that occupations began to be recorded for children aged ten and over, who were then legally allowed to leave school to take up paid jobs.

Some workers slept under the same roof as their employers, and will be listed as lodgers or in a separate part of the building. Others would have lived nearby, generally no more than a day's return walk (about 14 or so miles in all), before cheap wheeled and motorized transport made longer distance commuting possible.

Totals of people sleeping in places deemed not to be dwelling houses, for instance in barns, sheds, tents or even in the open air, were merely counted in 1841 and 1851, and as the 1841 census was taken in summer there must have been many seasonal harvest workers whose names do not feature at all. In 1861, these temporary visitors appear in a 'list of persons not in households', and from 1871 in whichever named road or street they slept on census night.

Travellers by coach or train and on the move were enumerated in whatever hotel or house they lodged in the morning after their journey, or if they alighted, wherever they slept during census night. As they might arrive late and leave early their given personal details may be sparse in the extreme.

People in institutions, not in a dwelling

There were special enumeration pages for households exceeding 100. These might be an army barracks, public and endowed schools, colleges, certified reformatories and industrial schools, workhouses (including pauper schools), hospitals for the sick, convalescent or incurable, public and private lunatic asylums, prisons and houses of correction. The returns are filed at the end of the relevant town, registration district or hundred (an administrative division of a county). These are indicated in the FRC 'Reference Books' by a coded number corresponding to the nature of the institution. Staff, their families and servants were listed first, and normally only the initials were noted for inmates of gaols, houses of correction and asylums.

People at sea or on inland waterways

Commanding officers of Royal Naval and merchant vessels in harbour or putting into port within a prescribed period filed special schedules to customs officers. The first surviving Royal Navy ships' enumerations date from 1861, to which there is a complete personal name index available on microfiche. The indexed returns for 1881 can also be searched at **www. familysearch.org**, on CD-ROM and on microfiche, and those for 1901 at **www.census.pro.gov.uk**. There are a few, earlier, 1851 returns of British merchant shipping in port and at sea engaged in the home trade around the United Kingdom, Channel Islands, Isle of Man, and Europe from the Elbe to Brest. The schedules list all the crew and passengers, setting out the name of the vessel, the names, rank or rating where appropriate, marital status, age and birthplace of all on board.

These returns are worth searching if you are trying to trace passengers on ships sailing to and from the Continent, transmigrants changing ship for an ocean-going vessel or intending emigrants already on board in the port of departure on census night. It is also worth trawling the hotels, guest houses and boarding houses for intending or newly-landed passengers. The returns fill a few of the gaps left by the years before 1890 when ships' passenger lists began to be preserved.

The earliest known returns of fishermen relate to boats putting in to port during April 1861. These are filed with the Royal Naval and merchant shipping returns, and have been indexed with them as described above. The 1871 and 1881 schedules cover a slightly shorter enumeration period than for merchant vessels, but in 1891 and 1901 they were the same, and include returns made by foreign fishing boats landing their catches at United Kingdom ports.

People on canals and inland navigable waterways were listed too, under the enumeration or sub-district where they were moored on census night, using similar schedules to ships'.

Scotland

Access to indexed digitized images of the 1891 and 1901 and indexes to the 1881 census returns of Scotland is available using the charged service run by **www.scotlandspeople.gov.uk**. You will need a credit or debit card to pay for this. At the Family

Records Centre the computerized ScotLink to the General Register Office, in Edinburgh, includes personal name indexes to the 1881, 1891 and 1901 census returns for Scotland. You can book a seat at one of the two computer terminals by paying a half-hourly fee, up to a maximum of two hours per session. You cannot print out any of the entries, or display the digitized images of the census pages on these screens. The online indexes will give you the district or parish details and call number for the microfilm copy of the returns in Edinburgh. Copies can also be hired for a small fee in a family history centre.

The 1841–1901 Scottish census returns can not only be seen on microfilm in the General Register Office, in Edinburgh, but hired in for use in family history centres too, and copies are held by many regional libraries throughout Scotland. The Gibson guide to census returns on microform will provide you with a location list. It is planned to provide paid access to the indexed digital images of returns from 1841 to 1881 at the above website soon. You can search the indexed transcriptions for 1881 on CD-ROM.

A search pass is necessary to use the GRO search room in Edinburgh, for which a fee is payable, but as you can also glean the indexes and registers of births, marriages and deaths from 1855, and the online earlier Old Parochial Registers of births, baptisms, marriages and burials from 1553 to 1854, you can achieve a good deal in a day. It is planned to make indexed digital images of all these online too.

Census arrangement and indexes

The Scottish returns are organized by district or parish, to which there are street indexes for larger burghs and cities, with the volume number being indicated against the appropriate entry in the census indexes. If you cannot find a particular place, look at *Gazetteer of Scotland*, edited by F. Groome, which will identify the parish to which it belonged.

Passengers and crews at sea

Returns of Royal Naval and merchant shipping from 1881–91, and 1861–91 respectively, are unlisted in the indexes, but are available on request. Online indexes and digital images of the Royal Naval and merchant shipping returns for 1891 and 1901 are available at **www.scotlandspeople.gov.uk**. The schedule content is similar to that for vessels putting in to English and Welsh ports.

Ireland

A few returns for 1841–71 only are known to exist for certain places in Ireland. A number of transcriptions of 1841 and 1851 entries, produced as proof of age in applications for old age pensions, are held by the National Archives of Ireland, in Dublin, and in the Public Record Office of Northern Ireland, in Belfast, to which there are personal name indexes, arranged by county. Other copies, including some for 1861 and 1871, are catalogued under pre-1901 census items in the National Archives. The whereabouts of known extant material is listed by county in *Local Census Listings, 1522–1930: Holdings in the British Isles*, by J. Gibson and M. Medlycott, and in J. Grenham, *Tracing Your Irish Ancestors*. You can inspect the filmed returns for 31 March 1901 and the original documents for 2 April 1911 in the National Archives of Ireland, in Dublin, and filmed copies for 1901 are available for the six northern counties in the Public Record Office of Northern Ireland, in Belfast. Microfilm copies of the 1901 returns can also be hired in to search in family history centres and you can find out which are available online by searching the county by county listing at **www.census-online. com/links/Ireland** and at **www.cyndislist.com/ireland.htm**.

The way the census was planned and indexed

Ireland was organized for census purposes under county district electoral divisions, and then by townland. The relevant 1901 return can be found from the *1901 Alphabetical Index to the Townlands and Town, Parishes and Baronies of Ireland*, which notes each division name and number. There is no corresponding index for 1911. County books list sequentially the numbered district divisions and townlands from which you can requisition the volumes for 1901, or loose paper schedules for 1911. There are street indexes for Belfast, Cork, Dublin and Limerick.

Census content

The 1901 household returns contain the forename and surname of all occupants, relationship of each to the head, religious affiliation, level of education, age, sex, rank, profession or occupation, marital status, Irish county or city or country of birth, whether bilingual or Irish- or English-speaking only, and if deaf and dumb, dumb only, blind, imbecile, idiot or lunatic. The number of rooms and windows in the main dwelling and in any outhouses was also specified, and the roof fabric. There may be contemporary photographic evidence to convey what the houses looked like, from which you can gain a rough idea of people's living conditions at that time.

The 1911 census returns disclose the number of years of marriage for each married woman, unless widowed, her total live-born children, and how many of them were still living. From this you can calculate approximately when she married, the minimum number of her confinements, and learn about her family's housing.

Copies and extracts from previous censuses

Unlike returns for other parts of the United Kingdom, the Irish 1841 census gave by household the name, age, occupation, relationship to the head of each person sleeping there on census night, the date of marriage where appropriate, level of literacy, and names of absent family members and of those who had died since 1831. You can thus distinguish who in the family unit was then still alive though not at home on census night, and who had died within the previous ten years.

From 1851, a person's religious denomination was indicated, with the names of family members who had died since the last census; from this you can identify which kind of church or chapel they are likely to have attended, taken their children for baptism, relatives for burial and their spouses for marriage. Since civil registration of births and deaths began in 1864, the loss of these remarkably instructive returns is a tragedy.

Earlier censuses

A number of incidental parish lists of householders have survived from the four previous censuses of Great Britain taken on Tuesday 10 March 1801, and Mondays 27 May 1811, 28 May 1821 and 30 May 1831, and including Ireland from 1821. Their known whereabouts are listed by county in *Local Census Listings, 1522–1930*. Many of the English and Welsh lists are deposited in county record offices. Mostly prepared by clergymen, schoolmasters or overseers of the poor, who served as census enumerators, these scraps of paper were originally stored in parish chests for safekeeping. Usually only the head of the household was named with the number and ages of other occupants, though for 1821 you might be lucky and find their names too, and in 1831 details of their occupations. Such lists shed light on people born in the late- or mid-eighteenth century.

For Scotland, there are some earlier lists for 1821 and 1831 among the Old Parochial Registers, held in the General Register Office, in Edinburgh, kirk session records in the National Archives of Scotland, in Edinburgh, and in local archive collections. These too are included in *Local Census Listings, 1522–1930*.

A few returns remain for the first two Irish censuses, taken in 1821 and 1831, arranged under county, barony, civil parish and townland, giving, as instructed, all inhabitants' names, their relationship to the householder, their ages and occupations, and the acreage of each landholding. The number of storeys in each house was noted in 1821, but excluded from the 1831 lists. These can be searched mainly in the National Archives of Ireland, or the Public Record Office of Northern Ireland. Look in *Local Census Listings, 1522–1930* for details.

Additional listings to try

Other inhabitants' lists were drawn up from time to time to meet various civil or ecclesiastical purposes. Examples are parish lists of assessed tax- and ratepayers, of men of an age to serve in the county militia, lists of landowners and householders subject to payment of the tithe, rentals of manorial tenants, names of parish contributors and recipients of poor relief, those of householders liable to serve as parish officers or jurymen, lists of communicants, and of suspected and known Catholics.

Such lists, by their very nature, were limited to individuals of some social or financial status, people over a certain age, to householders or defined groups, but nonetheless they are a guide to the whereabouts, responsibilities and existence of local residents at a particular date. They may fill in gaps where other records are deficient or silent. They may demonstrate the continuity, geographic spread and density of certain surnames within an area at a particular time. Sometimes they can only serve as circumstantial evidence of a family's local presence or continuance.

Census surveys overseas

Similar population counts have been undertaken at frequent or irregular intervals in almost all countries of the world; some, for the first time only in the twentieth century. They are not all thorough surveys, nor have all of the records been preserved, or are open to public inspection. In the future, it is likely that many of the historical returns will be made available as indexed digital images. When civil registration began later than the census, and church records are unreliable or absent, such lists assume great genealogical importance, providing evidence of settlement, occupation, approximate year and place of birth, and of close family relationships.

United States of America

In the United States of America, the first decennial federal census was undertaken on Tuesday 2 August 1790, in the 13 States then belonging to the Union. The other dates were 4 August 1800, 6 August 1810, 7 August 1820, 1 June 1830, 1840, 1850, 1860, 1870, 1880, 2 June 1890, 1 June 1900, 15 April 1910, 1 January 1920 and 1 April 1930.

Once the returns reach 72 years old, they are made available to the public, so those for 1930 have been accessible on microfilm since 2002. Many of the 1890 returns were destroyed. The schedules for 1790 have been printed and where places are deficient, inhabitants' names have been inserted from other contemporary sources. Microfilm copies of all the returns up to 1930 can be inspected in the National Archives, in Washington, DC, its branch Regional Archives, in State archives, and in family history centres. You can also search indexes and digital images of the following federal census returns: for 1790–1850, and 1920 and 1930, a partial index and digital images for 1860, images only for the years 1870, 1880, 1900 and 1910, and indexed images of the remaining fragments of the 1890 returns at **www.ancestry.com** which offers a subscription service. Online access is free both in the National Archives and the Library of Congress. You can also search the index and transcriptions of the 1880 returns (plus those for Canada in 1881) at **www.familysearch.org**. The 1901 census of Canada is available at **www.archives.ca**, plus the 1871 returns for the Province of Ontario, and the 1906 census returns of the North West (prairie) provinces of Manitoba, Saskatchewan and Alberta. For these, except for 1871, you do have to know the district or place where someone was, since they are not indexed by personal name. You may be able to find people who crossed into Canada or vice versa in these entries.

Indexes to the census

There are personal name indexes for each federal census to 1850. These are arranged by State, then by county. Many of these are printed or in microform and are widely accessible in State archives, public and research libraries, but to use them you need to know your ancestor's full name, or that of the head of household and the State or county of residence. The best indexes are the microfilm copies relating to the 1880 State schedules, but which encompass only households containing children aged ten or less. These give the name, age and birthplace of each member. It is not a complete index, so you cannot rely solely on it for all that was included in the census, but it offers a clue to the state-wide distribution of that surname at a specific date. This and the later indexes adopt the Soundex system, running alphabetically by first letter of the surname, then phonetically by sound using a number code, followed alphabetically by every householder's forename. Each householder's index card includes other family members listed with him or her in the census.

Miracode index cards are used for some States in 1910, enumerators' household numbers rather than the Soundex system of page and line references linking them to the original census entries.

Tips

- All the indexes are subject to omissions and errors, so consult every compilation for a given census year to pick up references missing elsewhere.
- Check every likely surname variant for others grouped with it, especially when the Soundex system is used.
- Whilst the 1890 index is complete, just over 6,000 schedules survive, so there is not much left to inspect.
- The returns are arranged alphabetically by State, and then almost always alphabetically by county, which you will need to know before you start.

You may be able to locate city and town addresses of people in census years from directories of the period. The Library of Congress, in Washington, DC, and many public libraries and historical societies have extensive runs. You can discover local holdings from **www.archives.gov** and from **www.cyndislist.com**.

How the census was organized and what it contains

The early returns are arranged by county and town of domicile, and up to 1840 merely identify the head of household and number of other occupants by their ages and sex. Only from 1880 are individual streets and houses numbered or named. Starting in 1850, the returns are far more expansive, as every free person was named, specifying age, sex, and colour, the profession, occupation or trade of males over 15, to 1870, the value of any real estate (and personal estate from 1860), the State, Territory or country of birth, whether attending school or married within the previous year (the latter up to 1890 only, in 1870 giving the actual month), educational level of everyone over 20 years of age, and if deaf and dumb, blind, insane, idiot, pauper or convict. Given natal months of infants born during the 12 months prior to the 1870, 1880 and 1900 censuses facilitate searches for their registrations or baptisms.

The 1880 and later census schedules give marital status, the relationship between everyone in the household to its head, and number of months of any unemployment during the past year More proving questions about the nature of employment were posed from 1910. From 1890 to 1910, you can discover the number of a mother's surviving children, and in 1900 and 1910, the length of the current marriage of every married woman, plus the number of children it had produced. Age at first marriage was recorded in the 1930 returns. After 1890, too, you can find out if the head of the house or farm was its owner or tenant, or had mortgaged it. The 1880 and 1890 census returns recorded any current illness or disability too. Ownership of a radioset was indicated in 1930.

In 1870, you can learn for the first time whether each named person's parents were foreign-born, about naturalized immigrants qualified to vote, and then track them down in naturalization records. The parents' state or country of birth was invariably included from 1880. The number of years' residence in the United States was specified from 1890, and whether the person had already been naturalized, or was applying for naturalization. The year of immigration, and current nationality of first-generation settlers over 21 can be traced in returns from 1900. The years of naturalization began to appear in 1920. The 1890 census onwards also indicate ability to speak English, from 1910 citing their native languages. What is missing are the exact birthplaces of immigrants, but family tradition or other clues such as surname distribution in the home country elicited from their records, published name directories and current phone books, may help pinpoint where they came from. Consult **www.cyndislist.com** for links to those online. Try searching **www.infobel.com/teldir** for present-day listings of telephone subscribers worldwide. Local newspapers of the day published at the time of the census may provide information about the origins of new arrivals. You can also search **www.ellisislandrecords.org** for details of ships, names, ages and dates of arrival of passengers arriving in the Port of New York between 1892 and 1924, and the Mormon Immigrants Index, 1840–90, on CD-ROM, for personal information about ships' passengers bound for America. You can find out who else was on board the same ship from both databases. Even if their own origins are not stated or unclear, those of their companions might lead you back to where your ancestors came from. There are links to other online lists of ships' passengers at **www.cyndislist.com**. You might also like to visit **www.archives.ca.** for details about online indexes to ships' passengers landing in Canadian ports between 1925 and 1935.

Special uses of the census

The census schedules also help plot the overland migration routes taken by individuals and family groups, starting in the 1840s, particularly along the lengthy and treacherous established overland trails west to the North West Pacific coast, California, or to Utah, or simply into neighbouring states or territories in search or work or new opportunities. The local press might announce new arrivals and report the births, marriages and deaths of travellers or recent settlers. Many of these peoples' journals, diaries and letters mention other migrants they met up with, so State libraries and historical societies and Pioneers' Museums are well worth consulting for any which have been deposited. Even if your own ancestor doesn't feature, you will get an idea of what the experience must have been like from the accounts of contemporaries. When the Intercontinental Railway was opened in 1869 it made possible a swift and easy crossing from coast to coast, so the census details can be invaluable for tracking people back along their route to their staging posts and starting-off point. Surviving records from these places may help you to build up a picture of your family's activities.

Slaves

Details about slaves are recorded on the back of the main returns under the name of the householder with whom they lived. Special schedules of slave owners were also filed in 1850 and 1860, listing only their number, age, sex and colour and these can be linked to wills and probate inventories of the period in which slaves' names were mentioned.

Veterans

You can use the census as a springboard for finding out more about men who fought in the Revolutionary War and Civil War from their service papers and pension claims. Veterans' schedules, listing names and ages of Revolutionary War pensioners (including women) alive in 1840, were filed by county and place of residence on the back of the main returns, under the name of the householder with whom they lived. Their names and ages were published in 1841. *A General Index to a Census of Pensioners for Revolutionary or Military Services*, relating to the 1840 census returns, is available on microfilm.

Another, incomplete, series of Veterans' schedules dates from 1890. These are in the National Archives, in Washington, DC, and relate only to States running alphabetically from Louisiana to Wyoming, about half of Kentucky and for Washington, DC. The microfilmed schedules concentrate on Union veterans and their widows, arranged by State or territory of abode, and then by county or sub-division. Current postal address, rank, company, regiment or ship, date of enlistment and discharge, length of service and any medical disabilities are recorded. The names of deceased veterans are written alongside those of their widows. You can link the numbered schedules to those in the federal census, where they might be listed as living with married daughters or other relatives. The 1910 returns also indicate if a person was a Union or Confederate veteran, and in 1930 if the veteran was military or naval, and of what war or expedition.

Ancillary surveys

In 1885, a census was taken in some of the frontier States (Arizona, Colorado, New Mexico, Nebraska, Florida, North and South Dakota) which partially compensates for the loss of the 1890 returns. In a period of rapid migration and population growth, these form an important directory of immigrants and their families, plotting their ages and origins.

Mortality schedules of returns of deaths during the 12 months preceding each census, starting in 1849–50, supply by State and county each person's name, age, sex, colour, marital status, birthplace and month of death, occupation, the cause of death and duration of the final illness. These form a vital genealogical resource, because they pre-date civil registration, supplement under-registration by local churches, make up for a total lack of official records in remote communities or settlements, and tie in with the decadal census returns. They also reveal why certain people were missing on census night, or eliminate one of the ten years needed to search for their deaths since the previous census enumeration.

In 1870 they disclose if the parents were foreign-born, in 1880 length of residence in the US and the parents' birthplaces. The original documents are dispersed in State archives, the National Archives, and the library of the National Society of Daughters of the American Revolution, both in Washington, DC. Copies and indexes to these are also available in many libraries. The National Archives probably possesses the best collection of microfilm copies, and you can also hire them for study in family history centres.

State and local censuses were also undertaken periodically from 1623 to 1918, usually as a pretext for taxation or military purposes. They have been listed, with their whereabouts, in *The Source: A Guidebook of American Genealogy*, by L. D. Szucs (ed), A. Eichholz and S. H. Luebking (ed), and *The Red Book: American State, County and Town Sources*, by A. Eichholz (ed), and in *State Census Records*, by A. S. Lainhart (ed). A number have been printed.

General advice on tackling the census

The census offers a rich seam of information for family historians to mine. The British returns offer a ten-yearly snapshot spanning 70, or in the case of the United States of America, a much longer period of a family's life. It tracks the changing size, composition and age structure of a household. A sequence of returns will track someone from cradle to grave, from parental home to independence, marriage and family responsibility, through working life, from one part of a town to another or from a rural to an urban environment, or even from one end of the country to the other or out of it altogether. The census returns set your family among its neighbours, and against a broader social and economic backdrop. The neighbourhood might alter as people came and went, and you can find out where they all originally came from. You can discover what kind of work the community was engaged in, and if there was a dominant local industry.

You can roughly estimate when people married, see where their spouses came from, and from the given birthplaces and birth years of their offspring learn the frequency, direction and distance travelled by a family. What you may not learn is the reason why, and how gradual or sudden each movement had been. Present-day inhabitants' recollections of former residents, contemporary newspaper articles and local histories may provide clues about why people left or were attracted there, so don't forget to work forwards as well as backwards. A little knowledge about the local history of the area is an advantage, because it will give you a better understanding of how particular places developed and of their underlying dynamics. It is also a sound idea to visit the place if you can, and to root out any surviving old photographs and maps of the period. The Local Studies Collection or Local History Museum is probably the best place to start looking for these. In the United States, you will find Pioneers' Museums contain a host of artefacts and memorabilia which bring early settlers' experiences vividly to life. Old maps, personal diaries, journals, letters and copies of birth, baptism, marriage or death certificates are often deposited there, not all of which are on public display. By studying these you can appreciate what life was like in a way unparalleled by scouring formal, official records, which were not designed for genealogists anyway. Contemporary maps and street plans show how the human and natural landscape changed over time.

- If you fail to find someone at a specific address always search the other streets and roads within the same enumeration district and those on either side of it. The same applies to villages surrounding the one where you expected your forebear to be. Write down their names and plot them on a map to see their proximity to each other.

- If you have no address near a census year, buy a copy of a birth, marriage or death registration of another member of the family around then, and use this as your starting point. However, there are now an increasing number of county databases of personal names for some census years, in addition to the countrywide ones for 1881 and 1901, thereby making it possible to discover the whereabouts of people with minimal information beyond knowing their county of residence.

- By relying merely on a street or personal name index to take you straight to the household entry of your family, you risk overlooking what else was going on in the neighbourhood. No family has ever been truly insular: the neighbours might have been workmates, employers, employees, friends, enemies, playmates, future partners or kinsmen.

- Note down details about people of your surname, as their given birthplaces may lead you to an earlier census return or to a contemporary one containing your own ancestor.

- Family relationships should be precisely given, and connect each member of the household to its head. Look out for children of the same father but different mothers. Illegitimate children might be described as a 'nephew' or 'niece'.

- The census will not tell you how long a lodger or boarder had been in a particular household. A 'visitor' usually indicates an overnight or slightly longer stay. People described as lodgers, boarders or visitors might actually be related to the head of household or by marriage.

- If you have failed to locate the birth certificate of your direct ancestor, and you find him or her in the census along with parents and siblings, a copy of one of these brother's or sister's birth registrations will put you back on the trail.

- Children born and dying before adulthood may be recorded in the census. Others might disappear, only to resurface later in someone else's household as a foster child, apprentice, or domestic servant. Fostering was more likely in big families or where a relative had no children. Large gaps between children's ages may indicate departure from the parental home, temporary absence, or childhood mortality. There may be children who were born and died between census years and for whom there will be no census record at all.

- A wife may have moved with her parents before her marriage. Whilst her birthplace reveals where she originally came from, once you know her maiden name it is worth looking for the rest of her family near her marital home. The birthplace of her eldest child may also be an indicator of her parents' whereabouts, since daughters often went back to their mothers for their first confinement.

- Given ages and birthplaces of aunts and uncles may be the key to the baptism of a direct ancestor dead by the time that census was taken. Look at the returns of the same census year of given birthplaces for family members, in case other relatives can be found there. Look at the returns of these places in the census years closest to the given birth years too.

- Sometimes a person was enumerated a long way from his or her native home, so the nearest town might be given as the birthplace simply because the head of household or the enumerator could not spell an unfamiliar or strange sounding name. Place names might also be written phonetically, close to the local dialect pronunciation. Occasionally the dialect may defeat you altogether so you may have to resort to a gazetteer, or to the relevant county volume produced by the English Place-Name Society.

- The census will give you clues as to when and where people were born, married and died, but apart from the Irish returns of 1901 and 1911, it does not reveal their religious denominations. You may have to rely on family knowledge or a marriage certificate for this.

- The handwriting of census returns often leaves a lot to be desired. If you cannot decipher the name of a street or road, look at a nearby census page where the word is written more clearly. Otherwise, try and build up the word letter by letter, by finding similar ones written elsewhere on the page, and eventually you may be able to work out what it was. The capital letter is key to sorting out difficult place-names, since this will reduce the number of possibilities. You can then check your interpretation against a contemporary town plan or directory entry, having noted down the streets and roads surrounding it to use as checking points.

- Try writing a difficult word as you see it. Sometimes enlarging or reducing the microfilm image, or sitting under different lighting can help. A photocopy of the relevant page may sometimes make it easier to read. If you are at the Family Records Centre, or in a record office, you can ask a member of staff to examine the page on the screen with you. Staff in the FRC may then authorize you to search the original census enumerator's book for yourself in the National Archives, Kew, or request one of the staff to do this for you and send you details about who was at a given household address.

- The Registrar General's clerks made numerous marks over the census entries, sometime obliterating the handwriting or numbers underneath, making them difficult to read on microfilm. Ask the FRC staff for advice.

- Sometimes pages were filmed twice, or missed out altogether. If you are in any doubt, ask a member of the FRC staff for authorization to search the original enumerators' books. There are a lot of missing pages for the 1861 census returns of London, and FRC staff will again be able to advise on this.

- There are numerous people whose names do not feature at all in the census. The reliability and accuracy of given information depended on the honesty and knowledge of the heads of household. This may explain why some details about age and birthplace appear so contradictory or misleading.

- If you are relying on personal name indexes to get to the census, bear in mind that no copy is perfect. Names may have been omitted or misread, so search the filmed census returns as a double-check if you know roughly where certain people should have been.

- In Wales, you may come across names which obviously relate to the same person, but were recorded differently over the decades. This may be explained by the patronymic naming system, still prevalent in some remoter communities in the nineteenth century. As rural populations were relatively small and scattered, such individuals should be readily identifiable from their farmsteads and localities, and from the names of others sharing their household.

08

other name lists

If you fail to find people where expected in the census returns, there may be other lists of names to help you locate them then or during inter-censal years.

Registers of voters

Annually published electoral registers theoretically record the name and address of every adult male after about 1884, but alas the surviving series is not fully continuous nor complete, as many were destroyed. Registers of voters in Parliamentary elections have been printed each year since 1832, except for 1916, 1917, and 1940–4. In 1832, the franchise was widened from forty-shilling freeholders to include copyholders and leaseholders of property worth £10 a year, tenants at will (i.e. dependent on the goodwill of the landlord) paying £50 a year in rent in the shires and £10 householders in boroughs. This meant that the enfranchised embraced tenant farmers and shopkeepers. Later statutes of 1867 and 1884 extended the right to vote even further, until virtually all men aged 21 and over were included. Similar acts were passed for Scotland and Ireland.

By their nature, the earlier registers are therefore selective, and not until 1918 were women over 30 able to vote, the age limit being lowered to 21 in 1928; in 1918 the property qualification was abolished, the right to vote being based on six months' residence or occupation of business premises worth £10 a year. From 1951 people reaching the minimum age during the year are listed too, and starting in 1971 the registers include the birth date, when the age threshold was lowered to 18.

The most complete series of electoral registers for the United Kingdom is held in The British Library, in London. These are listed in R. H. A. Cheffins, *Parliamentary Constituencies and their registers since 1832*, and you will need a reader's ticket to consult them. The early holdings are patchy, though there is a complete set for 1937 and 1938, and then from 1947 onwards. Many are on microfilm. Some copies of electoral registers can be searched locally in record offices and libraries. Look in J. Gibson and C. Rogers, *Electoral Registers since 1832; and Burgess Rolls* for a county by county list of their whereabouts. This includes names of people entitled to vote in local government elections from 1888, and in borough elections from 1835. Names of married women qualifying as occupiers to vote in local elections are included after 1869. There are electoral lists of Irish voters in the National Archives of Ireland, in Dublin.

To 1915, the electoral registers are arranged by constituency, ward and polling district, then township, naming alphabetically by qualification the allotted number, surname, forename, actual and qualifying address of each voter. From 1918, they are organized alphabetically by street or road, and then by voter's name, making them more difficult to use. You therefore need to know the town or parish where a person lived or was qualified to vote in order to locate his address, which may be incompletely recorded, whilst lodgers and other short-term residents may not appear at all. Men aged 19 and serving in the armed forces were listed as 'absent voters' in their home Parliamentary constituency divisions after 1918. You will also find graduates listed under their respective universities, until their parliamentary representation was abolished in 1948.

The qualifying date for inclusion into the register was October and it was published in February. Entries were valid until the next edition, during which time voters might have died or moved away. It is a good idea to look at the register both for the year of the census and the year after for any changes of address or family circumstances. You can see from these how many of the family were living together or in the same neighbourhood at any one time.

Constituency boundaries changed from time to time, so a specific address may come under different electoral divisions. Changes up to 1971 are plotted, with maps, in F. W. S. Craig, *Boundaries of Parliamentary Constituencies, 1885–1972*.

Where electoral registers are deficient you may be able to fill the gaps by consulting county and borough poll books, which were published after every Parliamentary election. Before the secret ballot was introduced in 1872, these lists of names and addresses of qualified persons relate only to those who actually voted, and for whom. Many were non-residents of the qualifying properties, so you can find out where they actually lived as well as who owned land. Most of the extant poll books date between about 1696 and 1872, an excellent collection of which is in the Guildhall Library, in London. Look in J. Gibson and C. Rogers, *Poll Books, c.1696–1872: A Directory to holdings in Great Britain* for their other whereabouts.

Another useful directory of addresses around a census year is the *Return of Owners of Land of One Acre and Upwards*, published in 1875 for England and Wales, in 1874 for Scotland, and in 1876 for Ireland. Copies can be found in many libraries of the county listings of owners' names, addresses, extent and nature of the land, and its gross estimated rental. These are useful because they reveal the whereabouts of absentee owners.

Trade and commercial directories

Trade and commercial directories were published as an outlet for merchants, professional people, craftsmen, traders, farmers and publicans to advertise their services through circulation to potential suppliers, distributors and customers. They also helped promote local industry and commerce. The earliest directories, mainly confined to naming private residents and merchants, were printed in the late seventeenth century, and within the next 100 years almost every county and large town had been served. Prominent among these was the annual *Post Office London Directory*, dating from 1800. The first telephone directory was issued in 1880.

Good runs of London and provincial directories are held by the Guildhall Library in London, and the Society of Genealogists. Local record offices and libraries generally have copies for their own areas. Scottish directories were compiled less often, but may be seen in the National Archives of Scotland in Edinburgh, and in regional offices, those for Ireland are in the National Archives, and the National Library of Ireland, in Dublin. A number of CD-ROMs, microfiche and facsimile copies of county and city directories are widely available. At least one digital copy of a directory for each country and city during the 1850s, 1890s and 1910s is being made available online at **www.historicaldirectories.org**.

You can discover the background history, function, dates of publication and scope of known directories from J. E. Norton, *Guide to National and Provincial Directories of England and Wales, excluding London, published before 1856*, G. Shaw and A. Tipper, *British Directories: A Bibliography and Guide to Directories published in England and Wales (1850-1950) and Scotland (1773–1950)* and P. J. Atkins, *The Directories of London, 1677–1977*.

How they were compiled

Some of these directories had a short life, as they were expensive to produce and market, ruining their promoters before their investment could be recouped. The printing costs were partly borne by local advertisers and subscribers. The publishers generally relied on local agents to collect the information, and no payment was asked for a single entry, though further ones might attract a charge.

Each edition was about a year out of date, and, although regularly revised and updated, a number were often little more than reprints. Although rival publishers lifted from each other's work, you can still find diverse entries in those years when several publishers produced volumes for the same places. Some of the stolen names and addresses were themselves out of date, so the reliability of the entries may be questionable, the range and quality of the content dependent on the purpose of the compiler, the integrity of his agents, and the response of the public.

Directories can be frustrating to search as they are listed only householders, and not every one at that, particularly if they were away when the agent called, failed to provide information about their business or did not come within the ambit of the relevant social or commercial statuses. Often it is an agricultural labourer, a domestic servant or lodger you want to track down, and these are the very people who were excluded. Some addresses were omitted altogether, and where street names or numbering of properties were altered, this can present difficulties. Most directories contained a throwaway map, and that is exactly what happened: they were generally thrown away. However, many directories will show which streets and roads crossed or abutted each other, so that you can try and find these marked out on other surviving town plans of the era.

Provincial directories

Each county volume was divided alphabetically into hundreds or wapentakes, and then into their constituent parishes, towns, villages and hamlets. Other directories consisted of a single city and its hinterland, and still others combined several contiguous counties in one book. Each place was prefaced by a short topographical description, the distance from the nearest market town, a summary of the type of farming or industry conducted there, and the population total. Names of major landowners, the descent of relevant manors, church history, patron and present incumbent of the living, income from the tithe and glebe, foundation dates of any chapels, local charities and trust funds, and of endowed schools, were all chronicled. Names of local public and parish officers, details of postal, transport and carrier services, market days and the annual fair, were followed by a list of names and addresses of private residents, giving their rank and profession if applicable, plus the names and addresses of professional and tradespeople, farmers and innkeepers.

As might be expected, directories of larger towns and cities are much more detailed. The first to be published, for the City of London in 1677, was succeeded by regular editions from 1734. The earliest provincial town to be covered was Birmingham, in 1763. These directories often take in the countryside around, so check the table of contents for places outside the town or city boundaries.

London directories

The bulky *Post Office London Directories* were divided into sections. The *commercial directory* listed alphabetically the names, addresses and employment of people in the professions, a trade or craft; the *court directory* listed both the town and country seats of private residents; the *official directory* set out alphabetically the names of people in government or legal offices; the *street directory* listed the principal London streets and roads in alphabetical order, with the names and occupations of householders ranged under house number, and indicating where each street intersected with others, sites of public or church or chapel buildings; the *trade and professional directory* was also arranged alphabetically, according to their title, and cross-referenced to related occupations. Where two trades were carried on by the same person, usually one only entry was listed, an asterisked note explaining duality of occupation. The *law directory* contained names and business addresses of judges and official staff in London and the provinces, including the police, barristers, solicitors and attorneys, proctors, notaries public, patent agents, district registrars, sheriffs and their officers, shorthand writers, law booksellers and stationers; the *Parliamentary directory* listed peers and members, their country and town residences, constituencies and clubs, with a corresponding index of constituencies; the *city, clerical and parochial directory* recorded the names of civic officials, parish churches and other denominational places of worship, the names of incumbents, officiating ministers and parish clerks, the titles of Poor Law Unions and their officers; finally, a *banking directory* outlined titles and registered offices of banks in London and throughout the United Kingdom. A map, on the scale of four inches to the mile, was usually attached for use with the street directory. There was also a section for 'too late entries' to encompass details from forms returned after the deadline.

What you can learn

Such directories provide a fascinating time capsule of communities, tracing their changing social and commercial structure, growth and development over time, as well as enabling you to trace continuity of residence, migration, local and regional surname distribution. You can plot a person's movements and occupations, bearing in mind that not everyone lived where they worked, and may have undertaken several types of employment at the same time, particularly in rural areas.

People in public life

Annual court directories, such as *Kelly's Handbook to the Titled, Landed and Official Classes*, published since 1874, *Who's Who*, from 1849 and *Who was Who*, from 1897, contain potted biographies, current addresses, clubs and hobbies submitted by people prominent in social, academic and political life. A cumulative index to the last two up to 1996, is available on CD-ROM.

Occupational directories

Professional and occupational directories began to appear in the mid-nineteenth century. You can find out about these from *The ASLIB Directory of Information Sources in the United Kingdom* and S. A. Raymond, *British Genealogical Bibliographies: Occupational Sources for Genealogists*. Annual professional directories, listing practitioners in the law (from 1775), the Anglican church (from 1836), and medicine (from 1847) were imitated during the course of the nineteenth century by the issue of similar volumes for newer professions such as dentistry and civil engineering. The foundation dates and registered offices of professional and craft associations can be gleaned from *Associations and Professional Bodies of the United Kingdom*, and *Directory of British Associations and Associations in Ireland*. Each of these should have good runs of past and present directories of members' names, but their libraries are not always open to the public, though the staff may be willing to undertake short searches for you among these and other sources. Limited collections are held in the Guildhall Library, and the Society of Genealogists.

Each profession or trade, on forming its regulatory organization, determined qualification for membership and fellowship and a code of conduct; candidates might be admitted on passing professional examinations, be nominated or elected, or pay an annual subscription to belong. The preface to the directory will normally give an outline of terms and conditions of membership. The entries are usually arranged alphabetically and summarize each member's education and relevant training, career and current address, based on his own submission. When a name disappears, look at the end of the entries for a list of deceased members, which may disclose the date of death. However, parentage is not generally included, nor date of birth, information which may be forthcoming from the records of the professional organization, the place of education or formal training.

Newspapers

If you know when a locally prominent or professional person died, check the local newspaper for an obituary or funeral notice. Consult *Willing's Press Guide* or *The Times Tercentenary Handlist of English and Welsh Newspapers 1620–1920* for details of the contemporary press. Microfilm copies of local newspapers may be found in the reference library or record office serving that area. There is an excellent collection of old national and provincial newspapers and periodicals for the United Kingdom and Ireland (and many from overseas) from 1801 in The British Library Newspaper Library, in London. Newspapers also tell you what was going on, what people were reading about, and what notices and advertisements were being placed.

Rate books

The name and address of every householder has been listed in parish rate books from the mid-eighteenth century. Rates were levied for a variety of purposes at a fixed amount in the pound, based on the yearly value of occupied property. Surviving books are now mainly in county record offices or reference libraries in large cities, but they are rarely street-indexed or complete.

The books are arranged by road and street, and include under column headings each assessed property number, the names of the occupier and owner, a property description, its name or site, estimated extent, gross estimated rental, rateable value of the occupied land and buildings, the rate payable in the pound and the date of the annual or six-monthly collections, annotated with details of any arrears.

Because occupiers are identified with their properties in these books, they may give street addresses not specified or unclear in the census. Deaths and changes of occupancy or ownership since the previous collection are indicated by marginal notes against the entries. Fluctuating values suggest property alterations, demolitions and enlargements, houses divided up into apartments or consolidated under a single occupancy. The books can also be utilized to date newly constructed houses, street developments and name changes.

Although street numbering was introduced in the City of London in 1767, it was not customary in provincial towns and cities until about 1847. Where a street name was altered or the numbering scheme changed, it may be unclear if a person continued to occupy the same premises or had moved. By noting down the names of the immediate neighbours and finding them in previous and subsequent rate books, you can gain a fairly reliable impression of continuity as it is extremely unlikely that all of them would have moved away. Houses on street corners may also prove difficult to identify, because they might be listed inconsistently under one street or the other.

Rate collectors sometimes varied their routes, so the order in which streets were listed may not be the same from one year to the next, and because they lack street indexes, you may have to examine books covering several districts when boundary adjustments occurred.

Maps and photographs

Electoral registers, directories and parish rate books can be used in conjunction with maps and town plans to plot exactly where your ancestors lived. It is worth seeing if there are any contemporary photographs to see what the property and its neighbourhood looked like, and compare it with how it is today. Most local libraries and record offices have substantial collections of local photographs.

Maps worth looking for

There are three main series of maps of especial genealogical value: tithe maps, Ordnance Survey maps, and Valuation Office record sheet plans. Until the second quarter of the nineteenth century, most parishioners in England and Wales contributed a tenth (tithe) of the annual produce of their land or stock nourished by it to the tithe owner (usually the parish priest). On agreement between most of the landowners or by resolution of the largest landowner, a number of parishes had already commuted this payment in kind to money when the common land had been enclosed. A list of Parliamentary enclosure awards and maps can be found in W. E. Tate, *A Domesday of English Enclosure Acts and Awards*. The remaining parishes (about 79 per cent, or over 12,000) converted the tithe to an annual rent charge after the Tithe Commutation Act of 1836.

Between 1836 and 1852, professional tithe commissioners and their assistants visited each parish, hamlet and township to confirm voluntary agreements reached by local landowners about commutation, or to draft a compulsory award which they had to accept. The commissioners drew up triplicate maps and plans of each place so that the rent charges could be assessed, based on land valuations and a seven-year average of the price of wheat, barley and oats. The occupiers were the tithe payers, but the landowners were ultimately responsible if they demurred. A list of surveyed districts can be found in R. J. P. Kain and R. R. Oliver, *The Tithe Maps of England and Wales, A cartographic analysis and county-by-county catalogue*. One map and accompanying schedule (also called an apportionment) was lodged with the Tithe Office, and was later transferred to the National Archives, another was given to the bishop's diocesan registrar in case of any future dispute, and the third copy was kept in the parish church. These last two copies are now usually available in county record offices, to which were attached any later revisions or revaluations, which may not always be appended to that in the National Archives. A complete set of Welsh tithe maps and schedules can be found in the National Library of Wales, in Aberystwyth. It may be more convenient to look at local copies, and where one is in poor condition, another might be better.

The dated maps were not all drawn to the same scale, but most were 26½, 20, or 13 inches to the mile, showing the roads, woodland and waterways, and on which were marked out the various sizes and shapes of every affected plot, each with its own unique number. If you do not know exactly where your ancestors lived, it is best to look first at the schedule, which sets out the date of agreement or award, and then lists alphabetically the names of the landowners, their chief tenants, their plot numbers, the title or description of the land or premises, their state of cultivation, extent in acres, roods and poles, and amount of the annual rent charge. Then find the plot number on the map. From these two documents you can discover the concentration, dispersal, central or marginal location of a

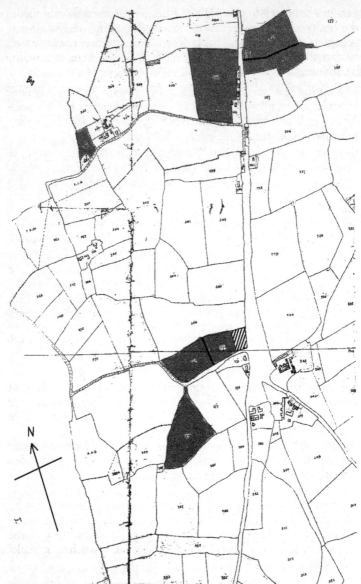

figure 6 tithe map of Great Finborough 1841, Suffolk
Meshech Chaplin farmed here until his death in 1849, aged 61 (reproduced by
permission of Suffolk Record Office)

properties occupied by Meshech Chaplin

Meshech Chaplin's house

person's property in the parish, what it was used for, its value, proximity to communications and water, the names of the occupiers of adjoining properties, whether the person was an owner/occupier or tenant, and identify who were the major landowners.

The entries are annotated with references to any subsequent annexed amendments of altered apportionments, for instance when land was taken to construct railways or make way for suburban expansion.

In 1936, the rent charge was converted into a 60-year annuity, paid by the landowner, and further maps were commissioned, which are now in the National Archives. The annuity was abolished in 1977.

As the tithe commissioners' survey was undertaken close to the census years of 1841 or 1851, the maps and plans can be used to track down exactly where your antecedents lived, the latter census returns recording the current farm acreage and number of men and boys employed on it. Unfortunately, not every occupier's name appears in the schedule, especially if he or she was a sub-tenant or shared the property with several other tenants. Secondly, property boundaries are not always accurately marked out, but the 'first class' maps, certified by the commissioners, and in the National Archives, will be of higher quality than their working record sheets.

The map and schedule complement surviving parish lists of householders assessed to pay the Land Tax. These are particularly good from 1780 to 1832, when the assessments were used to find out who was qualified to vote in Parliamentary elections. The lists are usually in county record offices. You can also check their whereabouts in J. Gibson and D. Mills, *Land and Window Tax Assessments*. The tithe material can also be used in conjunction with parish rate books, and manorial rentals of tenants. The whereabouts of known manorial records can be elicited from the Manorial Documents Register of the Historical Manuscripts Commission, in the National Archives, Kew. Some of the catalogues to these are available at **www.hmc.gov.uk/ mdr/mdr.htm**.

Scotland

The survey starting in 1836 did not stretch to Scotland, where teinds (a form of tithe) were levied in kind or money on proprietors of heritable property until abolished in 1925.

Records of teinds may be found among family and estate papers, disputes and adjusted payments settled by the Teind Court and Commissioners in the National Archives of Scotland, in Edinburgh.

Ireland

As in England and Wales, a tithe was collected in kind in Ireland until the second quarter of the nineteenth century. Tithe applotment books, dating from about 1823–38 cover every barony, civil parish and its townlands, recording commutation based on the average price of wheat and oats over the seven years up to 1823. The original volumes are in the National Archives of Ireland in Dublin, those for the six northern counties being in the Public Record Office of Northern Ireland, in Belfast, and on microfilm in the National Archives in Dublin. Microfilm copies are available in the National Library in Dublin.

The tithe books are incomplete surveys, because certain types of land were exempt, but they enumerate the names of tenants in each townland, and in many cases the names of their immediate landlords. There is a surname index in the National Library, in Dublin (**www.nli.ie**), giving county by county the barony where a name was located, but you will then need to find the civil parish yourself. As they long predate surviving census returns, central registration of births, marriages and deaths, and in some instances parish registers of baptism, marriage and burial, the tithe books are an important key to fixing people in time and place, and offer a guide to surname distribution and densities.

Ordnance Survey maps and town plans

The tithe was the first large-scale study of landownership and occupancy to be undertaken. The Ordnance Survey, set up in 1791, began to issue a series of official maps for England and Wales based on a standard scale of one inch to the mile, starting with Kent in 1801 and ending with the Isle of Man in 1873, when a thorough revision was commenced. Facsimiles of the first edition have been published by one or two commercial firms, and original maps may be held in county record offices, local libraries, as well as the special map collections of the National Archives, The British Library, and the Bodleian Library, in Oxford. A relevant reader's ticket is necessary to visit the last three. The maps are immensely useful in showing place-names of villages, hamlets and towns, the geographic contours, topographical features, water and road networks of an area with which you might not be familiar, or whose landscape has since been drastically changed by urban encroachment, but they are not sufficiently detailed to permit identification of individual field-names and boundaries.

For individual field-names and boundaries, you will need to find a larger scale map. In 1840 and 1853, the survey was extended to produce maps and town plans using scales of six inches and 25 inches to the mile respectively, so that particular properties and field-names could be easily picked out. They were adopted by the Registrar General to demarcate census registration districts and sub-districts, but the other main purpose to which they were put was to assign hereditament (plot) numbers to every property during the general land valuation of England and Wales undertaken between 1910 and 1915. This was in preparation for a proposed (abortive) increment value duty to be collected when ownership changed. The resulting record sheet plans of income tax districts, and the accompanying field books, are in the National Archives, Kew, though there are some gaps.

Because the plans and books relate to the years immediately before the First World War, and to every piece of private property, they tell us about contemporary town and village layouts, urban and rural housing conditions and the current values of each. The precise location of a building can resolve any problem of change of name. They form a bridge between the tithe maps and schedules of the 1830s, 1840s and 1850s and the communities we know today. You can link them to photographic evidence, estate agents' sale particulars, sale catalogues, and auction notices in the local press, all of which may now be in county record offices. Used in combination with the 1901 and earlier census returns, you can determine the family's length and continuity of occupancy, the number of people who lived there at a specific date, the nature of any business conducted on the premises, and any change of land use since the tithe survey. You can determine how much property in a parish was concentrated in the hands of one or more families, and to whom it was let and at what rent, and who was responsible for payment of rates, the Land Tax and any other outgoings.

The scale of the record sheet plans, dating from 1880 to 1915, depended on population density, larger scale ones specifying street and road names as well as identifying larger buildings, and many plans were new revisions of urban and industrial centres. Occasionally you will find even bigger maps, up to 127 inches to the mile for some city centres, whilst others are enlarged for certain parts only. There are index sheets in the National Archives to help you identify the number of the correct record sheet. Each hereditament was demarcated, shaded in and allocated a unique number in red ink, except for exempt Crown property and land owned by statutory and public utility companies such as for railways and canals.

The parish field books are organized sequentially by hereditament number, cited at the top of the page with the record sheet plan reference, plus any related hereditament number. The valuation officers used parish rate books to extract the names and addresses of owners and occupiers, the extent and rateable value of the properties, to which were added any unrated sites. There is a street index to the London books, but otherwise you need to find the appropriate record sheet plan first, then find the hereditament number and link this to the field book.

Besides recording information taken from the rate books, the type of tenure was included (freehold, leasehold, yearly tenancy), annual rental, liability and amounts due for Land Tax and tithe, responsibility for rates, insurance and repairs, and the purchase price of the property if sold within 20 years up to 30 April 1909. There was a floor by floor description of the layout and function of each room, a list of outbuildings, sometimes sketched on a plan before 1912. Construction materials, including the roofing, the approximate age and present condition of the premises were also written down, as well as any recent expenditure on improvements or extensions. The property's gross market value, that of the site less buildings and timber, and its total worth less any fixed charges and encumbrances such as a mortgage, were listed, from which the assessable site value was calculated.

The valuation (Domesday) books, prepared before the field books, are held in county record offices, with many of the initial working papers and draft record sheet plans, except for volumes covering the City of London and Paddington (Westminster), which you can inspect in the National Archives. They duplicate the field books, though the building descriptions are omitted, and the properties are listed under the names of the landowners in the same way as the tithe schedules of the previous century. They may give more specific addresses for non-occupying owners too.

National Farm Surveys

If the land was a farm, you can also have a look in the county record office for land minute books kept by surveyors on behalf of the government between 1916 and 1918. Executive committees appointed by county War Agricultural Committees throughout England and Wales reported on the state of cultivation and efficiency of local farms and smallholdings. Correspondence, petitions and soldier labour books mention names of people who were tenant farmers, labourers, or in 1918 those deemed suitable for army recruitment or exempted because they were required for essential work. Tenants threatened with eviction, fine or imprisonment for failing to raise their standards of husbandry or to convert grassland to arable are also referred to, as well as women, aliens, soldiers and prisoners of war taken on to help.

The National Archives, Kew, holds corresponding National Farm Survey material for England and Wales between 1940 and 1943, similarly collected with the intention of increasing wartime food production. The maps are of six inches or 12½ inches to the mile, onto which were marked the numbered plots of farms and farmland over five acres. The returns, arranged by county and then alphabetically by parish, identify every farm, its owner's name and address and length of occupancy, with details of fruit, vegetables, hay and straw stocks, crops and grass, livestock, horses and employed labour. You can also discover whether there was electricity, water supplies and access to main roads. A representative from the Ministry of Agriculture then made an inspection. His report commented on the condition and management of the farm, before grading it. Personal remarks on the farmer's age, health and ability were often added. There are also parish lists drawn up in June 1941, giving the farm's full postal address, its acreage and owner's name. You can compare the two sets of wartime records for information on acreage, type of cultivation and manning levels a quarter of a century apart.

Scottish Valuation Office records

Scotland was divided up into 12 valuation districts by the Valuation Office in 1910, and the record maps and field books are in the National Archives of Scotland, in Edinburgh, where you can also search the yearly Scottish valuation rolls beginning with 1855. These are arranged under county or burgh, and list the landlord, tenant and occupier, the name and value of each property, and some have been indexed. You can use these to trace changes of occupancy and ownership.

The Primary Valuation of Ireland

In Ireland, the Tenement Act of 1842 led to a countrywide valuation of every property as a prelude to assessment of tenants' contributions towards the relief of paupers in Poor Law Unions. The resulting *Primary Valuation of Ireland, 1848–64* (also called Griffith's Valuation) can be searched as an indexed database at **www.irishorigins.com** which offers a charged service, at **www.otherdays.com** on subscription, or on CD-ROM, whereas the printed county volumes and microfiche copies have to be trawled through for entries of names.

The county books, organized by barony, Poor Law Union and civil parish, give under headed columns a map reference number, the name of each townland and its householders, their immediate lessors (landlords), a tenement description including its extent, the rateable and annual value of the land and buildings. Although every landlord and householder is listed, they do not include anyone else. Householders of the same name residing in the same townland are, however, distinguished from each other by the name of their father being written alongside in brackets.

Because there are so few extant 1851 and 1861 Irish census returns, this documentation is invaluable as a guide to surname distribution and location of individuals, supplementing the tithe applotment books of a quarter of a century earlier. As neither the 1901 nor 1911 census reveals exact birthplaces, the books can be utilized to show where a name was found within the county of birth 50 years before. Conversely, surname distribution in these two sets of books may enable you to find later family tenants of the same properties in 1901 and 1911. As they pre-date civil registration, the townlands and civil parishes indicate which churches and chapels might be appropriate places to seek for family baptisms, marriages and burials. You can also dig for title deeds for more information about sales and leases.

The National Archives of Ireland, in Dublin, has an incomplete set of the valuation surveyors' original notebooks, house books, field books and tenure books for southern Ireland, whilst those of the six northern counties are in the Public Record Office of Northern Ireland, in Belfast. They all contain map references, the house books noting occupiers' names, the field books the size of each holding, and the tenure books the yearly rent and nature of the occupancy (dated lease, or tenancy at will), which help anyone investigating estate papers or records in the Registry of Deeds, in Dublin. They also record any residential changes between the valuation and final publication.

Other Valuation Office records

Subsequent cancelled land books and current land books, at the Land Valuation Office, in Dublin, or in the Public Record Office of Northern Ireland, also mention any changes of ownership or occupancy since the Primary Valuation. Likewise, any variations in the size and nature of the premises affecting the valuation are noted in the regular revisions. The books can help you establish approximate year of death, movement out of the area, or even emigration of the owners and occupiers. During the last decade of the nineteenth century, a series of Land Acts allowed tenant-farmers to apply for subsidies to buy their land, so that it could be passed on to the next generation, and you may therefore still be able to trace descendants living there today.

09

finding your way to the records

In this chapter you will learn:
- how to plan your research
- what and where archives are
- how useful libraries can be

A great English genealogist, Sir Anthony Wagner, wrote that 'The prospects of success in solving problems of genealogy depend on many factors, but chiefly, I think, on four: property, continuity, name and record. The possessors of property, other things being equal, are better recorded and more easily traced than those with none, and the more so the greater their possessions. Those who from generation to generation maintain a continuity, whether of dwelling place, of trade, or of anything else, are, other things being equal, more easily traced than those who break with family tradition. Some names are rare, some common and the genealogical advantage is all with rarity, whether the question be of surname or Christian name or the two combined or of a pattern of names of brothers and sisters recurring in a family. Finally there are areas, both geographical and social, where the records are good and full and others where they are poor ... Sometimes all four factors are favourable, sometimes one or two or three, sometimes none, but the presence of any one may compensate for the lack of another' (*English Genealogy*, p. 411).

We are not all going to be lucky enough to have ancestors who were large landowners and whose estate ownership can be traced in deeds and wills down many generations; sometimes it is the person at the bottom of the social ladder who will be far better recorded. It might be a family on the verge of poverty whose father or mother had to establish a legal place of settlement so that if he or she fell on hard times and was unable to work, the parish would support them financially. It might be a person in trouble with the law, tried and sentenced, and appealing against the sentence, or locked on board a prison hulk or ship bound for the colonies. Records abound for both these sets of people. Continuity of residence brings its own problems, because you will discover that the pool of forenames used locally in past times was small, unless new forenames were introduced from outside the community, there was a passing fashion for particular names like those of the patron saint of the parish, popular national or literary figures of the day. Surnames used as forenames can help identify specific family descents. The nightmare scenario for most family historians is continuity of settlement in a rural parish with relatively few surnames and several inhabitants of the same forename having children baptized with identical names at the same time. Certain families may become extinct, to be replaced by other branches moving in, or by people of the same name but no blood relationship from neighbouring parishes. Some apparently distinct variant names may actually stem from the same ancestor, the spellings having evolved by different local pronunciations, depending on the place where they were recorded. Seemingly rare surnames may not be as unusual as appear at first glance. Conversely, common surnames may be densely concentrated in certain parts of the country. Some surnames today can be associated with particular parts of the country for their origin. Recent surname studies have led to the creation of databases plotting geographic surname distributions in various periods. DNA testing offers an exciting way of tracing the common genetic codes of people with variant surnames.

So far, most of your research will have been in nineteenth- and twentieth-century centralized records, but as you progress further back in time you will inevitably have to tap into sources kept in lots of different places. At present there are no consolidated or fully comprehensive personal name indexes, or any uniform or consistent scheme of reference to these.

What you have learned so far

Firstly, look at your family tree, and all the additional information you have been able to insert onto it from various birth, marriage and death certificates, and from the census returns. Have you found the answers to your original questions? Are you now ready to move on, or do you need to spend some more time among these records? Are there any contradictions? If so, how can these be explained, or do you think you may have made a copying mistake, or attributed information to the wrong ancestor? Do people in the family seem to have moved around rather a lot? Have a look at a map to see if these migrations are reasonable in the given timescale, or should you discount them as similarly named people from an entirely different family? Have some family members remained elusive? Have you written down full details about the years you searched, for what events, and surname variants? Are there any gaps? You may need to plug these first before going any further, or repeat searches where you are uncertain you extracted all the required information or understood what the document was saying.

Drawing up a checklist

Think about the particular line you now wish to pursue beyond centralized records, and list, in no special order, sources you think may contain the answers. Then do some background reading about them, to see if they really are the most appropriate, and if they are linked to other archives which may help you build up your family's history. Try the seach engine **www.ixquick.com** to hunt for what may be available on the Internet on specific subjects. The subject-index in your library catalogue should help too. Always search published bibliographies and footnotes in books and articles for ideas on further reading. Feature articles in the family history and local history press also shed light on sources and the problems in using them. Most libraries will have copies of current and previous issues of journals like *Family Tree Magazine*, *Practical Family History*, *Family History Monthly*, and *Ancestors*, *The Local Historian, Local History Magazine* and *Local Population Studies*; for American family historians, *Everton's Family History Magazine*, *Family Tree Magazine*, and *Family Chronicle* are packed with articles about specific sources and research methodology, new databases, search tips and reviews. The *National Genealogical Quarterly* and *New England Historical and Genealogical Register* contain much advice passed on by genealogical experts. This is available online from 1847 to 1994 at **www.newenglandancestors.org**.

Have a look at S. A. Raymond's *British Genealogical Bibliographies,* and *British Genealogical Periodicals: a Bibliography of their Contents*. The Gibson guides, now produced by the Federation of Family History Societies, focus on a number of sources of value to family and local historians. Each guide contains a full introduction to the records, explaining their historical background and purpose, as well as their content and limitations, before a county by county listing of their whereabouts, and those of any transcriptions, copies or indexes.

Prioritize the sources most likely to tell you what you are looking for. Restrict yourself to researching one generation at a time, and an upper limit of ten sources. You will then need to check the whereabouts of the material for the period and place you want.

Hunting down your chosen sources may take time, but a disciplined approach to your research will save wasted hours later. You will need to put in some groundwork and to devise a plan before you embark on a research trip to a record office such as that at Kew, or to a local record repository.

What archives are

Archives are records which are no longer in active use by their creators or those people for whom they were intended. Some may still be called upon from time to time for reference purposes, and many will have their own finding aids which were compiled when they were created or in active use, to make them speedily retrievable and easily understood. We are likely to create documents to record decisions and activities or to keep track of expenditure. Those of communities, organizations, and local and central government were stored where they were created for reasons of convenience, and were kept in their original arrangement. They are therefore most likely to run chronologically by date. Through time the sheer volume of accumulated records might become overwhelming, the majority of which were no longer useful, so they might be weeded and only selected items chosen for more permanent preservation, and the rest disposed of elsewhere or destroyed. For example, the 9½ million or so administrative and departmental records deposited by central government and by the English and Welsh central courts of law in the National Archives in Kew, represent merely two per cent of what was ever created, which is a sobering thought.

How archives are grouped

Archives fall into three main groups: state, ecclesiastical, and private. State archives embrace both central and local government and courts of law. Ecclesiastical archives include not only those of the Established Church but of other denominations too. Private archives, cover semi-official public bodies, families, estates, and businesses.

National archives of the United Kingdom

The 'public records' (government and legal) of the United Kingdom government departments and agencies, and of the central courts of law of England and Wales, can be inspected in the National Archives in Kew. A number of Welsh records have now been transferred from Kew to the National Library of Wales. There are similar national archives offices for Scotland, Ireland, and Northern Ireland. Access to each is by a renewable reader's ticket, which can be issued when you first visit, on production of a current UK driving licence or banker's card, or a valid passport. Each has its own website, all of which except the National Archives of Ireland (**www.nationalarchives.ie**) can be reached via **www.familyrecords.gov.uk**, a government portal. The sites provide online guidance for family historians and a series of leaflets to help you plan your visit, and have an e-mail address for enquiries. The Kew, Aberystwyth and Edinburgh sites have online catalogues to their holdings.

The National Archives in Kew contains material representing continuous record-keeping spanning almost 1,000 years, including the Domesday Book, dating from 1086. The public records here are usually made available to searchers when they are 30 years old. Exceptions to the rule are the census returns, which are closed for 100 years, personnel records of the armed services, and records involving national security. Others may become immediately available. The government department concerned decides which records are to be selected for permanent preservation and when they should be released to the public. They are transferred to the National Archives to be catalogued before being made available.

Surrogate copies of some of the most popular public records for family historians are kept in the Family Records Centre, in central London. These include indexes to divorces in England and Wales between 1858 and 1958, the Registrar General's Miscellaneous Non-statutory Foreign Returns from 1627 to 1965, deposited non-parochial registers of births, baptisms, marriages and burials, wills and administration grants from the chief church court (Prerogative Court of Canterbury) from 1384 up to 1858, and death duty registers, 1796–1857, and indexes to 1903, all of which are described in this book. The FRC is the only place of the two where you have access to microfilm copies of the census returns of England and Wales between 1841 and 1891, though you can search the 1901 census online and on microfiche in both places. There are a number of online family history databases at both sites, including indexed digital images of the Prerogative Court wills. You do not need a reader's ticket to use the Family Records Centre, and unlike the National Archives, it is open on Bank Holiday Saturdays, except for Easter and Christmas. Copies of the above microforms are widely available elsewhere, especially in family history centres, making these records searchable throughout the world. Such copies protect the original documents from further wear and tear.

How to find what you want

There is no personal name index to all the public records, none of which was created or intended with the genealogist in mind, though some may be indexed. The documents are kept in their original arrangement and are catalogued using letters representing their department of origin. Each set of records is given a series number, and each document, box, book or bundle a unique piece number. The catalogues help you find these references, which you need to cite when ordering documents for use in the search rooms. The paper catalogues have now mostly been dumped into a computer memory bank called PROCAT. Try PROCAT, by keying in a phrase, name, place or subject you are interested in to see what references are displayed on the screen. If you want to trace service records about soldiers, sailors, merchant seamen, Royal Marines, airmen and women, land girls, nurses, teachers, medals, gallantry awards, coastguards, dockyard personnel, customs and excise officers, lawyers and others appointed by the Crown, records about the Metropolitan Police, the Royal Irish Constabulary to 1922, railway company staff up to 1948, dissenters, emigrants, immigrants, Huguenots, naturalization certificates, changes of name by enrolled deeds poll, bankrupts, divorces, coroners' inquests, trials in the Assize courts or Old Bailey Sessions and Central Criminal Court, civil litigation from Medieval times onwards, tax lists, Poor Law Union records after 1834, enrolled land deeds, tithe and enclosure maps and awards, Valuation Office maps and field books, the National Farm Survey of 1940, and correspondence from and to the colonies and foreign countries where the government was represented, then this is the place for you. There are online leaflets covering all of these, with direct links into the appropriate part of the catalogue.

A number of the Welsh legal records have been removed from the National Archives, in Kew and transferred to the National Library of Wales in Aberystwyth. The National Library is the place of deposit for Welsh public records, being mainly those of the civil, criminal and equity proceedings of the Great Sessions. It also holds copies of the Welsh census returns, parish and Nonconformist registers and records, diocesan material such as marriage allegations and bonds, and bishops' transcripts, wills proved in the local church courts before 1858, later registered copies of wills, manorial documents, maps, deeds, personal, family and estate papers, pedigrees, and newspapers. The website address is **www.llgc.org.uk** which you can also access via **www.familyrecords.gov.uk**, the UK government's national archive portal.

There are two branches of the National Archives of Scotland, based in HM General Register House, and West Register House, Edinburgh. The Historical Search Room, in HM General Register House, holds legislative and administrative records of Scotland before the Union with England in 1707, those of the central and many local courts, kirk session minutes relating to Church of Scotland congregations, archives of other denominations, testamentary material from all of the Scottish commissariats, registers of sasines and deeds, valuation rolls, taxation lists, burgh records, those of customs and excise officers, and military musters, pedigrees, family, business and estate papers. An online personal name index to 350,000 digital images of testamentary records running between 1500 and 1875 (soon to be extended to 1900) is available at **www.scottish-documents.com** which is a charged service.

The National Archives of Ireland, in Dublin (**www.nationalarchives.ie**), and the Public Record Office of Northern Ireland, in Belfast (**www.proni.gov.uk**), are the places of deposit for material relating to their jurisdictions. Besides housing surviving census returns for the whole of Ireland, the National Archives of Ireland holds some parish registers of the Established Church of Ireland, marriage licence bonds, wills and administrations, tithe applotment books, Primary Valuation and various taxation lists, army and militia papers, pedigrees, and microfilmed copies of material located in other repositories or in parish churches. The Public Record Office of Northern Ireland covers the six northern counties and contains microfilm copies of sources relating to them before 1922 and held in the National Archives of Ireland, as well as some parish registers, wills, land and manorial records, army and militia lists, family, business and estate papers.

National archives of the United States of America

The National Archives and Records Administration (NARA), in Washington, DC, (**www.archives.gov**), holds the following freely accessible federal material: census returns 1790–1930, mortality schedules, records about Indian tribes, slaves, land transactions and awards, maps, naturalizations of immigrants after 1906, ships' passenger lists, passport applications, births, marriages and deaths of American citizens abroad, details about federal government employees, military and naval personnel to the end of the First World War and veterans, their widows and dependants, coastguards, and wills of residents of District of Columbia. These are subject to a 75-year closure rule, and many lack personal name indexes. There are self-service microfilm facilities on a first-come first-served basis, but many of the microfilms can be inspected in 16 National Archive Regional Archives, each of which serves several States. You can arrange to borrow them for more convenient use in other State libraries and research institutions within each region. Details about services and holdings can be found at **www.archives.gov**, which also lists those online. There is a special genealogy section, with feature articles about certain records, and a State by State, county by county list of vital records, with contact addresses. You will need to obtain a search card to gain access to these.

English local government records

Records of English and Welsh local government are preserved in county record offices, observing pre-1974 boundaries. As well as offering a safe place of deposit for historical material, like the National Archives they continue to receive new acquisitions from councils and numerous local bodies and organizations, parishes and individuals all the time. Many now have insufficient accommodation to admit searchers without an appointment, so branch offices have sprung up, making archives of the immediate area available there, with microform copies of other popular sources in the county record office. There is generally access to the Internet, though you may have to pre-book to use a computer terminal. Their opening hours vary, some having a late-evening extension, or a Saturday service.

Admission to many county record offices is by reader's ticket, issued on production of personal identification either as part of the County Archive Research Network (CARN) and valid at any of the contributing offices, or on an individual basis. You will generally need to show or relinquish your numbered ticket each time you visit and order documents. As with tickets giving access to the National Archives, these reader's tickets are valid for a certain period, and are renewable. A few offices charge for a ticket, and you may need to take along two passport-sized photographs of yourself. It is a good idea to phone first to find out what is required. Occasionally you may find that all you need to do is sign the visitors' book on arrival. J. Gibson and

P. Peskett's *Record Offices: How to Find Them*, contains information about search regulations, opening hours, addresses, and phone numbers and handy maps indicating car parking facilities. It is advisable to ring first to confirm these details and to check if you have to book a seat in advance.

County record offices

A typical county record office will contain the following:

- filmed copies of census returns for the county;
- *International Genealogical Index, British Isles Vital Records Index, National Burial Index*;
- church registers of baptism, marriage and burial, and other parish records;
- Nonconformist chapel records;
- marriage licence allegations and bonds;
- published indexes;
- parish histories;
- typescript and published studies about the area;
- Poor Law Union material since 1834;
- wills and administrations;
- collections of family and estate papers;
- local authority cemetery registers, transcripts;
- maps;
- directories;
- electoral registers;
- poll books;
- newspapers;
- school records;
- rate books;
- tax assessment lists;
- county police records;
- county council minutes;
- manorial documents;
- pedigrees and biographies;
- Petty and Quarter Sessions records;
- coroners' records;
- County Court files;
- old deeds and charters;
- estate agents' sales catalogues;
- deposited records of local businesses, societies and

organizations;
- hospital records;
- personal name and topographical indexes to various deposited series of records.

You can discover more about their holdings from their websites. Try **www.google.co.uk** and insert the name of the record office you want, or use **www.genuki.org.uk** or **www.hmc.gov.uk/archon** as the link. You can search a number of their catalogues online at their websites, or at **www.a2a.pro.gov.uk** County record offices and other places of deposit of original manuscripts are listed in *Record Repositories in Great Britain* and in *British Archives, A Guide to Archive Resources in the United Kingdom* by J. Foster and J. Sheppard. The various Gibson guides list county by county holdings, indexes and transcripts of a number of the above sources (census returns, name lists and indexes, marriage indexes, specialist indexes, Poor Law Union records, wills and administrations, electoral registers and poll books, newspapers, certain tax lists, Quarter and Petty Sessions records, coroners' records), together with an introduction to their background history, content and limitations for family history researchers.

Some county record offices also contain a local studies collection of photographs and books about the area.

A number of county record offices operate a limited research service. Most offer free handouts about their principal holdings, and some publish family history guides.

Corporation and borough archives

Corporation and borough record offices contain civic and town administrative and judicial material. You would expect to find deeds, charters, maps and town plans, apprenticeship and freedom registers of guilds, livery companies or of burgesses, books recording payment of rates, tolls and taxes, and minutes of court sessions. Some of these sources stretch back to the Middle Ages. Access to them may be restricted or only by appointment.

Scottish regional centres

Scottish regional archive offices and libraries cover an area wider than a county; they contain records of local administration. Transcriptions, indexes and microform copies of local census returns, Old Parochial Registers of birth, baptism, marriage and burial, and other parish material can be consulted here as well as school records, papers about the distribution of poor relief, local newspapers, electoral registers, maps, and local history.

Local Irish resources

Ireland is served by a government-funded network of local history, genealogy and heritage centres. They hold computerized indexes of parish records, and offer a commercial research service, since public access is not permitted. The parish records mostly relate to those of Roman Catholics. Other sources included are tithe applotment books, the Primary (Griffith's) Valuation, civil records of births, marriages and deaths, gravestone inscriptions, and the 1901 and 1911 census returns. You can find out more about the county centres at www.irishroots.net.

American regional facilities

Individual American State archives, county courthouses, local libraries and historical societies, concentrating on local sources like land deeds and wills, as well as microfilm copies of church registers, gravestone inscriptions, and other parochial material, often overlap in their catchment areas, so that you do not always have to travel to the State capital to carry out your research. State archives are likely to hold copies of national archives, their own administrative and State government records and copies of sources in county courthouses. Try www. archives.gov or www.google.com for a link to the website of the State archives you are interested in.

County courthouses contain indexed civil registration records, some naturalizations granted before 1906, deeds of purchases and divisions of estates among heirs, wills, probate and guardianship records, mortgages, marriage material, civil and criminal court records, taxation lists and family papers. Unfortunately, political boundaries changed over time so have a look at *Map Guide for the US Federal Censuses, 1790–1920*, by W. Thorndale and W. Dollarhide, to trace their evolution. Another problem with courthouses is that many of their contents were destroyed by fire, flood, neglect or vermin. If you cannot locate a particular ancestor in surviving records, search for details about neighbours and associated families for clues. Try www. archives.gov or www.google.com for a link to county courthouse websites. The Church of Jesus Christ of Latter-day Saints has an ongoing programme of filming selected records from county courthouses throughout America.

Local historical societies are well worth contacting because they focus on their own community and the people who lived there. The website **www.cyndislist.com** should provide links to their websites.

Church records of England and Wales

Most diocesan record offices have now joined with county record offices. Unfortunately, diocesan boundaries do not always correspond with those of counties, so some ecclesiastical archives will be held in a county record office away from their immediate area. They were the custodians of records of ordinations of clergy, licences to schoolmasters, physicians, surgeons and midwives, the church courts, bishops' and archdeacons' visitations of parishes, wills, and bishops' transcripts of parish registers. Lambeth Palace Library, in London, is the place of deposit for archives for the Province of Canterbury (except for probate material, which is in the National Archives, Kew), and the Borthwick Institute of Historical Research, in York, is responsible for the archives of the Province of York.

Denominational libraries

Denominational archives include collections about the history and development of the relevant religious Movement and individual chapels or congregations, and biographies about clergy and prominent members.

Churches and chapels

Churches and chapels keep their current registers of baptism, marriage and burial, and occasionally those which are no longer in use. Records of parish or congregation business, like church-wardens' accounts of expenditure on church maintenance, and receipts of church collections, the minutes of vestry meetings, overseers of the poor rate books and payments of relief, highway surveyors' and constables' accounts, tithe map and apportionment and trust deeds gifting money or income from land to the parish, were all stored in the parish chest for safekeeping. Most of these are now in county record offices, but the more recent books of parish meetings and churchwardens' accounts will still be in the church. Chapel elders kept similar administrative records, and membership rolls. These tend to be held in the same place as their registers of birth, baptism and burial.

Private collections

Specialist archives include those accumulated by large public or limited companies and businesses, assurance societies, places of learning and professional training, trade and professional associations, private clubs, charitable foundations and trusts, historical and genealogical societies, and museums. Not all of these are open to the public, or grant only limited access. Nevertheless, specific searches can generally be undertaken on your behalf. You can find out about records of many of these from **www.hmc.gov.uk/nra**, which consists of catalogues to private collections of company, business, family and estate records. *The ASLIB Directory of Information Sources in the United Kingdom* provides a directory of addresses and contact details, which also tells you when each organization or society was founded, and services offered to members. Each organization is listed alphabetically by its title, and there is a subject index at the back of the book. You can also try J. Foster and J. Sheppard, *British Archives*, which is listed alphabetically by repository, under the name of the relevant town or city. This too contains a subject index.

Society of Genealogists and family history societies

Organizations you ought to find helpful are the Society of Genealogists, in London, and your local family history society. The Society's library is mainly self-service. Non-members are required to pay an hourly, half- or whole-day fee to use the library, which is offset against the joining fee if you decide to apply to become a member. There is an online catalogue to the library, and you can find out more about the collections by visiting **www.sog.org.uk**. Some of the indexed collections are being made available on the Internet at **www.englishorigins.com**, which is a charged service. To date you can search over 5 million entries in Boyd's Marriage Index (see the next chapter on parish registers) which covers the period 1538 to 1840, the marriage licence allegation index for the Vicar-General's and Faculty Offices of the Archbishop of Canterbury, 1694–1850, the Prerogative Court of Canterbury wills index 1750–1800, and Bank of England will extracts from 1717 to 1845 (see the chapter on wills) plus other databases.

It is well worth paying for a half-day's rummage around the collections, because there are gems to be excavated if you are prepared to dig around for them, particularly among the personal name indexes.

Family history societies focus on material connected with their own and contiguous counties. They often have a collection of microform copies of centralized records like the GRO birth, marriage and death indexes, National Probate Indexes, and the census returns, as well as the *International Genealogical Index* and *National Burial Index* for their own county. Many societies operate a reference library at their meetings or which you can use by arrangement. Several are attached to county record offices or local libraries. Consult their websites for details of services and contacts. The portal for societies belonging to the Federation of Family History Societies is **www.ffhs.org.uk.**

Family History

In Salt Lake City, Utah, the library of the Church of Jesus Christ of Latter-day Saints, founded in 1894 by the Genealogical Society of Utah, is open to the public without restriction. It is the largest genealogical library in the world, and is almost entirely self-service. Newcomers are invited to view a short presentation about the Society, its history, work, and library. You will be handed an interactive orientation pack to help you focus on what you are doing as you build up your family tree using its resources.

Absolute beginners may be directed to the FamilySearch Center nearby, where you can use the LDS website **www.familysearch.org** to look for your family name in the various databases. You can help yourself to the catalogued published family histories, and deposited family group sheets. You can search the library catalogue by personal or place-name or by subject, and if you do not have time, you can order up items for consultation in any of the 3,700 family history centres worldwide, by paying a small hiring-in fee.

Each floor of the Family History Library is devoted to a region of the world: there is one for printed material relating to the USA and Canada, another for microforms for these two; another floor covers the British Isles, Australia and New Zealand, and the fourth concentrates on the European Continent and rest of the world. You are able to move freely from one floor to another in search of your ancestors, and there are staff on hand to give advice and help you decipher copies of records in unfamiliar handwriting or languages. You can access the LDS website at one of the many computer terminals on each floor. You can do printouts directly from the screens, and you can also make photocopies of any other material in the library for a small fee.

There are daily classes for visitors if you want to learn more about family history research or particular types of records. You can also help yourself to one of the many free or inexpensive *Research Outlines, Resource Guides* and *Genealogical Word Lists*. There is also a growing series of inexpensive interactive leaflets, focusing on no more than four major sources per country, which take you through them step by step. All of these leaflets are designed for use in family history centres worldwide, and can also be ordered through your local centre, or using the online service.

A complete list of family history centres can be found at **www.familysearch.org** or in the phone book under 'Church of Jesus Christ of Latter-day Saints'. No reader's ticket is required, but it is essential to phone first to make sure of opening hours, and seat availability.

National Register of Archives

The National Register of Archives, part of the Royal Commission on Historical Manuscripts, which is now joined with the Public Record Office, Kew, to form The National Archives, is a central clearing-house of information on the manuscript holdings of local record offices, national and university libraries, museums, other organizations and private collections in the United Kingdom and elsewhere. From this you can discover the whereabouts of private archives, family and estate papers of major landowners and public figures. You can search the online catalogue at **www.hmc.gov.uk/nra** for personal, family business or corporate names. The Manorial Documents Register for England and Wales is a list of the known whereabouts of manorial material, which is cross-referenced to the parish or parishes over which each manor had jurisdiction. At present only details concerning those manors in Hampshire, the Isle of Wight, Norfolk, Yorkshire and Wales have been loaded onto the website at **www.hmc. gov.uk/mdr/mdr.htm**.

The Scottish Historical Manuscripts Commission is in the National Archives of Scotland, West Register House, in Edinburgh and the Irish Manuscripts Commission is in Dublin.

Using your local library

Try a large local library for general reference works and publications about your area, current local electoral registers, United Kingdom phone books, and back-numbers of certain national and local newspapers and magazines. A number combine a local studies collection with the main library service, so will additionally offer microform copies of centralized sources such as the census returns, birth, marriage and death indexes, access to the Internet and various databases such as the *International Genealogical Index*, as well as having a good collection of old directories, local maps and photographs. You can request books from other libraries using the inter-library loan service, and there should be an online catalogue for you to key in the subject, title or author of your choice. The opening hours of libraries tend to be longer than those of record offices, and of course you can borrow most of the books. Everything is generally self-service. You can undertake a lot of preparatory work in your local library using its published genealogical guides and sources, before you embark on a trip to the record office. Sometimes its contents will be sufficient to supply the answer to your problem. Many local libraries subscribe to **www.familia.org.uk** which lists their holdings of copies of the following genealogical sources: GRO registration indexes, census returns, trade directories, electoral registers, poll books of voters, the *International Genealogical Index*, any unpublished indexes relevant to the area, parish registers, and other materials. Unfortunately, county libraries and local studies collections may not always be in the same town as the county record office.

Always be on the lookout for local or themed museums, especially those featuring the industrial or rural past, since these can shed a lot of light on what it must have been like to live in the area when your ancestors were there. J. Cole and R. Church's *In and Around Record Repositories in Great Britain and Ireland* contains details of many of these, and you can also contact the local Tourist Information Centre for up to date information on opening hours, events and activities.

Regimental, Maritime and RAF Museums are also well worth visiting. You should be able to discover more about these by using a search engine and keying in the name of the regiment or title.

National and internationally known libraries

National libraries, like The British Library in London, the National Library of Wales, those in Edinburgh, and in Dublin, and the Linenhall Library in Belfast, require you to obtain a reader's ticket. Each of these has its own website. The British Library catalogue is available at its website **www.bl. uk/collections**. The British Library, National Library of Wales, Bodleian Library, Oxford, Cambridge University Library, and Trinity College, Dublin, are copyright libraries, in which a copy of every book published in the United Kingdom is supposed to be deposited. Besides its printed books, The British Library has sections devoted to official publications (including surviving electoral registers for the United Kingdom), manuscripts, prints and drawings, maps, the Oriental and India Office Collections, and the National Sound Archive. The National Newspaper Library is based in Colindale, although a part of The British Library. The National Library of Wales has a fine department of prints, drawings and maps.

The American Library of Congress, in Washington, DC (also a copyright library), has an excellent local history and genealogy room, to which there is a family name index. You can access the library catalogue at **www.loc.gov/catalog**. Books can be hired from here using the inter-library loan service. The library contains a notable series of current and old telephone, city and reverse telephone (criss-cross) directories for the US and overseas.. The Newberry Library, in Chicago, at **www.newberry.org/** and the New England Historic Genealogical Society also have renowned family history collections. State libraries are another good resource, and many have websites, which you can find via **www.cyndislist.com**.

A few words of warning: transcripts, catalogues and indexes do not escape error, abbreviation, inaccuracy and omission. They may be incomplete versions of the original source from which the information was copied or extracted. The compiler may not have really understood the significance or limitations of the material he or she was working with. Always find out what the compiler's objective was in selecting the material to copy or index, its scope, and what was excluded. A catalogue is a descriptive list of record office or library contents to help you find specific items. A transcript or index is no substitute for the original, but rather acts as a signpost to the original record, making it easier to access and read. Listed alphabetical strings of names are meaningless or misleading if you do not know the background to and purpose of the records from which they were lifted. Don't forget that the names have been plucked out of their original context in order to compile the index, and some of their significance lost in the process. Online and CD-ROM databases conceal information in a computer memory bank. It can only be retrieved in response to your commands, and this may differ if you interrogate it in different ways. With a book, or microfiche index or transcript, what you see is what you get, but it may take longer to find what you want.

Preparing for your visit to a record office

Time will inevitably be a constraint when you do your research. Plan ahead what you want to achieve, list those places and records you think most likely to contain the answers, and work out the most efficient and cost-effective way of setting about it.

- Find the present whereabouts of the record office, library, or family history centre you plan to visit. Study its website, or give it a call to check on opening hours, search regulations and if you need to reserve a seat or parking lot.
- Is it the right place to search the documents for the period and place you want? If not, can staff recommend where you should be? Can you order any in advance, and if so how many?
- If you want to use a microform reader or Internet access Point will you need to book?
- Is there anything else you need to know?

It is not recommended that you take a friend. The chances are their interest in your family will not be as riveted as yours, and they can prove a distraction and a nuisance to others.

When you get there

Always take a minimal amount of paperwork with you, since many repositories will insist you leave bags and papers locked up outside the search room. This can be massively inconvenient, and a waste of effort if you have carried them some distance. Limit yourself to a search checklist, a working family tree chart, plenty of A4 narrow feint file paper, a magnifying glass or sheet, a map of the area you are interested in, a good supply of sharpened pencils, soft drinks and a packed lunch in case the record office or library is not close to any shops or cafés. You want to maximize your time, not squander it hunting around for somewhere to eat. Don't forget to take any necessary personal identification or reader's ticket, plus loose change for the lockers and cloakroom.

Once in the search room you will normally be asked to sign the daily register, and show or be issued with a reader's ticket.

Many record offices and libraries supply explanatory leaflets to help you find your way around the system. If in doubt, ask the staff to help you locate your first document reference so your order can be processed immediately. Some archives are now only available in microform, so while you wait for original documents to be produced you could spend some time helping yourself to these. Make sure that you do not leave a microform reader unattended with your film or fiche still in place when going to collect an original document, because this may deprive someone else of a machine. You cannot be in two places at once!

Browse through any personal and place-name indexes, and if you come across any promising references, write these down and consult the main catalogue from which the information was taken before ordering the documents themselves. You will be surprised how often family history treasures lie hidden in such indexes.

Note down the title, author and date and place of publication of any books or guides and where you consulted them, in case you do not have time to read them in full, so you can find them again or order them on inter-library loan.

Try not to be too ambitious, and take regular, short breaks to offset mental fatigue and eye strain. The mind switches off unawares, and you may catch yourself turning pages or winding on reels of film totally oblivious to their content. If you miss that crucial entry of a name which will not appear anywhere else, you will end up with a needless gap in your family's history. If your attention starts to wander, take a walk, have a cup of coffee, browse the shelves, and then come back, turn back some pages or frames, and repeat the last part of your search. You will be amazed at how new this information seems.

Avoid being too hasty. If your expectations of yourself are too high, and you are running out of time, you will be tempted to rush. The longer the day gets the more tired you become, and the more careless your efforts. If you read slowly and steadily and plan another visit, your day will be far more productive. You will make fewer mistakes, your handwriting be easier to read, and your copying more accurate and complete.

Review and evaluate what you have found as you go along and add any new information onto your working pedigree chart. You may want to cross certain items off your search list, juggle them around or insert new ones. It may take a few minutes to identify their whereabouts, which may not be where you happen to be.

Avoid acting on assumptions and speculative searching, jumping from one random source to another in the hope of proving a hunch, or in pursuit of every reference to your surname in the relevant period in the hopes that eventually you will find the right person. Work carefully step by step, using your pedigree chart and checklist as your guide, focusing on one individual and one problem at a time.

Every stated or suggested family link should be capable of standing on its own merits without need of more research. Every new piece of evidence should corroborate or expand your existing knowledge. If not, then any discrepancy or conflicting assertion should be resolved before you go any further.

If your family seems to have moved around a good deal, look at your map to see if your conclusions about them are reasonable, or if you should be searching records of places closer to where your ancestors were last known to be. There may be a published local and parish history which could explain the background and patterns of regional movement in that area.

Plan B

Have a contingency plan in case you reach a dead end; if you have travelled a long way you may never return to that record office again, so make ample use of all relevant resources and seek out any special local collections which might assist in your research.

If you have a lot to do or run out of time or energy, plan for a two-day research trip. Many record offices will reserve material overnight for collection next morning. If there is a late-night opening and you are coming a long way this would be a good day on which to begin. It takes a while to understand the system, identify documents, order them, and then to read and take notes from them. If you know that you can work beyond normal office hours you will avoid the rush hour traffic, and feel more relaxed. If you cannot spare two days, many record offices are happy to tell you about any paid search service or give you names and addresses of independent professional researchers to complete the job.

Try if you can to combine visits to several repositories in a town on one day. This requires careful planning, and must be realistic. Having moved into the countryside, I frequently underestimate walking distances between London record repositories and how long I can spend hanging about for public transport. If you know their various opening hours and overlapping copies of material, you may be able to juggle your time to leave these till last and search them in the place staying open longest. However, your search priorities may preclude this. Don't stockpile everything until the end of the day when mental and physical tiredness are taking their toll. Your research should remain a pleasure not become an endurance test. You may even have to go backwards and forwards between venues, adding further to your time.

Handling documents

Paper, parchment or vellum documents are unique and irreplaceable. Many will be very old, decayed, fragile or faded, and were never created for frequent handling. They have been carefully preserved in controlled storage conditions, so deserve the utmost respect.

Be sure you have enough space to spread out large documents, and if wedges and weights are supplied, use these to support tender spines and keep the documents flat. Never lean on a document, mark it in any way, or write your notes on top of it. Try not to touch it more than absolutely necessary, and never lick your fingers when turning pages. If you have to sharpen a pencil record offices will usually provide pencil sharpeners, so you avoid transferring graphite onto documents. Never use a rubber, because its dust can erase the contents of a document. Some record offices will provide gloves for you to wear when handling their material. If the document is a large one, with little or no punctuation and lots of repetition, you may find a ruler or place marker helpful in scanning its many lines. Always turn a document over to see what is on the other side, and uncurl folded corners for concealed information. When you have finished, replace the document as you found it, and return it to the production desk if required.

Using microforms

Cramped workspace and poor lighting conditions pose special hazards in designated microform areas. You may also find that the magnification is insufficient to make the images readable on the screen. Ask the staff if you can move to another machine if you have to book one. They may be able to authorize you to examine the original document if the microform copy is indistinct or illegible. While it is very annoying to be able only to search copies of the original, remember this is intended to preserve the originals from constant wear and tear and deterioration. Besides, the very existence of such copies usually means they can be consulted simultaneously by many people in different places, whereas the original document is unique and can only be searched by one person at a time in the place where it is kept.

Problems with handwriting

Handwriting styles change dramatically over time and place. Working steadily back in time your eye becomes attuned to the ways in which letters and words were formed. Some Victorian documents can be more awkward to decipher than Tudor ones, compiled three centuries earlier, and there have been good and bad scribes in every epoch. You will also find that certain types of document had their own style of handwriting, shorthand and abbreviations.

Spelling was also haphazard until standardized by Johnson's *English Dictionary* in the eighteenth century. A single document might contain a person's name spelt in a several different ways. If in doubt about a word, pronounce it, as it may have been written phonetically. Words were often abbreviated by contractions or suspensions, especially when office copies were constantly being made of the same type of document, to which only new names, places, dates and other details were added. Examples of contractions, where vowels or part of the middle of a word are omitted, are usually indicated by a horizontal line drawn over the top. Where only a few letters of a word are written, the suspension of the rest is shown by a curved line over or through the last letter, by a flourish, or by a full stop. Other words may run together, have double vowels or letters in superscript. Some letters were interchangeable, such as 'c' and 't', or were written in a different way, like the reverse 'e' and the long 's'.

If a specific word presents problems, its context may help. Look for its occurrence elsewhere in the same document where it may be written more clearly or its meaning known from the words or phrases surrounding it. Use a magnifying sheet, increase or reduce the magnification, or move your seat to a different lighting area. Try to construct the word letter by letter, by identifying each one in other words on the same page or in the same document; leave a gap for letters you cannot recognize. Eventually you may be able to guess what the word is supposed to be. Leave a gap if you are attempting a word by word copy of a document, and come back to the missing words later. Write the word as it appears. As a last resort, ask a member of staff for help to decipher an odd word for you. You gain valuable practice by reading facsimiles and transcripts of a range of documents which build up your expertise and tell you about their content so you can predict where names and dates will usually appear. Don't forget that nineteenth- and twentieth-century documents can be hard to understand! A photocopy of a microform page perused at leisure, with an old alphabet for guidance will sometimes be easier to read.

Meanings of words

You may need to consult a specialist glossary or dictionary to understand archaic or obsolete words, or those which have changed their meaning over time. Some may be regional dialect words or written phonetically, especially when describing domestic furniture or work tools.

Understanding Latin documents

Formal legal documents follow a set pattern of content and terminology, so you can usually predict the whereabouts of stock phrases, names, relationships, and dates. This is indispensable when the document was written in abbreviated Latin, which was the language of legal court records until 24 March 1732/3, though English was used between 1653 and 1660. Read printed examples in translation first if Latin is not your strong suit. A rudimentary knowledge of Latin grammar and vocabulary is helpful, but you should be able to get by with a dictionary and Medieval Latin glossary. Often the original clerk's own grasp of Latin was shaky, so English words were given Latin endings. Be careful with proper names in Latin. In Medieval documents people may be described by their occupations or parentage rather than surnames, which until the fifteenth century were by no means fixed let alone hereditary. You can find out about Latin proper names and their English equivalents from *The Record Interpreter*, by C. T. Martin. Try the translation exercises in *Latin for Local and Family Historians*, by D. Stuart.

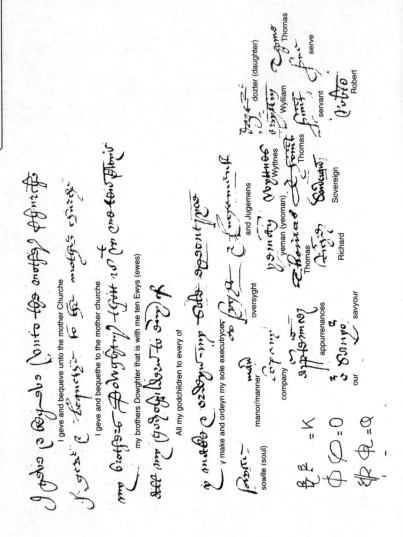

figure 7 samples of handwriting, showing capital letters and small characters, common contractions, abbreviations and suspended letters, found in sixteenth- and seventeenth-century documents

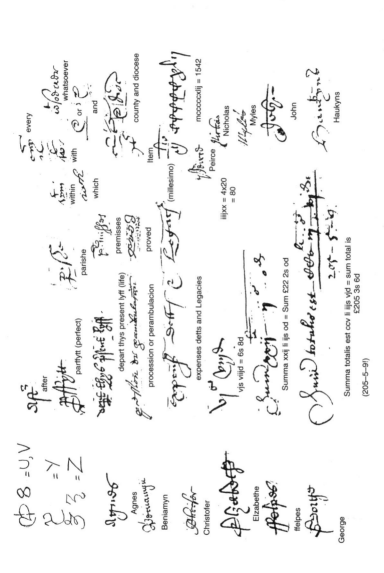

8 = U, V

= Y

= Z

after

parfhytt (perfect)

depart thys present lyff (life)

procession or perambulacion

parishe

premisses

proved

expenses detts and Legacies

every

within

which

with

whatsoever

and

county and diocese

Item

(millesimo)

mccccxlij = 1542

Peirce

Nicholas

Myles

John

Haukyns

iiijxx = 4x20 = 80

vjs viijd = 6s 8d

Summa xxij li ijs od = Sum £22 2s od

Summa totalis est ccv li iijs vjd = sum total is £205 3s 6d

(205-5-9l)

Agnes

Beniamyn

Christofer

Elzabethe

ffelpes

George

Working with numbers

Arabic numbers were not common in English documents until the late sixteenth century, Roman numerals being used, with pounds '*li, libri*', shillings '*s, solidi*' and pence '*d, denarii*' written in superscript to indicate sums of money. A score (20) was indicated by 'xx' in superscript above the appropriate number. Where numbers ended in digits, each one was dotted, and the final one indicated as 'j'. You can calculate money values today from *How Much is That Worth?*, by L. M. Munby.

The dating of documents

Before 1752, in England and Wales, Ireland and the Dominions, according to the Roman Julian Calendar, the first day of the year was 25 March (Lady Day). In 1582 Pope Gregory XIII introduced our present Gregorian Calendar. This was more quickly adopted by Continental Roman Catholic than Protestant states, Scotland using it from 1 January 1600. Thus a traveller passing from one country to another might go backwards and forwards between calendars.

Until the end of 1751, the whole of March was counted as the first month, and February as the twelfth. An unwary searcher might be lured into thinking a baptism entry in January 1741 followed by a burial in October 1741, related to the same infant. The latter event had actually taken place several months before in 1741 under the old calendar, and the baptism in 1742 under the new. If you write down January 1741/2, the conversion is clear to any reader. Occasionally months are numbered, particularly in records of the Religious Society of Friends, so the seventh month in 1741 was September, and the eighth October, rather than the ninth and tenth months they became from 1752. Old and new dating schemes present difficulties for users of the *International Genealogical Index*, where you may come across a mixture of original and modernized dates. If in doubt, go back to the original document.

Documents of a legal and fiscal nature were dated by regnal year. Since 1307 each new regnal year has commenced on the date of the current monarch's accession, and is numbered sequentially on each anniversary, ending on the day of death. Deeds and charters were often dated using the number of days or day in the week before or after a fixed religious festival or feast day, whilst others were tied to moveable Holy Days such as Easter and Trinity. Consult a perpetual calendar, or

A Handbook of Dates for Students of English History, by C. R. Cheney, to work out their precise dates.

Taking notes

When taking notes, use separate numbered sheets of file paper for each source and write only on one side. Head each with the document reference number or catalogue mark, its title, the period or date searched, and its whereabouts. If continuation sheets become detached such referencing makes it easier to reunite them. The first sheet should also record the period actually searched, any gaps, and name variants checked. Even if a search was negative, always record it to avoid repeating it. Try to avoid abbreviated or shorthand notes which may seem obvious at the time but are open to later misinterpretation. Keep extracted information in its original order, leaving unaltered the spelling of names and places (in Latin if necessary). It helps to pick out people's names in capital letters. Retain descriptions of family relationships as they were written, using 'my' in preference to 'his', to guard against later confusion. Indicate any part of a document which was too indistinct or illegible, or queried words, names and dates, which can be double-checked another time or against information in other sources.

There are commercial standard record sheets and workbooks which you can use to write in information from documents, which are arranged under headings. Their major drawback is that the headings take no account of any idiosyncracies of recording, and as a result information may be copied up out of sequence and out of its original context. For instance, an illegitimate child's surname may not be clear from a baptism register giving the surnames of the parents, but not of the child. If you write down the entry exactly as you saw it you will avoid jumping to the wrong conclusion.

Some record offices permit you to use a Dictaphone or laptop computer to help with your research, which speeds matters up somewhat. There is usually a quiet area set aside for laptop users, so enquire about this rather than face the ire of other readers. Always be sure to cite document references as described above. If you are using a Dictaphone you will need to spell out names and this can be irritating to other searchers; remember to do this as quietly as possible.

You may prefer to purchase photocopies or scanned images of documents for consultation at home. This will save you precious search time, but will cost you money. If you do this yourself follow any given instructions on how to operate the copier. Always write down on the back of any copy the document, microfilm or microfiche reference, what it relates to, and where you copied it. Some places, such as the National Archives, Kew, permit you to bring your own camera to photograph documents under supervision. Ask about this facility.

Interpreting your findings

At this stage you are sifting and gathering information, extracting names, relationships, dates, places, occupations and other given details. Your assessment of its relevance and genealogical value comes afterwards. Sometimes you will look at the wrong document or in the wrong place, search too short a period, overlook a key source, or miss documents which would have expanded or completed the story. You may misread, misunderstand or miss vital details. Be prepared to study a document again when it does not appear to make sense the first time. It is up to you to appraise your sources effectively and accurately.

Do not read into a document what is not there. Your evaluation of its value will be modified by its scope, period, and purpose, the knowledge, honesty and accuracy of its author. It may not tell you all or indeed any of what you want to know, or may tantalize you with its ambiguity. Any document should be capable of being corroborated or amplified by evidence from other documents, especially if written by someone else. Ask yourself who was providing the information, what was his or her role: as official recorder, participant, or witness? How contemporary was the person to the event or activity described, as a time lapse may indicate the source was secondary? Is the given information consistent with that in other records of the same period and place? Does it contain clues to other events and activities, or documentation? Does it clarify relationships, or name other people and places? If there are discrepancies, are these due to clerical error by the original author, a later transmission to writing of an oral record, or poor copying, or has there been a mistake on your part? Perhaps the document does not relate to your family branch at all, or to a different generation. And discarded information should be set aside and reviewed again from time to time.

Analyse your findings critically and carefully and write up each new fact onto your pedigree. This is only possible if you have sufficient relevant, valid information, regularly filed and easily retrieved. Do not be tempted to leave your filing until you have amassed so much that the task becomes overwhelming.

Filing and storage systems

Having transferred your discoveries onto your pedigree chart, file away your notes carefully and safely. Keep your system simple, and stick to it. The best test of a filing system is: can a total stranger understand it unaided, and can you quickly and easily retrieve information from it? Never destroy any notes, however negative, for they may come in useful later. Place file paper in a ring-binder, under subject or date order, with a checklist or search log at the front. Keep a separate correspondence log.

You might want to store information about individual people in an alphabetical card index, or record a couple and their children on family group sheets. Place the card or group sheet for the latest born person of the same name in front of earlier ones, and accord each one a unique number. Identify them by including their parents' names and date and place of birth. This number is linked to the correspondingly numbered person on your pedigree chart. A card can record much more than is disclosed on the chart.

You can feed your data onto computer, using a specially devised program. You can buy or hire commercial demonstration videos featuring a variety of programs to help you make your choice. Look also at the regular reviews and updated lists and titles of packages, with contact details and purchase prices in the family history press. Some of the packages have inbuilt support systems which warn you of impossible connections, so you can recheck your sources. They may offer alternative pedigree layout styles. What you buy is a matter of personal choice, but by chatting to other family history computer buffs you will discover which ones come highly recommended. Computers are more versatile than card indexes, and will produce more professional-looking printouts of information. You can download copies of data to share with others, and of course you can edit, correct, add, move and merge information. Always copy and save your updated information onto disk, and regularly save the data you are inputting in case of electrical breakdown or failure. Disks take up far less storage space than card indexes or files of paper, but you do have to spend time keying-in information. Each time you make a copy you stand the risk of making mistakes or omitting something, so do not attempt to do too much at one sitting, and always check your data against the paper version before disposing of the original notes. You may wish to keep these as back-up.

Never store original material such as photographs, newspaper cuttings or other family treasures in airtight containers, but keep them in dark, cool, dry conditions or under cover above floor level and away from direct heat and the fading effects of direct sunlight. Ventilation is important as it prevents mould. It is worth investing a little money to ensure safe preservation of your family's archives and photographs. Acid-free high-strength corrugated self-assembly archive boxes are ideal for storing loose papers and documents. Unique items and photographs kept in transparent acid-free or Melinex sleeves will guarantee their condition does not deteriorate and obviate the need for handling. These can be filed in an album. Avoid using polythene bags and brown envelopes, as the former are prone to sweat and absorb ink and print from the very items they are supposed to protect, and envelopes leave a brown stain and cause deterioration as they degrade. Remove any rusty clips, elastic bands and pink tape attached to documents, and replace them with brass clips and white tape if necessary. Damaged items should be repaired with wheat starch or special archival tape, not glue or Sellotape, which are not suitable long term and cause further harm. If in doubt, seek expert help first from your record office to avoid costly mistakes. Staff there should be able to give you details of suppliers of the above materials, too.

searching parish registers

In this chapter you will learn:

- what parish registers are
- how you can find and interpret them
- what copies and indexes exist and how to use them

Census returns tell you approximately when and where people were born. If the birth occurred after civil registration began, you should be able to find it. Sometimes, however, births remained unregistered or prove impossible to trace in the indexes, perhaps because the mother's confinement took place away from home, or the child was registered under different names from which it was later known, or as an unnamed male or female. If you know where the parents were usually resident, it may be easier and cheaper to look for the child's baptism in the local church registers. Before the start of civil registration on 1 July 1837 (1 January 1855 in Scotland, and 1 January 1864 in Ireland), it is to these records that you must turn for evidence of birth and parentage. A child's birthplace was not necessarily where it was baptized, nor does the census indicate religious denomination. You may therefore have to look not only at registers of the Established Anglican Church of England, but at those of Nonconformist chapels as well. Baptism did not always promptly follow birth, and might be delayed until the family was complete, so that all the couple's offspring were baptized together, perhaps years after the eldest child was born – so the given year of birth is no guarantee of year of baptism. By the early nineteenth century baptism was by no means invariable.

Formal registration of church baptisms, marriages and burials began in England and Wales in September 1538. Every church preserved a written record of them, the previous week's entries being read out during the Sunday service. These records were intended as a form of reference, to prevent disputes about age, parentage, inheritance and lineage, and to determine whether a person was the monarch's born subject.

Baptisms and marriages are still registered today. Since 1853 (1852 in London) there have been fewer interments in churchyards for reasons of public health and hygiene, so the burial registers represent only a sample of the true total, for the vast majority of burials were recorded by the local authority or a private company responsible for the cemetery concerned, or from 1902, the crematorium.

Where to find them

Originally stored in a locked chest in the church for safekeeping, completed parish registers are now mostly deposited when full in the local county record office, the incumbent retaining those still in use. If you want to consult these, or later register volumes, you will need to write to the church concerned for an appointment. Always enclose a stamped self-addressed envelope with your request. Addresses of Anglican clergy can be found in *Crockford's Clerical Directory*, but do not write to a named individual, who may have moved to a different living. There is a fixed scale of fees for searching the registers. If you are unable to examine the registers yourself, the incumbent may be willing to do it, although he or she is not obliged to, and the fee will be different. An offer of a reasonable donation to church funds may be welcomed as an alternative. Always check in advance how much you are likely to have to pay. An urban register crammed full of scrawled yearly entries will take much longer to search than a rural volume, so you may have to limit the period to be searched. Always write and thank the incumbent for his or her help.

The Phillimore Atlas and Index of Parish Registers, edited by C. R. Humphery-Smith, contains county parish maps for England and regional maps for Wales and Scotland, showing the date of the earliest known surviving register for each parish church. The indexes tell you the whereabouts of the registers at the time of publication. Most record offices have published lists of their current holdings and a phone call will give you up to date information on the whereabouts of specific church registers. You can also find out about parish registers in record offices by searching the relevant county at **www.genuki.org.uk**.

Because of their fragile state and heavy use, many original church registers are no longer accessible to the public and can only be viewed on microform. If your ancestors came from a different part of the country, it may be easier to inspect filmed or microfiche copies of parish registers at a family history centre near you. There are more than 3,700 of these worldwide, whose addresses and contact details can be found at **www.familysearch.org** where you can also search the Family History Library catalogue for details of filmed copies. There is a small hiring-in fee. Baptism and marriage entries have been extracted from many of these for inclusion in the *International Genealogical Index* (available at **www.familysearch.org**, on CD-ROM and on microfiche) and *British Isles Vital Records Index* (on CD-ROM). You can find out which parishes, events and dates are covered from both databases. However, not all the register content was incorporated in either index, so they are not perfect. It would be unwise to rely on them alone for your research. Check a filmed copy of the original register to be really sure you have every scrap of information you need, and to verify the indexed entry.

Thousands of parish registers have been transcribed or indexed and these should be available in the local record office or library. Probably the most comprehensive collection of transcriptions is that held by the Society of Genealogists, in London, and some can be borrowed by members. Its published catalogue, *Parish Register Copies in the Library of the Society of Genealogists*, is integrated into the *Atlas and Index* mentioned above. *The National Index of Parish Registers: Parish Registers of Wales*, edited by C. J. Williams and J. Watts-Williams, lists the whereabouts of Welsh originals, copies and indexes. A series of English county volumes published by the Society of Genealogists under the title of *National Index of Parish Registers* similarly lists the known whereabouts of original registers, copies and indexes, and some of these volumes cover Nonconformist chapel registers too. Have a look at S. A. Raymond, *Births, Marriages and Deaths on the Web* (in two parts) for details of parish register transcripts on the Internet.

The history of parish registers in England and Wales

Although parish registers were introduced in 1538, in practice very few survive from that date, but where they do they represent over 460 years of continuous record keeping. The histories of few families are likely to be traced through the registers of any one parish from their inception to the present day, because like now they moved around, even if just for a generation or so before returning to their roots, and because few of the registers are a continuous record from their beginning to the present day. In 1598, each parish was ordered to purchase a parchment register book into which all preceding baptisms, marriages and burials were to be copied up, particularly those after the start of the Queen's reign in 1558. This meant that many older books were discarded and the first 20 years of record keeping ignored. A professional scrivener was often employed for the task, so the handwriting for at least those 40 years is neat and consistent, even if the entries are often truncated, may be erroneous versions of the originals, leave out some entries altogether or mix up two to make one.

Parish record keeping was disrupted during the Civil War and Commonwealth period, between 1643 and 1660. A special officer, called a 'parish register' was elected by the parish ratepayers, and given custody of the registers from 1653, when the Established Church was Presbyterian. Some register books were removed from the church into private homes, were not returned at the Restoration of the Anglican Church in 1660, and so vanished. From 1645 to 1660, the registers recorded births and deaths as well as baptisms and burials, and between 1653 and 1660, the publications of intent to marry. Weddings during this period were performed by local magistrates rather than a priest, so were civil ceremonies. Some registers therefore have complete gaps of almost a generation, whilst others combine entries with those from other churches in the vicinity. After 1660, Anglican clergy retrospectively and incompletely wrote up details of baptisms, marriages and burials from the hiatus years, possibly to provide evidence of age and paternity for inheritance purposes. Thus the erratic under-registration of these years may truncate many family trees unless other contemporary sources can be utilized to show evidence of continuity and relationship with people of the surname recorded there prior to 1643.

After the Act of Toleration in 1689, dissenting congregations were permitted to erect their own places of worship, and as a result began to keep their own records of birth, baptism, marriage and burial, so not every inhabitant of a parish will be registered in the Established Church registers. From 25 March 1754, the marriages of everyone, regardless of creed, became mandatory in the Anglican Church until 30 June 1837. Thenceforward to 1837, only the Quakers and Jews were allowed to continue to perform their own weddings and keep their own marriage records.

Registration was also affected by a tax on births, marriages and deaths, imposed between 1694 and 1706, and by a stamp duty on baptisms, marriages and burials between 1783 and 1794.

In Wales, poor record keeping and ineffective supervision of remote country parishes with thinly scattered settlements led to a patchy survival of parish registers.

The arrangement of the entries

At first, details about baptisms, marriages and burials were written up in one book, but from 25 March 1754 marriages were recorded in a separate printed volume, and baptisms and burials followed suit after 1812. Until then, the entries might be arranged chronologically by date, list all the baptisms, then the marriages, and finally burials during each month, record baptisms on one page, or at the front of the book, and burials on the facing page or running from the back, with marriages scattered among each. They soon ceased to be contemporaneous if baptisms exceeded the number of burials, or vice versa. Occasionally, stray entries were inserted out of date order, or baptisms mixed in with burials. From 1813, separate printed baptism and burial registers were employed and the entries became standardized.

Baptisms

Until 1812, the content of the baptism entries reflect the whim of the clerk. At best they provide the day, month and year, the child's baptismal name, surname and parentage, the father's abode (perhaps even naming the farm, house or locality in the parish) and his occupation, at worst merely the exact date and name of the infant. There is often no cohesion in the way the entries were written, the surname coming after the child's or parents' names, making searching laborious. Between 1798 and 1813, parish registers in the diocese of Durham and some other places note not only the names of the child and his or her parents, his or her date of birth, and birth seniority, but the birthplace of each parent, grandparents' names and the occupations of the father and paternal grandfather, with the result that a single entry can extend the family's history back a further two generations beyond the child itself.

From 1813, baptisms were copied into pre-printed books, under headed columns, giving the exact date, forename of the child, the names of both parents, the surname, parents' place of residence, father's occupation and the signature of the officiating priest. These entries are much easier to read because all you have to do is scan down the surname column for your surname.

Special points concerning baptism

Although baptism was supposed to be on the first Sunday after birth, or on the next Sunday thereafter, you will find that in the few instances where dates of birth are given, this was rarely so. It may have been strictly adhered to at the outset, but weeks, months or years often elapsed before baptism. It seems too that there was a falling-off of baptism in the nineteenth century, so

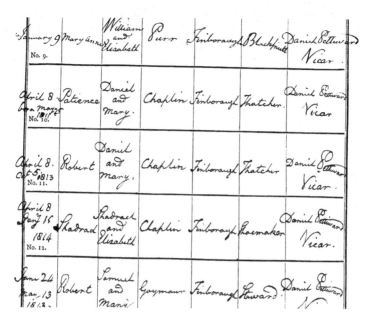

figure 8 baptism register of Great Finborough, Suffolk, 1814
the birthdays of the Chaplin children were also included, and the fathers were
brothers (reproduced by permission of Suffolk Record Office)

the registers are not an accurate record of all births within the parish. Sometimes, with the onset of civil registration in 1837, parents elected to register the births of their children with the district registrar in preference to their being taken to church for baptism, or vice versa, especially before 1875, when the civil registration system was tightened up.

Dual entries were occasionally made in the registers for children 'privately baptized' at home by a licensed midwife, surgeon, physician or priest, and later 'received into the church' or 'publicly baptized'. This may indicate that they were sickly and not expected to survive, or there were severe weather conditions, no resident priest, or the church was temporarily closed, particularly if several similar baptisms occurred in the same period, or the number of them was drastically fewer than usual. Such an entry may also relate to a Roman Catholic family, the public baptism confirming the birth and parentage to conform with the law, since Catholics were persecuted until the late eighteenth century.

Whenever possible, the putative ('reputed') father of an illegitimate ('base born') child was named, to enable the vestrymen or local magistrates to enforce maintenance payments against him, and thereby avoid the ratepayers having to provide support. Before 1813, the entries are frequently ambivalent about the surname adopted by the child.

How best to utilize the registers

If you are undertaking a specific search, broaden the period to 15 years surrounding an ancestor's possible birth in case of faulty information, late or missing baptism, so that you can detect the family's presence in the parish from entries relating to siblings.

If you extract every entry of the surname and its variants from the beginning of the register, particularly in rural areas, entire generations, family groups and unconnected strays will reveal themselves. When you have completed other searches in neighbouring parish registers or in other sources of the period, these people may fit into your family tree, the strays being returners or visitors from nearby.

When people cannot be linked, or vanish, consult a local map and look at the registers of parishes within walking distance (about 14 miles in a day), as many families did not move far, often in a series of circular movements spread over one or two generations. You may find the direction of travel was towards the nearest market town, which might be as close as seven miles away. In an urban centre you might have to examine the registers of a cluster of parishes serving a small and densely populated neighbourhood. An itinerant family might have offspring baptized in a number of parishes along the route of travel. Try the *International Genealogical Index* and *British Isles Vital Records Index* for isolated references to your surname in case any are relevant to your migrant ancestors. The 1901, 1881 and earlier census indexes can also yield clues as to birthplaces before civil registration of people of the same surname and put you back on track in a locality you had not yet considered.

A large-scale Ordnance Survey map showing contours, natural features, field names, local communications, and proximity of settlements to each other is helpful where a change of domicile is apparent. But it may be a homestead had been renamed, or a person may have disappeared from the registers merely because the family was complete. Sometimes this movement out coincides with the appearance of a newcomer or new parent of an identical name, who might or might not be related to the former resident.

Parish boundaries were also redrawn and new churches built in response to new housing to cater for a burgeoning population. A family staying put might therefore be recorded in the registers of more than one church serving their neighbourhood. Conversely, the clerk of a mother church frequently noted baptisms in outlying chapelries in both sets of registers.

Some likely obstacles

Several couples with identical given names producing children of the same name in the same period, place or locality present a special problem, particularly in rural communities where there were relatively few surnames. Sometimes the registers will distinguish between them as 'senior', 'junior', 'elder' or 'younger' or connect them with their township, farm, house or occupation. A search of the burial registers and the contents of wills may eliminate a few. Parental demise may be indicated when the adjective is dropped, but it may not be the older person who died first. Posthumous offspring should be so described. Another explanation might be that one had moved away, or had ceased childbearing rendering the distinction no longer necessary.

Look for forename patterns over successive generations or within your wider family. In the past a fairly limited range of names seems to have had currency. Systematic naming of children after the father, paternal grandfather, maternal grandfather and so on are clues to filiation, birth seniority and possible gaps in recording. Sometimes a younger child was named after one who had died or several were given the same forename as older surviving siblings as a form of insurance policy for the continuation of that name. By the early nineteenth century, surnames, especially maternal maiden names, were often adopted as forenames, and two or more given names were common. The patron saint of the church, biblical figures, names from popular contemporary literature and heroes of the day were chosen too.

Continuity of occupation within a family may be a clue, the eldest son being the most likely to follow his father's trade or work. If there were too many following the same trade, then younger members might be forced to branch out into neighbouring towns and villages or further afield, sometimes acting as agents for the main concern.

If you cannot find the baptism of a child it might have been by the mother's previous marriage. Having taken on the stepfather's name, his or her original identity was lost. Young children taken into the families of married older sisters, or childless relatives, might also adopt their surname. This may partially explain the use of aliases.

Points to bear in mind when using Welsh records

In Welsh parish registers, you will find patronymic strings of first names prefaced by 'Ap' or 'Ab', which trace the genealogy of a person over three or more generations. The names drew on a small pool of biblical and saints' names, so it is the identification and continuity of homestead which is all-important, rather than heredity of surname. Place-names and personal names were recorded in the native language, the rest of the entry being in English.

Marriages

Once you have tracked the baptism of the earliest known child of a couple and there are no earlier entries during the previous 15 years, you can then start searching for the parents' marriage. As many as a third of all marriages began with the bride already pregnant, some taking place after the child was already born. If the birth was before marriage, the child would be baptized using the mother's surname, so once you have located the wedding entry and thus her maiden name, have a look in case this has happened. It may be that her future husband's name was inserted as the father in the baptism entry for such an infant.

The wedding usually took place in the bride's parish, so search for the eldest child's baptism there too, because the baptisms you have already found might have been in the parish where the couple settled down. New mothers often returned to their parental home for their first confinement. Sometimes couples chose the nearest market town or ecclesiastical centre to marry, the baptisms of their children being in a number of churches in and around the town.

What the registers reveal

Until 1754, the precise date, forenames and surnames of both partners may be found, or merely those of the husband. Where

figure 9 marriage of George Chaplin at Great Finborough, Suffolk, 1771
he was a widower, and whilst he signed the register his bride, Susannah Bacon, made her mark
they were the parents of Daniel and Shadrach Chaplin, whose own children were baptised at the church there (reproduced by permission of Suffolk
Record Office)

one party was widowed or came from another parish this might be mentioned as well. From 25 March 1754 however, marriages were written up in a printed book, so the entries became standardized. Thereafter the name of each party, their current marital status, parish of residence, date of the marriage, whether after the reading of banns or by licence, and the signatures or marks of each of them, together with those of at least two witnesses and the officiating priest were recorded. The witnesses might be churchwardens, relatives and friends of the couple. Witnesses who were kinsfolk may guide you to your ancestor's previous or later whereabouts, should you get stuck.

From 1 July 1837, marriage registers were kept in duplicate, one being sent to the superintendent district registrar when full; these duplicates are identical in every detail to the certified copies you can pay for, except that the actual registers contain signatures. You can pay to examine the original registers at the church or see them in a county record office free of charge, whereas only the Registrar General's indexes are free.

Clandestine and irregular marriages

Before 25 March 1754, there were two other ways of getting married, both of which were legal, though frowned upon by both the church and the courts of law. One was by contract, whereby each party clearly stated their intention to marry the other either now or in the future. If the latter, the marriage was regarded as valid from the moment of consummation. The second type of marriage was one performed in secret (clandestinely) by an ordained priest in front of two or more witnesses.

A number of urban and rural centres earned a reputation for clandestine and irregular wedding ceremonies. The registers of such 'lawless churches', which claimed exemption from ecclesiastical control, contain far more wedding entries than can be justified by their number of inhabitants. A clandestine marriage was one without banns or licence, usually performed by a clergyman in a church or chapel of a place where neither party was a resident, or in a marriage-house, tavern or prison. An irregular marriage was also without banns or licence, but in the parish church of one of the couple; it might also be in a church other than where banns had been read, or for which a licence had been granted when neither party was a local or had not already been living for the obligatory four weeks.

Many surviving registers, notebooks and indexes of clandestine marriages at marriage-houses, taverns and prisons, compiled by clergymen or register-keepers, are now in the National Archives, in Kew. They can be searched on microfilm there and in the Family Records Centre, London, and in family history centres. A number were destroyed, found their way into other repositories, were filed as evidence in legal proceedings, or remain in private hands. Some of the registers have been published in a series edited by M. Herber. The authenticity of these register books is dubious because entries were fabricated, duplicated, pre-dated, recorded incompletely or mixed up out of date order. Occasionally baptisms were included too. Places of abode and occupations might be mentioned as well as the wedding date, names and marital status of both parties, providing vital clues as to where they came from, but some of the names and places are fictitious. This kind of ceremony particularly appealed to runaways from disapproving parents, couples from different social backgrounds, intending bigamists, women in search of a protector from creditors, military and naval personnel with no permanent fixed abode or about to go on service abroad, and preying suitors of vulnerable heirs.

It has been reckoned that in the early eighteenth century between a quarter and a third of all weddings were contracted in such places. After 25 March 1754 clandestine marriages continued in the Scottish border country until declared illegal in 1856, unless one party had been a resident for at least 21 days. Eloping couples from England journeyed over the border to marry in places such as Gretna Green, and to the Channel Islands, where the law did not apply.

As a result of an act passed in 1753 (known as Lord Hardwicke's Act), marriages in England in Wales were legal only if performed according to the Anglican rites, by banns or licence. This meant that marriages by contract or in secret were illegal, except for those which had already taken place. The only exceptions were Quaker and Jewish ceremonies which were allowed to continue, and they kept their own records.

If you find a marriage entry after 1754, but no baptisms of any children, it may suggest that one partner was Nonconformist. Another possibility is that it may have taken place out of the couple's normal residential area, and was intended to be in secret, or 'clandestine', because one of the couple was under age and was unlikely to obtain parental consent, or they wished to marry away from the gossip of neighbours. In a densely populated city parish they could lie about their background and sit tight for the necessary period of residence to qualify them to marry there.

Banns books

Banns, signalling a couple's intention to marry, were read out during the services in their home parish churches on the three Sundays preceding the ceremony. If any of the congregation knew of a legal impediment like a pre-contract, existing marriage, or minority, they had ample time to object, or the parents of minors could express dissent. The dates of the banns and the names and parishes of both parties were recorded in each church, either as part of the marriage registration, on separate pages in the same volume, or in a special banns book. If you cannot locate a particular marriage, have a look at the banns, because these may contain that vital clue of where the other party lived and married. Even if banns were read, it does not always mean that a wedding followed promptly, if at all.

The alternative to the reading of the banns was for the couple to apply to the diocesan registrar or his surrogate for a marriage licence, which cost money, but was private. Until 1822, the period of residence required in the parish of the intended marriage was four weeks, thereafter 15 days. The marriage register will indicate marriages by licence as 'by Lic'. The groom and his intended bride alleged under oath that there was no impediment to the marriage in civil or canon law. They confirmed that they were either over 21 or that parental consent had been given if they were under age. Before 1822, the groom was required to enter a bond offering a large sum of money as security for the truth of the allegations, with a friend or relative acting as surety. The information from these allegations and bonds can help you to trace a marriage which was out of the expected area. Between 1822 and 1823 a certified copy of each party's baptism entry was attached, too.

Indexes, transcripts and extracts

Besides the *International Genealogical Index* and *British Isles Vital Records Index,* county marriage indexes and *Pallot's Marriage Index* can prove invaluable. Not all are fully comprehensive, some may be limited by period or area, others may be privately held. Look at *Marriage and Census Indexes for Family Historians,* by J. Gibson and E. Hampson, for details about your county of interest.

In the Archdeaconry Court of Suffolk.

The 27th day of October 185

Appeared personally Spencer Chaplin of the parish of St Margaret in Ipswich in the County of Suffolk a Bachelor of the age of 19 Years but under the age of 21 Years and prayed a License for the solemnization of Matrimony, in the Parish Church of Saint Margaret in Ipswich aforesaid in the County of Suffolk between him and Ellen Smith of St Nicholas in Ipswich aforesaid in the County of Suffolk a Spinster of the age of 19 Years but under the age of 21 years and made Oath that

he believeth that there is no impediment of Kindred or Alliance, or of any other lawful Cause, nor any Suit commenced in any Ecclesiastical Court, to bar or hinder the proceeding of the said Matrimony, according to the Tenor of such License. And he further made Oath that he the said Spencer Chaplin hath had her usual place of abode within the said Parish of St Margaret in Ipswich aforesaid for the space of Fifteen Days last past. And he further made oath that the consent of Shadrach Chaplin the father of the said Spencer Chaplin and also the consent of william Smith the father of the said Ellen Smith hath respectively been obtained to such marriage

Spencer Chaplin

Sworn before me

License issued same day
Charles Steward
Registrar

figure 10 Spencer Chaplin's marriage allegation, 1854
because both he and his bride Ellen Smith were under twenty-one, their fathers, Shadrach Chaplin and William Smith, were required to give their consent to the wedding (reproduced by permission of Suffolk Record Office)

Printed transcriptions of some marriage registers end in 1812, principally those of W. P. W. Phillimore and E. A. Fry, leaving a gap of 25 years to civil registration. Before his death in 1955, Percival Boyd used printed copies, extracts, marriage licence allegations and bonds to compile a marriage index for England between 1538 and 1840. Almost 7 million names, representing between 12 per cent and 15 per cent of total marriages in 4,300 English parishes, are recorded in the indexes, which are organized in three series. The Main Series is divided into 16 county runs, then under ten 25-year periods (except for 1538–1600, and 1801–40), with double entries for men and women excluding Yorkshire, which is indexed only by males. Just the year, surname and abbreviated forename of each person, the place of marriage or licence issuing office are recorded, so you will need the original source for full details. The First Miscellaneous Series extends from 1538 to 1775 (double-indexed only as far as 1700), drawing on published marriage entries in other areas, and contains additional entries for counties in the Main Series. The Second Miscellaneous Series, 1538–1837, relates to marriages from all English counties, with double entries in strict alphabetical surname order. The first two Series are phonetically indexed, for example names beginning with GN- and KN- appear under N-, so caution is required. The indexes do not extend to every county, nor are dates consistent, or run from start to finish, unbroken, for each parish, but *A List of Parishes in Boyd's Marriage Index* outlines the percentage of coverage for each county as well as dates and places. The 534 volumes are lodged in the library of the Society of Genealogists, and these are gradually being loaded, county by county, onto the Internet at **www.englishorigins.com**, where they can be searched for a fee. You can also search these on microfilm at family history centres.

Another important marriage index for family historians is *Pallot's Marriage Index*. If you have totally lost track of your ancestors it may be that they had found their way to London, not necessarily to stay there, but at least to pass through, and they may have left some record of their time there. This index contains double entries for each wedding in all but two of the 103 City churches between 1780 and 1837, making it a prime genealogical source. It includes some entries from other counties too, and there is a less extensive baptism index for the same period. It is available on CD-ROM, from which you can discover which parishes and periods are covered. To view the original images of the entries you will need to subscribe to www.ancestry.com, if you don't own the CD-ROM itself. Details of parish coverage are also listed in *The Phillimore Atlas and Index of Parish Registers*. This index can save you many hours of fruitless research on the off-chance you might locate a missing marriage in one of the London churches.

If you know the approximate year of a male ancestor's birth, but have failed to locate his baptism or marriage, indexed wedding entries of females of the same surname and generation can often lead you back to where he came from too, as brides tend to marry in their parish of birth. Marriage indexes can also be used to plot surname distribution over geographic area and time, as well as enabling you to pick up stray references to people marrying out of their usual area of domicile.

What to do next

Having found a marriage, your next step will be to locate the groom's baptism, taking his given parish of residence first, deducting ten years off the year of marriage to get a start date. This allows for delayed baptism and entries relating to younger siblings. You will need to cover a broad period if you do not have an approximate birth year from other sources like the census returns, a death certificate, gravestone inscription or family knowledge. If he died after 1812, the burial register will invariably record his age. In the past, people were frequently uncertain about their true ages, so you will still have to search several years around the estimated year of birth.

Burials and what the registers may tell you

Burial registers are frequently neglected by family historians. Up to 1812, at best they yield the precise date, deceased's name, abode, occupation and age. If the deceased was under 21, parents' names may be mentioned, and whether death occurred in infancy. If a woman, her current marital status and husband's name help place her in her family context. At worst merely the date and name appear.

In time of crisis or epidemic such as 'pox' or plague, under-recording was inevitable, the reason for increased mortality usually being noted. Some late eighteenth- and nineteenth-century registers in and around the City of London and other parishes note cause of death, exact place of interment in the church or churchyard and age of the deceased. 'P' was written against the names of people given a pauper's funeral, probably with latitude when stamp duty was payable on burials between 1783 and 1794.

From 1667 until 1814, corpses were by law to be wrapped in sheeps' wool to keep the wool trade buoyant. The burial registers therefore note ('by Aff') when an affidavit was sworn by a member of the deceased's family to confirm this had been done. These were sometimes accompanied by the person's name and relationship to the deceased. Where the burial registers are deficient, notes about affidavits can prove invaluable as they were sworn within eight days of interment.

Some entries record bodies that were 'hurled', 'interred' or 'tumbled' into the ground, indicating the burial of a dissenter without benefit of Anglican funeral rites, or of an unbaptized person, excommunicant or suicide. Burials of executed felons abound in parishes where the county Assize Sessions sat.

From 1813, the printed burial registers are arranged with standard headed columns. Into these were written the date of burial, forename, surname, age and abode of the deceased, plus the signature of the officiating priest. The given ages are often unreliable, marital status and family relationships invariably omitted, because they were not required, making positive identification difficult. Other nineteenth-century sources like a death certificate, gravestone inscription or will may help you to identify the person to whom such a burial entry relates. Conversely, you may find a burial for which there is apparently no related death certificate.

From 1853 (1852 in London) only burials actually in the churchyard are recorded in the church registers, so if you know when and where a person died you may have to track his or her burial to a public or private cemetery. Many of the cemeteries were originally run by Burial Boards, and their records are now in county record offices. The entries tell you the date of burial, name, abode, occupation, age and plot number, and whether the person was interred in consecrated or unconsecrated ground, the latter being used by non-Anglicans. You can find the whereabouts of many cemeteries and crematoria run by district councils and private companies in R. Blatchford, *The Family and Local History Handbook*. For London, consult P. S. Wolfston, *Greater London Cemeteries and Crematoria*, and H. Meller, *London Cemeteries, An Illustrated Guide and Gazetteer*. You may not be able to inspect the registers yourself, and a fee may be charged for the disclosure of information from them. Always ask about the plot number and how to find a particular grave, since the headstone may contain details lacking in the burial entry itself.

Indexes of burials

Attention has now turned to indexing burial registers. The Federation of Family History Societies has produced a CD-ROM containing 5.4 million names extracted from almost 4,500 church and cemetery registers, to form the *National Burial Index,* which you can search by keying in the name of the person you want. The database will tell you which places and periods have so far been covered, since the start and end dates are not invariably 1538–2000, not every county is included, and some much better than others. The most complete years are between 1812 and 1837, the vital generation preceding civil registration. A new updated edition will appear soon.

Percival Boyd's index of over a quarter of a million London burials between 1538 and 1852 includes interments of Protestant dissenters in Bunhill Fields from 1823. This is available on microfiche, the original books being held in the library of the Society of Genealogists in London.

Why burials are important sources

Burials complement baptisms and marriages in a variety of ways:

- They round off a person's life, and may tell you how old they were at death.
- They may disclose where someone was last living and their last occupation.
- They may mark the end of one attachment and the availability of the surviving partner to form a new one.
- They provide a start date at which to begin looking for a will or administration grant.
- They may eliminate candidate(s) of the same name as future bridegrooms, parents or beneficiaries in wills.
- They may indicate where newcomers had come from.
- They may provide a clue to residential continuity where the registers are defective, and certainly in the early years after 1538. This will enable you to search other contemporary documents for references to the name in that place which may contain their kinships.

Gravestone inscriptions

Burial registers should be used wherever practicable in conjunction with gravestone inscriptions. Because the majority of parish registers have been removed from churches to county record offices, this may involve a special journey to an outlying churchyard or cemetery. Many churchyards have been cleared but generally a plan of the numbered plots and a transcript of the inscriptions was made. Copies of these may be found in the county record office, the church itself, or in the library of the Society of Genealogists in London, (for which there are published lists). Details of inscriptions copied years ago from gravestones which are no longer legible or in place, or are in a crowded or overgrown churchyard or cemetery are indispensable. No gravestone inscriptions are included in the *National Burial Index*. Consult S. A. Raymond, *Monumental Inscriptions on the Web* for details of searches you can do online.

Headstones in churchyards, bearing engraved inscriptions, became popular and widespread from the late eighteenth century, using local stone, metals or wood. Each headstone style was chosen by the family, erected and inscribed maybe some years after the first interment, since whole families might be buried in the same or adjoining plots and share a gravestone. At best dates of birth and death, residence, occupation and names of the grave's occupants will be given, setting out their relationships as husband and wife, as parents and parents-in-law – information lacking in the burial registers. At worst only the name, age and date of death may be recorded. Occasionally the inscription does not correspond with the burial register entry, perhaps because the gravestone was erected some years after the death. An inscription before 1813 may, however, be the only evidence you have about a person's approximate year of birth.

Earlier church illuminated tombs, wall memorial tablets, floor slabs, brasses and stained glass windows commemorate local nobility, gentry, wealthy merchants and clergy. Many sarcophagi lie in inaccessible family vaults, and other memorials are inconveniently sited inside the church. The Tudor and Stuart monumental tombs are often enriched with coats of arms, striking and colourful effigies of the deceased and their immediate family, and provide a range of detail about the deceased, his or her forebears, family connections and near descendants which would otherwise be difficult to reassemble. Many of the inscriptions were written in Latin. A short printed guide to the church will usually translate these for you.

Bishops' transcripts

The earliest church register copies are the yearly or biennial parchment or paper bishops' transcripts of baptisms, marriages and burials sent by English and Welsh parishes to the local diocesan registrars from 1598 until the early part of the last century. At first, the reporting year began at Easter, but from 1603 became fixed at 25 March (Lady Day). The transcripts are now lodged in county or diocesan record offices, but there is no complete unbroken run for any diocese through to about 1936, neither are there any English returns between 1645 and 1660 when the diocesan courts were suspended. From 1837, there are no returns of marriages.

Some transcripts pre-date 1598. Duplicate archdeacons' transcripts (or register bills) can sometimes fill gaps. The transcripts are usually arranged in parish bundles, but the Norfolk and Suffolk register bills for the archdeaconries belonging to the diocese of Norwich are organized by year, then by deanery and parish. If you know when, but not precisely where someone was born, this arrangement allows several neighbouring parishes to be tackled at once, but you must take care to note those places for which years are missing. In Wales, transcripts extant only from 1661 are in the National Library in Aberystwyth, though many commence in the late eighteenth century.

Bishops' and archdeacons' transcripts can be a good substitute if you want to search a number of parishes whose registers remain in the church, no longer exist or are too indistinct for the required period. They are often complementary to the registers, as the churchwardens or clerk often corrected errors or omissions in the original registers or added extra information. However, they also missed out or shortened entries, so the transcripts are not entirely reliable. Surnames and forenames may be spelled differently, names, dates and occupations vary from what was in the register itself, possibly because the copyist was not the original scribe. You cannot always be sure which of two conflicting entries was actually correct without checking other sources.

Other copies to look for

Modern, printed, typescript or manuscript copies and indexes of parish registers are the products of someone else's interpretation of old handwriting, making widely available records which are perhaps now too badly decayed or damaged to be read, or are held a long way from where you live. Transcribers make mistakes, misread names, omit, mix, transpose and abbreviate entries, so use such copies and indexes as a guide only and consult the originals wherever possible. Some 'copies' may amount only to selected extracts rather than a complete transcription. Remember also, that just because a copy or index is on the Internet this doesn't imply it is any more perfect. There are filmed copies of thousands of original registers which you can hire in to search and check out for yourself in family history centres for a moderate fee, using the Family History Library catalogue at www.familysearch.org.

International Genealogical Index

Two examples of extensive indexes of births, baptisms and marriages extracted from parish registers and other sources are the *International Genealogical Index (IGI)* and the *Vital Records Indexes* of various countries and regions of the world, produced by the Church of Jesus Christ of Latter-day Saints (LDS). The *IGI* was first launched on microfiche as the *Computer File Index (CFI)* in 1968, with updated editions in 1976, 1978, 1981, 1984 and 1988 under the title of the *International Genealogical Index* (IGI). It consists of hundreds of millions of names up to about 1885. The 1992 edition and later addenda are available on CD-ROM and at **www. familysearch.org**. The 1992 and earlier editions are on microfiche. From 1992, the entries include church members' deposited family history sheets ('compiled records'), whose contents are unverified. You may thus come across several entries relating to the same individual which have been submitted by different relatives, and not all of whose details exactly coincide. The *British Isles Vital Records Index (BIVRI)*, at present available only on CD-ROM, has reverted to the original format before 1992 of 'controlled extraction program' entries only, and includes entirely new information not in the *IGI*. There is a *Vital and Parish Records Listing* of dates and places attached to each edition.

The microfiche versions of the *IGI* are organized by country, then by county for England and Wales, Scotland and Ireland. For Ireland there is a set of 'All counties' microfiche as well as for individual ones. The indexes run alphabetically by surname using a standard phonetic spelling, though retaining the original variant, cross-referenced where appropriate; this means that similar sounding, though distinct surnames, may be grouped wrongly together. Given names appear strictly alphabetically as taken from the records, for example 'William', 'Willm', and 'Wm'. Some will be written in Latin rather than their modern English equivalents, for instance Egidius for Giles, will appear under 'E' not 'G', Gulielmus for William will appear under 'G' rather than 'W'. For Wales there is an additional separate series of microfiche arranged by given name. These are straightforward after 1813 as surnames were written in printed columns in parish registers, but before this the *IGI* may mistakenly assume that the child took the given name of the father as his or her surname, the entries ignoring the longer patronymic string of names. If you know the approximate year and parish of birth it may be simpler to search this given name index, whereas if you know the father's name, the surname index might be better used.

Each entry will give alphabetically the surname, forename of the person to whom the event relates, plus the names of parents or spouse, sex or relationship between the parties, the type of event, its date, the town or parish where it took place, followed by details of the date and the Church temple where special ordinances were performed for that person with living descendants acting as proxies. The entries run sequentially by date, the earliest first, for people of the same surname and forename. The final two columns indicate the batch or film number from which the information was taken for the index, and the serial or sheet number of the compiled family record.

The online and CD-ROM versions allow you to quickly retrieve details about other children with the same parents' names as well as the birth or baptism entry of the person you want. This is useful if you do not know who they were. However, the screen will only display exactly what you ask of it, so if the same set of parents are identified in one entry as 'Jn and My', in another as 'John and Mary', and yet another as 'John and his wife' you will have to try every permutation to be really sure you have retrieved all the relevant information. You can request a baptism search or a marriage search, and you can request details of every entry extracted from a specific batch or film number.

With microfiche indexes what you see is what you get, but their main drawback is the length of time taken trying to find all the children of the same set of parents if the surname is a common one.

Because the indexes contain only a limited amount of information you should always treat them merely as a finding

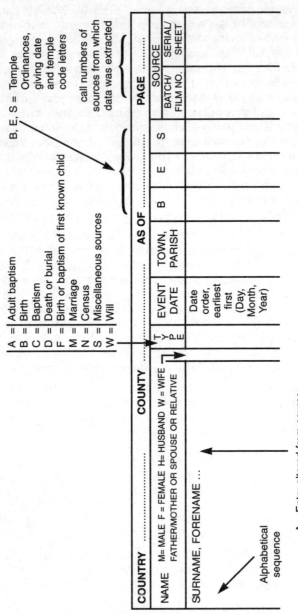

A = Adult baptism
B = Birth
C = Baptism
D = Death or burial
F = Birth or baptism of first known child
M = Marriage
N = Census
S = Miscellaneous sources
W = Will

B, E, S = Temple
Ordinances,
giving date
and temple
code letters

call numbers of
sources from which
data was extracted

COUNTRY .... COUNTY .... AS OF .... PAGE ....

NAME	TYPE	EVENT DATE	TOWN, PARISH	B	E	S	SOURCE	
							BATCH/ FILM NO.	SERIAL/ SHEET
M= MALE F = FEMALE H= HUSBAND W = WIFE FATHER/MOTHER OR SPOUSE OR RELATIVE		Date order, earliest first (Day, Month, Year)						
SURNAME, FORENAME ...								

Alphabetical
sequence

A = Entry altered from source
‡, 2, > = Relatives named in source

figure 11 what the *IGI* contains on microfiche

aid and not rely on them as your sole source for tracing the births, baptisms and marriages of your ancestors. Because they contain few burial entries you risk false matches with 'ancestors' who actually died young. Not every parish register, every entry from those included in them, or even the complete details of each extracted entry are embedded in the indexes. However, they have revolutionized the family historian's approach to tracking down ancestors who may have been born and married away from their home areas, and have revealed family linkages and surname distributions which might otherwise have proved undetectable. For people born after 1 July 1837, the indexes can occasionally help you locate the correct registrations when faced with several of the same name in the same district. You may also be able to locate a marriage whose date you were otherwise unaware of. You will still have to examine the original records or order a certified copy for full details, but your search time will have been drastically reduced.

Such indexes can help you to trace family and individual migrations. The most mobile group was probably aged 12–30. Movements of young unmarried people will not feature in parish registers at all until marriage or demise, perhaps many miles away from where they were born. If you are looking for apprentices, agricultural workers, domestic servants and professional people, they can be difficult to find, so it is well worth looking for their marriages in the *IGI, BIVRI* and the other marriage indexes described earlier in this chapter.

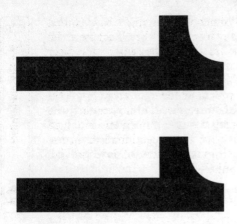

the Nonconformists

In this chapter you will learn:
- how the different religious groups broke away from the established church
- what alternative records there are to Anglican Church registers
- how to find births in two pre-1837 registries

An important and large group of people who might be excluded from the parish registers of the places where they lived were the religious dissidents. As successors to the Puritans of the later sixteenth and seventeenth centuries, parishioners dissatisfied with the practices of the Anglican Church began to meet together informally for worship. Known collectively as The Old Dissent, they soon ramified into three discrete movements, the General and Particular Baptists, the Presbyterians and Unitarians, and the Independents or Congregationalists. In the mid-seventeenth century the Religious Society of Friends also broke away from the Established Church.

So strong was their political and social influence that during the period 1643–60, episcopally ordained clergy were ousted and supplanted by Presbyterian elders. From 1646 until 1660 the authority of Anglican bishops and archdeacons was abolished altogether and replaced by that of self-regulating parish presbyteries. Beginning in 1662, after the Restoration of the Monarchy, there was a backlash and a series of enactments under the Clarendon Code led to the ejection of priests occupying a church living who refused ordination or acceptance of the Anglican Book of Common Prayer. Consequently many evicted clergy roamed around the countryside to preach, perform clandestine marriages, or chose to emigrate with their congregations.

Tolerance of Protestant dissenters

From 1672, nonconforming preachers and householders were permitted to apply to the local bishop for a licence to 'teach' or hold meetings in their homes within that diocese. A list of their names, addresses and denominations, taken from sources in Lambeth Palace Library in London, and from State Papers in the National Archives, Kew, has been printed in *Original Records of Early Nonconformity under Persecution and Indulgence,* by G. Lyon Turner. The Act of Toleration in 1689 went further, and henceforward meeting houses or chapels could be built by Protestant dissenters and used for worship, so long as they were registered with the archdeacon, bishop or county Quarter Sessions, thus conferring official sanction and a local focus.

Although many such chapels were established around this date, they did not all flourish. Originally most meeting houses served a wide radius, or were shared by different denominations which were locally too small to support a chapel of their own. As the number of adherents increased, daughter chapels might be founded, but births and baptisms might continue to be recorded by the mother chapel some distance away. Some preachers travelled around on circuit, whilst others became so popular that their fame attracted people from far afield. There was also a two-way flow of allegiance between the Church of England and dissenting congregations, and between the denominations themselves, especially between the Presbyterians and Congregationalists. Returners to the Anglican fold are frequently described in parish registers as 'Anabaptists' when baptized or buried, and in any event where they had no burial grounds of their own the parish churchyard was utilized by dissenters, performing their own funeral rites. Mostly, though, it is difficult to distinguish from parish register entries who was and was not a conformist.

Gradually, splinter sects, whose beliefs diverged from the mainstream, hived off to form their own meetings. From the mid-eighteenth century, Calvinistic (Primitive) and Wesleyan Methodist preachers travelling from one circuit to another, drew most of their converts from the transient and densely populated mining and manufacturing communities which had sprung up in ancient sprawling rural parishes, whose churches were situated far from their accommodation. Until 1790 these adherents still continued to be baptized and buried by the Established Anglican Church but worshipped in their own places. Each denomination had areas where its influence was particularly strong, depending on the evangelizing influence of the preachers and the enthusiasm of the congregations. In Wales, the spread of Nonconformity was slow until about 1780, after which it gathered pace.

Denominational registers

Because of their early persecution, the first known surviving English Protestant non-parochial register starts only in 1644, but few commence so soon. As all births and deaths were recorded in parish registers between 1645 and 1660, and marriages took place before a magistrate from 1653 until 1660, separate records were unnecessary when the Presbyterian Movement was pre-eminent. Under an act of 1695, up to 1706, births of Nonconformists were supposed to be notified and written into the parish registers. The advantage of mandatory registration was that such records could be produced in a court of law as proof of paternity or age, whereas their own could not.

In 1840 and 1857, the Registrar General of England and Wales ordered the surrender by every congregation of non-parochial registers up to 1837 for examination and authentication. Foreign Protestant congregations in England also deposited their registers. They are now in the National Archives, and filmed copies can be searched there, in the Family Records Centre, in London, and in family history centres, whilst county record offices often have microfilmed copies of registers for their own areas. The authenticated entries from the birth and baptism registers have been incorporated into the *International Genealogical Index.*

A large number of registers were kept back and may still be in the chapels, county record offices, the denomination headquarters, or elsewhere. The *National Index of Parish Registers* has attempted to track down their whereabouts in its series of county volumes. Most denominations publish *Yearbooks* of addresses of current local chapels and meetings, so it is worth approaching them if you cannot locate a specific chapel register, or want information from a date later than 1837. *Nonconformist Registers of Wales,* edited by D. Ifans, is a survey of the principality. The National Library of Wales holds an extensive collection of material generated by the Welsh Calvinistic Methodist Church (the Presbyterian Church of Wales), whilst the Glamorgan Record Office in Cardiff has records of Welsh meetings of the Religious Society of Friends from the 1660s onwards.

Points to consider

- The denomination at the time registers were surrendered may not have been the same as at the chapel's foundation.
- A chapel's foundation date and that of the first register entry may be many years apart.
- The books were not uniformly kept, with gaps, incomplete scrappy entries, retrospective baptisms jumbled up amongst those of a later era, and erratic recording of burials.
- Under-recording was least likely between 1785 and 1794, when stamp duty on baptisms and burials was extended to Nonconformist registrations. This was seen as a tacit acceptance of their records.
- Because the registers were regarded as the personal property of the minister, he might take them with him from chapel to chapel, entries from entirely different parts of the country being mixed up in his book.

Register content

The dated birth or baptism entries usually consist of the names of both the child and his or her parents, the mother's maiden name, where they lived, and the father's occupation, so are more informative than their Anglican counterparts. Of course there are fewer entries than in parish registers because the congregations were much smaller. Baptist registers record births and the adult baptisms of members. Certain family names may be dominant in a particular congregation. The inclusion of mothers' maiden names makes it simpler to trace their marriages in parish registers after 25 March 1754. As people travelled as much as 30 miles to have their infants baptized by their favourite priest, or in their nearest denominational chapel, their given places of abode are invaluable.

Burials

As already mentioned, oblique mentions in parish registers to bodies 'hurled', 'interred' or 'tumbled' into the ground may imply that they were dissenters, for whom the Anglican incumbent refused to perform funeral rites. From the eighteenth century, congregations began to set aside or purchase land for their burials, but the registers are often deficient until 1864, when all burial grounds were legally obliged to keep records of interments. After 1880, dissenting ministers were allowed to conduct funerals in parish churchyards too, which were then registered by the church.

The burial entries in Nonconformist registers state the date of interment and name of the deceased, sometimes accompanied by details of residence and age. Registers of public burial grounds of dissenters in large urban centres, for example in London, those for Bunhill Fields, 1713–1854, which are indexed to 1838, and the indexed registers for Bethnal Green Protestant Dissenters' Burying Ground, 1793–1826, contain references to people of all denominations, and some Anglicans. You can search these on microfilm in the National Archives, the Family Records Centre, and in family history centres. Nonconformist burials are included in the *National Burial Index*.

Gravestone inscriptions

Monumental inscriptions may fill gaps left by the registers, many of which they pre-date. Transcripts of a number of these have been published, and a good collection is held by the Society of Genealogists in London. Look also in S. A. Raymond, *Monumental Inscriptions on the Web* for online copies.

Other records kept by dissenters

Surviving minute books recording the conduct of church business and moral discipline, membership lists and church rolls should also prove helpful, as they may include details about members' baptisms and burials, addresses, dates of admission and cessation as members through death or migration to another congregation. When a person or family moved, their destination was often recorded. The church membership rolls were endorsed with women's married names. Trust deeds relating to chapel property may also be annotated with the dates of death of trustees and their replacement by new nominees. Denominational magazines and year books should be scanned for obituary notices and biographies of ministers and nationally or locally prominent members. All the foregoing may be found in the chapel, county record office or denominational headquarters.

Two London birth registries

In 1742, a centralized birth registry was set up for the three denominations of The Old Dissent at Dr Williams's Library, in London, in the hope that its certificates might be admissible as evidence in a court of law, and to make up for the recognized deficiencies of local record keeping. Anyone paying the requisite fee could register their children's births, and as it was not limited to Londoners, births of people from all over the British Isles and overseas can be found until the end of 1837 when the register was closed. Duplicate certificates, issued locally, were completed and signed by the parents and two witnesses to the birth testifying the date and parish where it occurred. The child's name, those of both parents and the maternal grandfather's name were written in, together with details about their places of residence, the father's and grandfather's occupations, and the name of the local Anglican clergyman. The certificates were then presented with the registration fee at the Registry, the details copied into the register, dated, and given a sequential number, which was endorsed on the duplicate certificates, together with the registration date. One of the certificates was handed back to the parents and the second was retained by the Registry. After 1768, you will frequently find dates of baptism recorded too. Registration might be deferred until a complete family's births were registered together, and thus given consecutive numbers. Parents might take the opportunity of registering their own births at the same time. The earliest registered birth occurred in 1717 and there are more than 50,000 entries.

Access to the registers is by an initial-alpha index to the numbered entries, arranged in tranches of years. Extracts from 80 per cent of the certificates have been incorporated into the *British Isles Vital Records Index*. You can search the filmed register books and certificates in the National Archives, the Family Records Centre, and in family history centres.

A similar scheme was set up in London in 1818 as the Wesleyan Methodist Metropolitan Registry. Its indexed registers, covering more than 10,000 registered births between 1773 and 1838, can also be consulted on microfilm in the National Archives, the Family Records Centre, and in family history centres.

Religious Society of Friends

A number of minute books of English and Welsh county monthly and regional quarterly meetings of the Religious Society of Friends, to which births, deaths and burials of local Quakers were reported, and of meetings at which public declarations of marriage were exchanged up to 1837, can be searched on microfilm in the National Archives, in Kew, and in the Family Records Centre, in London, in county record offices and in family history centres. Records of Welsh meetings are kept in the Glamorgan Record Office, in Cardiff.

An invaluable key to the minute books are the filmed county digests of births, marriages, deaths and burials in the Religious Society of Friends Library, in London. On payment of an hourly fee, you can extract all the references to your surname and its variants from the seventeenth century to 1837 in any chosen county before searching the minute books themselves. The birth and death digests are virtual copies of what you will find in the minute books, but the marriage digests omit the names of relatives and Friends who were witnesses. You will need to look in the digests under the surnames of both partners for details of their parentage. The digests do not record the occupations of their fathers either, which are given in the minute books.

Later central registers of births to 1959 (when birthright membership was abolished), deaths and burials to 1961, and of marriages of Friends throughout Great Britain to 1963, are also available in the Library, arranged chronologically by initial letter of surname. They may be used as an alternative to civil registrations, but are not fully comprehensive for births or marriages. From 1843, announcements in *The Friend* (discontinued after 1913) or *British Friend* may be better sources.

What the minutes tell you

The birth entries in the registers of minutes reveal the child's name, when and where born, parentage, place of parental domicile, and father's occupation. Some of the early minutes retrospectively record parents' births too, in the early part of the seventeenth century, before the Movement had really taken off. The death entries provide, in many instances, dates and places of both death and burial, name, age, residence, occupation and parentage. The dated marriage entries set out the names and abodes of the couple, their occupations, parentage and father's residence and occupation, followed by a list of names of everyone present, starting with relations.

As the same surnames constantly recur in the minutes, it is possible to plot out family networks extending over several generations and into collateral branches and families linked through marriage. From 25 March 1754, Quakers were not subject to the same restrictions as other dissenters, and were permitted to continue with their own marriage ceremonies and record keeping.

As Quaker burials were in private gardens, orchards, or in a parcel of land designated as a sepulchre, and headstones were denounced as idolatrous in 1717, memorial inscriptions are rare before 1850, when this rule was relaxed.

Some points about identifying dates

When using the digests and registers, you will see that the months and days are numbered rather than named. Before 1 January 1752, the first day of the year fell on 25 March, which was also the first month, February being the twelfth. Sunday was the first day of the week. The dates given in the digests are exactly as they appear in the minute books.

Details about Quakers in other sources

Look for baptisms in Anglican parish registers of adults who were born to Quakers, for marriages of Friends to outsiders, and their burials in the churchyard, especially during the first 50 years after the implementation of the second Burial in Wool Act in 1678.

You may find details about prospective marriages between Friends in the minutes of the men's and women's fortnightly preparative meetings and monthly meetings. These might be convened together or held separately. Couples were required to make two or three monthly notifications of their intention to exchange marriage vows. The meetings then made enquiries about their suitability as marriage partners, checking that they were not closely related, or remarrying in haste, and before 1859, that both were Friends. Parental consent also had to be assured. If one of the parties belonged to another meeting a certificate affirming suitability for marriage was produced, so you can find out where they came from. Occasionally these are the only extant record of a marriage, though it does not necessarily mean the wedding actually took place. You can also search the minutes for testimonies about recently deceased Friends which will tell you more about their lives and reputations. The minutes of county quarterly and London yearly meetings of elders and representatives also contain similar testimonies. There are indexes to the minutes of the yearly meetings for 1672–1906, in the Friends Library, in London.

Roman Catholics

If your ancestors were Roman Catholics, their baptisms, marriages and burials are likely to have taken place according to the rites of the Established Anglican Church until about 1791, because their own religious practices were proscribed by a series of punitive laws. From 1606, you may discover their private baptisms recorded in parish registers, thereby avoiding the necessity of actually entering a church. Catholic landowners' children were usually publicly baptized in the Established Church in order to protect their rights of future inheritance. Otherwise, Catholic recusants may be under-recorded or difficult to identify as such in Anglican registers, and their own early records were deliberately sparse in case they should be seized as incriminating directories of names.

Roman Catholic registers

Full Catholic emancipation did not come until 1829. Catholic recusants were forced to worship in secret in private chapels or houses of local Catholic gentry, many of whom were prominent landholders in the remoter northern counties of England. Although rough notebooks of baptisms were kept by priests and house chaplains, registers became prevalent only from the mid-eighteenth century, especially after the passage of the first Catholic Relief Act of 1778, and from 1791, when their places of worship began to be registered and thus became legal. Like their Protestant dissenting counterparts, non-resident Catholic priests treated their registers as their personal property, so many were lost or contain baptisms of people from different parts of the country.

Roman Catholic registers are mostly still in private hands, though a small number with entries running up to 1837 were deposited with the Registrar General in 1840 and 1857. These mainly relate to congregations in Yorkshire, Northumberland and Durham, and can be searched on microfilm in the National Archives, in Kew, Family Records Centre, in London, and in family history centres. Details from the entries in the authenticated registers have been incorporated into the *International Genealogical Index*. A few registers from other counties such as Hampshire and Lancashire have been published by the Catholic Record Society. Look for lists and whereabouts in England, Wales and Scotland of *Catholic Missions and Registers 1700–1880*, compiled by M. J. Gandy. There is a separate *Catholic Parishes in England, Wales and Scotland, An Atlas*, marking out their boundaries. You can obtain the names and addresses of parish priests from the current edition of *The Catholic Directory*.

What the registers disclose

The register entries are usually written in Latin, the dated baptisms setting out the name of the child, its parents, mother's maiden name, parental residence and father's occupation. They may also give the child's date and place of birth and indicate the birthplaces of the parents too. The entries invariably give the names of grandparents and godparents ('sponsors' or 'gossips'). Baptisms may have been retrospectively recorded, and surname spelling is idiosyncratic and often phonetic.

Marriages between Catholics may have been secret (clandestine), or by licence, followed by a private ceremony conducted by a Catholic priest, even after 25 March 1754, when they were obliged by law to marry in the Established Church of England.

Catholic registers of interments in their own consecrated burying grounds usually record age at death as well as name and date of demise of the person, though they were not legalized until 1852.

Other sources about Catholics

It is more common to find Catholic burials recorded in Anglican registers, unless refused by the incumbent because the person had been excommunicated by a church court. They may be described as 'papists', 'recusants' or 'privately interred', indicating that Anglican rites were not performed.

Monumental inscriptions on headstones in churchyards prior to 1830 are likely to belong to Catholics if they are incised with a cross or the monogram 'IHS', but thereafter their attribution is less certain.

At least one branch of your family may have had a connection with nonconformity, however brief. The above sources are the ones most likely to contain details about their births, baptisms, marriages, deaths and burials, but there are lots of other records to tell you more about their activities and whereabouts at certain dates, thanks to the legal restraints imposed on them and the government and the Anglican Church's need to keep track of their allegiances and movements.

12

parish registers in the rest of the British Isles, Ireland and the United States of America

In this chapter you will learn:

- what periods are covered
- online access to indexes and registers
- the whereabouts of original registers and what they contain

The Channel Islands

It is worth looking first at the *International Genealogical Index* for mentions of Channel Islanders. Indexed births, marriages and deaths of islanders between 1831 and 1958 are also included in the microfilmed Registrar General's Miscellaneous Foreign Returns, which you can search in the National Archives, in Kew, and in the Family Records Centre, in London, and in family history centres. A transcript of baptisms, marriages and burials of native Channel Islanders at the 'French Church', Southampton, running from 1567 until the eighteenth century, is in the library of the Society of Genealogists, in London.

On Jersey, the rectors of each of the Anglican parishes have custody of registers of baptisms, marriage and burials prior to civil registration (1842), the first entry dating from 1540. Manuscript copies and indexes in the library of the Société Jersiaise, St Helier, are open to members and bona fide searchers. Later marriage registers, up to the current year, are kept by the Superintendent Registrar, in St Helier, but there are no public research facilities. A microfiche index to marriages as far as 1900 is available at the above library. The Channel Islands Family History Society is preparing an index to entries in the registers of all 12 parishes and of the Methodist, Independent and Roman Catholic congregations up to 1842, all of which can be inspected in its research room in St Helier.

On Guernsey, you can search microfilm copies of parish registers for the island, Alderney and Sark in the Priaulx Library, St Peter Port, by appointment. Details about Roman Catholic residents are among the records of the Bishop of Portsmouth, on the mainland.

Isle of Man

Abbreviated details of pre-civil registration births, baptisms and marriages from deposited Anglican registers at the Civil Registry, in Douglas, are included in the *British Isles Vital Records Index*. For full details you will need to examine the original registers of baptisms, 1611–1878, marriages, 1629–1883, and burials, 1610–1878, or the bishop's transcripts of them, which cover the periods 1734–67, and from 1786 until the end of the nineteenth century, by appointment at the Registry. Microfilm copies of Anglican baptisms, marriages and burials between 1821 and 1964 are available to hire in family history centres for a small fee.

Scotland

Indexes to the Old Parochial Registers of births, baptisms, proclamations of banns and marriages kept by ministers and kirk session clerks of the Established (Presbyterian) Church of Scotland from 1553 until 1854 are available on CD-ROM, and online at **www.familysearch.org**. The index gives the surname and forename of the person, and those of the parents or spouse, as appropriate, the type of event, date and parish. You can also search indexed digital images of the actual records at **www.scotlandspeople.gov.uk**, using the charged service. It is planned to make the indexed burial entries similarly available at the same website soon. If you are visiting the Family Records Centre, in London, you can search the computerized indexes to births, baptisms and marriages in ScotLink on payment of a half-hourly fee.

If your surname begins with Mc- or Mac- be sure to check under both prefixes, as they are indexed separately. Interchangeable letters such as 'Qu' for 'W', and Gaelic renditions of forenames are other features to look out for. Where both the birth and baptism dates were recorded in the registers, the index entry relates to the baptism date, and only the first parish will be named where several were combined. You can identify which these were from the maps in *The Phillimore Atlas and Index of Parish Registers*, or a gazetteer.

The registers, to which the indexes are the key, and the burial registers, are available on microfilm and as indexed digital images in the General Register Office in Edinburgh. Local copies can be accessed in regional record offices and libraries, and copies can be hired in for a small fee at family history centres too. Births, marriages and deaths occurring between 1801 and 1854, recorded as 'Neglected Entries' when civil registration began in 1855 are found at the end of the appropriate filmed register.

Background to registration

Most of the Old Parochial Registers begin in the seventeenth century or later, but there may be lengthy intervals when there was no recording. Deaths and burials before 1855 may be omitted altogether. This may be explained by the custom of taking bodies back to ancestral or native burying grounds, or by the existence of several graveyards in a parish. The entries are written in English or Old Scots, the latest-starting and least complete registers seeming to have been kept by more remote communities.

Births and baptisms

The most informative registers are of dated births and baptisms, which usually contain the names of the child and its parents, the mother's maiden name, parental abode and the father's occupation. Birth seniority may be stated too, especially when baptism was delayed and several siblings were baptized together. There was a widespread custom of naming the eldest son after the paternal grandfather, the second after the maternal grandfather, the third after the father, whilst the eldest daughter took the name of the mother's mother, the second that of the paternal grandmother, and the third daughter her mother's name, though there were variations. This enables you to predict both the names of direct antecedents, and expected names of children in their birth order. Children might be named after the minister, or their sponsors (whose names and any blood relationship to the child might be written up in the register), though it has been suggested that sponsors were sometimes chosen because their names matched those of the grandparents. Surnames began to be used as forenames from the eighteenth century, but were not always associated with the family itself. A few male and female forenames were interchangeable, particularly in the Highlands, and Gaelic names, diminutives and latitude with forename variants were common, sometimes making positive attribution difficult.

Illegitimate children normally took the father's surname, in the nineteenth century the mother's. They were legitimized if the parents subsequently married, provided both were single or of widowed status at the time of the birth. The child then assumed the father's surname. The kirk session minutes, mostly in the National Archives of Scotland, in Edinburgh, reveal the outcome of parochial investigations into the paternity of base born (illegitimate) children so are worth exploring for more information.

Marriages

Dates of proclamation of banns or contract of marriage rather than the actual ceremony itself may be recorded in the register of weddings or kirk session minutes. Although banns may have been proclaimed, matrimony did not invariably follow. The kirk session minutes note the marriage money pledged by the groom as surety for the couple's good behaviour and wedlock within

40 days. The proclamation identified the parishes of each partner, the bride's father's name and groom's occupation, and if the groom was a minor, his paternity. If you look at the registers of the churches of both the bride and groom where the proclamations were made, you may find extra information.

Irregular marriages

Irregular, but nonetheless valid, weddings in Scotland took four forms until 1939. Since then, only unions by cohabitation and repute have been legally recognized, for which a declaration of marriage is required from the Court of Session in Edinburgh. The other three types of irregular marriage were by betrothal followed by consummation; by consent in the presence of witnesses; or without proclamation of banns though taking place in the Established Church. The payment of fines for the last are recorded in kirk session minutes. Irregular marriages were preformed at Tolls, such as those at Lamberton and Mordington, at Halidon Hill and Coldstream, and in matrimonial offices like Gretna Hall. These were frequently the resort of English residents who slipped over the border for a secret ceremony away from prying family and friends. From 1856, at least one of the couple had to have been resident in Scotland for 21 days prior to the ceremony, which was a deterrent for runaways. This traffic was not entirely one-way, for when Nonconformist weddings were forbidden in 1661, many Scottish dissenters crossed over into England to marry until Lord Hardwicke's Act of 1753 put a stop to non-Anglican marriages. Exceptionally, after 1712, members of the Scottish Episcopal Church could be married by their own clergy under certain conditions. Otherwise the prohibition on weddings in churches or chapels other than those belonging to the Church of Scotland was not removed until 1834. From 1834 onwards proclamations of banns of dissenters' intended weddings were recorded in the Old Parochial Registers. Conversely, after 25 March 1754, English Presbyterians travelled North to centres like Edinburgh and Haddington in East Lothian to be married until the law was relaxed in England in 1837.

Deaths and burials

The lack of death and burial entries may be partially resolved by looking for details of fees paid to the kirk session clerk for hire of the parish mortcloth or pall to drape the coffin, a luxury not extended to the poor or to children under the age of ten. In larger towns and burghs the registers of non-denominational burial grounds were better kept, and are in the custody of the municipal authority or the General Register Office in Edinburgh. The Association of Scottish Family History Societies is currently engaged in compiling a national burial index from these records, which will eventually be made available to the public.

Scottish memorials

The durable quality of many Scottish granite and slate headstones has ensured the survival of a surprising number from at least the sixteenth century. The Scottish Genealogy Society in Edinburgh holds an extensive collection of transcriptions of monumental inscriptions from all over the country and outlying islands, copies of which are also kept in regional record offices and libraries. Consult the Family History Library catalogue at **www.familysearch.org** for copies which you can hire in for a small fee to search in a family history centre near you. The inscriptions may record not only the name of the deceased but his or her dates of birth and death, occupation, place of origin, the croft, farm or town of domicile, parentage, spouse's full name and native parish, and the names of their children. The preposition 'of' before a place-name indicates a landowner, 'in' a tenant, and 'at' a landless person. Occupations are also visually represented by carved symbols.

From the Scottish civil registration records, you can discover the birthplaces and dates and places of marriage of the parents of people born after 1855, the parentage, approximate birth years and places of the bridal couples themselves, and information about births and deaths of older siblings. Because so many of the centralized Scottish records are now available online you can swiftly and easily move from one source to another following these clues about birth years and places, marriages and eventual year of death or burial, and locate them in their households in census years. When all the indexed census returns are available online, your Scottish ancestry will be at your fingertips.

As there are relatively few surnames in Scotland, the identification of both parents in post-1855 civil records gives you an immediate headstart. In the Border counties, nicknames and diminutives were often used to distinguish local inhabitants of the same name. In the coastal communities of the north-east the name of a person's boat might be tacked on to his surname. Patronymics were often used instead of hereditary surnames in the Northern Isles up to the nineteenth century. Siblings might be given different surnames, although of the same paternity. An alias might indicate a territorial Highland clan or sept name, a wife's maiden name, or a wife's maiden and married names, though women were usually known by their maiden names throughout their lives and were recorded as such at their burial.

Kirk session minutes record the dates when fees were paid by parishioners for baptism, proclamation of marriage banns and burial, but contain only the briefest information about the parent, groom and bride, or informant. These may be useful where the registers themselves are deficient.

Dissenters in Scotland

The Old Parochial Registers do record people of other denominations. For instance, the baptisms of many Methodists can be traced in records of the Established Church of Scotland. Unlike their English and Welsh counterparts, Nonconformist registers were never rounded up and deposited centrally. Incomplete series of baptism and burial registers of Episcopalians since the seventeenth century, of Methodists from a century later, of members of the Free Church from 1843, and of nineteenth-century baptisms and marriages of Roman Catholics are in the National Archives of Scotland, in Edinburgh, though a number are still in local custody.

The Scottish Established Church became Presbyterian when Roman Catholicism was outlawed in 1560, though from 1610 to 1638, and 1661 to 1689, it too was displaced by the Episcopalian Church. Sometimes births, baptisms and banns of marriage of Episcopalians will be found in the Old Parochial Registers, especially after their clergy were driven underground and their meeting houses shut down or destroyed in 1716 and 1746 after the two Jacobite rebellions. Toleration was only restored in 1788 on condition that the ministers swore to acknowledge the 39 articles and the Book of Common Prayer. Roman Catholics, however, continued to be persecuted until the first Relief Act of 1793. Few Catholic registers survive from before this for obvious protective reasons. Even when virtual full emancipation was granted in 1829, many Catholics continued to marry by cohabitation and repute. Consult *Catholic Missions and Registers, 1700–1880*, vol. 6, by M. Gandy for details of the dates and present whereabouts of known records.

The presence of English garrisons in Scottish forts led to the establishment of short-lived dissenting congregations which did not long outlast their stay. Nonconforming itinerant and seasonal workers from England and Wales after the Treaty of Union in 1707 made a more profound impression on the religious life of their communities. This exchange of labour is illustrated in the given birthplaces recorded in the census returns of the Scottish and English Border parishes. Catholic Irish arrived by sea from Donaghadee and Larne in large numbers during the nineteenth century to work as railway navvies and shipwrights. When the steamboat service started between Belfast and Glasgow in 1818 this gave added impetus, to the point at which the number of Roman Catholics was second only to the Established Church of Scotland. Unfortunately the registers fail to reveal their exact places of provenance in Ireland.

A comprehensive register of Quaker births, marriages, deaths and burials from 1622 to 1890 is held in the General Register Office, in Edinburgh. There is a microfilm copy at the Friends' Library in London, to which a Scottish digest up to 1837 serves as a handy key. Search the Family History Library catalogue at **www.familysearch.org** for references to copies of these which you may then pay to search in a local family history centre. The Society of Genealogists, in London, has a transcript of Scottish Quaker meetings recording births to members between 1647 and 1874, marriage ceremonies from 1656 until 1875, and deaths between 1667 and 1878.

A central register of Quaker births throughout Great Britain from 1837 up to 1959, deaths to 1961 and marriages to 1963, is held in the Religious Society of Friends Library, in London.

Ireland

Although a minority Movement, the Church of Ireland was pre-eminent until its disestablishment in 1871. The official keeping of parish registers of baptisms, marriages and burials began in 1634. However, very few start so early, and most start after 1770. Nearly a thousand of the registers of baptisms and burials up to 1870, and marriages to 1845, collected up as public records, were destroyed by fire in 1922. This left less than half the original total, fortuitously kept back by the clergy, any incidental transcripts made by priests surrendering their records in 1845, and compiled extracts by historians and genealogists who had used them before the fire. As civil registration of non-Catholic marriages was not introduced until 1845, and of births, deaths and Catholic marriages not until 1864, this was disastrous. There are no Irish bishops' transcripts, and few census returns survive before 1901. Mercifully, the 1901 and 1911 census returns record people's ages and counties of birth, though not precise places, and the 1911 returns indicate the duration of women's marriages. The ages may be unreliable, so you will need to broaden the sweep of years for birth registrations. You can find the distribution of surnames throughout Ireland by searching the *International Genealogical Index,* The Primary (Griffith's) Valuation of Ireland, 1848-64, on CD-ROM, and online at **www.irishorigins.com**, and the indexes to the tithe applotment books, 1823-38, over half a century before. As with Scotland, the limited range of surnames and forenames means you must be very cautious when trying to identify exactly who and where your ancestors were.

The present whereabouts of surviving registers

A list of all known surviving Church of Ireland registers is held by the National Archives of Ireland, in Dublin, and there is a published *Guide to Irish Parish Registers,* by B. Mitchell. Deposited originals, microfilm and other copies are dispersed in the National Archives, the Representative Church Body Library in Dublin, and for the northern counties in the Public Record Office of Northern Ireland, in Belfast, although some still remain with the clergy. The prior written permission of incumbents is necessary before you can inspect the filmed registers of the dioceses of Kildare, Glendalough and Meath, in the care of the National Archives of Ireland. Names and addresses of local priests can be gleaned from the *Church of Ireland Directory.* Indexes to parish registers can be searched for you by staff of county genealogical centres. These are listed at **www.nationalarchives.ie/genealogy_countycentres.htm**l.

What the registers reveal

The church registers were kept up erratically and badly written, the spelling being inconsistent or phonetic. You can expect the baptism entries to state the date, child's name, and those of his or her parents, and occasionally the townland where they lived, and from about 1820 onwards the father's occupation. The marriage registers contain dates and the names of couples, giving the parishes of those who were non-residents. Between 25 March 1754 and 31 March 1845, all weddings excluding those of Quakers and Jews had to be performed in the Established Church of Ireland by banns or licence, as in England and Wales, the entries being annotated accordingly. Irregular Irish marriages of dissenters during this period can be found at Portpatrick, in Wigtownshire, and Gretna Green, in Dumfries and Galloway, both of which were reached by the short sea crossing to Scotland. The burial registers usually provide the date, name, age and townland of the deceased, regardless of denomination.

Headstones commemorating the dead

Gravestone inscriptions are a vital source of information about birth, marriage and death of Irish people when parish registers don't help. Many have been copied and indexed. There is a surname and place-name index up to 1910, and integral indexes thereafter to those published in the *Journal of the Association for the Preservation of the Memorials of the Dead, 1888-1934*. Indexed details are held on computer at local heritage centres throughout Ireland, which offer a commercial search service. You can find their addresses and contact details at **www.irishroots.net/** the website of the Irish Family History Foundation. There are also extensive collections of transcripts in The Genealogical Office, in Dublin, and in the Society of Genealogists, in London. Try the Family History Library catalogue at **www.familysearch.org** for copies which you can pay to hire for searching in a family history centre near you.

Tracing Nonconformists

Baptisms, marriages and burials of Presbyterians are often found in Church of Ireland registers, though some records of individual congregations survive from the late seventeenth century. The Presbyterian register contents are similar to those of the Established Church of Ireland. The originals are in church custody (especially for the southern counties), in the Public Record Office of Northern Ireland, or at the Presbyterian Historical Society, in Belfast. The Public Record Office in Belfast also has microfilmed copies of most of the locally held registers for the northern counties, and a list of those deposited with the Presbyterian Historical Society. Unfortunately, the present local whereabouts of a register of a particular church may be difficult to ascertain as many congregations merged, moved or vanished.

Like the Presbyterians, early Irish Methodists will be found mentioned in Church of Ireland registers between 1747 and 1816, rather than in records of their own creation. During the split in the Movement between 1816 and 1878, Primitive Methodists continued to use the Established Church, whereas Wesleyan Methodist ministers began to keep registers of the baptisms they performed within their circuits, making it awkward to track down specific entries without knowing what routes the ministers took. As many county genealogical centres now have indexes to copies of known surviving registers, this problem has been alleviated somewhat.

Microfilmed minutes of monthly meetings, recording births, marriages, deaths and burials of Quakers in Ireland, are held in the Religious Society of Friends' Library in Dublin, and the Library in Lisburn, Co. Antrim, Northern Ireland. Some of these date from the seventeenth century, and the former institution has indexed records of births, marriages and deaths of Friends throughout Ireland between 1859 and 1949.

The earliest known surviving Roman Catholic register of baptisms and burials in Ireland dates from the 1680s, but many only start in the nineteenth century as a precaution against government seizure to discover the names of adherents. When civil and religious restrictions were relaxed from 1793, and full emancipation was granted in 1836, Catholic registers began to flourish. Burial registration was uniformly patchy, so you may have to rely on gravestone inscriptions as a substitute. Late start dates may also be connected to the creation of smaller parishes carved out of older sprawling ones to accomodate new burgeoning urban centres. In order to identify which Catholic church served a civil parish look at *Topographical Dictionary of Ireland*, edited by S. Lewis; county maps showing Roman Catholic parishes and the date of the first register entry are included in *Tracing Your Irish Ancestors*, by J. Grenham. Microfilm copies of Catholic registers at least to 1880 are held in the National Library of Ireland, in Dublin. The priest's permission is necessary to inspect them.

The registers are written in Latin or English. The baptism entries note the date, the infant's and parents' names, the mother's maiden name, where they then lived, and the names of godparents or sponsors. Marriage entries reveal the date, the names of the bride and groom and at least two witnesses, but may include the couple's addresses, age, occupation and paternity. The registers also record marriage dispensations, granted when partners were blood relatives (*consanguinati*), and specify their degree of kinship as first cousins (second degree), second cousins (third degree), or if the two families were linked by an earlier marriage (*affinitatus*).

United States of America

Because civil registration of births, marriages and deaths started as recently as the last century, church registers should assume a great importance as a genealogical tool in researching ancestors in America. The lack of any federal or State uniformity of worship, and myriad local sects reflect the creeds and native origins of the first settlers. Some of these religious assemblies soon withered away or could no longer financially sustain a chapel and preacher, so amalgamated. One of the problems of American genealogical research is that people moved vast distances, so any baptisms and marriages may have to be traced in records of churches and chapels along the route, whilst burials might have been performed where people died, with no formal record keeping. However, there were well-established and mapped overland trails, so if you know where the family eventually ended up you may be able to track them back over their journey. Mentions may be made of family events in surviving letters, diaries and journals of fellow travellers. A number of these have been published, whilst others are in county courthouses, State libraries and archives. There must be many still in private hands too.

Identifying a congregation

As with British dissenters, adherence to one denomination was not always strict, so names of settlers might be found in the records of a variety of local chapels and churches. Often though, the denomination is an indicator of the European State or locality of first-generation migrants who frequently sailed to the American continent as part of a larger regional group with their local priest; their place of origin can provide powerful clues to the provenance of others in the group. You should be able to identify the religious affiliation of your ancestors from their marriage and death certificates.

Tracking down the records

Original registers may be studied in State and local historical libraries and societies, or remain in the care of the church, where access may be restricted. You can obtain their addresses and contact details from online phone directories at **www.infobel.com/teldir** or at **www.cyndislist.com** Try a search engine such as **www.google.com** for links to library and society websites. Microfilmed copies and transcripts of many church registers may be hired for a small fee for consultation in family history centres. Consult the Family History Library catalogue for details at **www.familysearch.org**.

What the registers may tell you

The earliest registers start in the 1620s, each year beginning on 25 March until 1751 inclusive, and thereafter on 1 January, in line with the modern Gregorian Calendar. Written in the vernacular, baptism entries usually set out the date, child's name and those of the parents, together with their place of residence, and sometimes include the names of godparents, and the infant's date of birth. The content of the first registers tend to follow the format of the registers of the country or State of origin, so vary in their comprehensiveness.

As the early Puritan settlers were married in civil ceremonies, the parish clerk was not obliged to record them. Marriage details vary in fullness from noting merely the date and names of both parties to a statement of age and birthplace, where they were then living, the groom's current occupation, parents' birthplaces, and the couple's religious denomination. This is more likely to be the case with Catholics, Lutherans and German Reformed Church members. Irregular marriages were contracted in large American cities, so look for an elusive wedding in records of the one nearest to the place of domicile. The length of a woman's present marriage can be elicited from the 1900 and 1910 census schedules, and clues about marriage date and place extracted from veterans' and widows' applications for Civil War military pensions, held in the National Archives and Records Administration, in Washington, DC.

Burial registers frequently specify the date and place of birth as well as death, vital to people attempting to trace the overseas origins of immigrants, or newcomers trekking from other States.

Gravestone inscriptions

Where death registrations and burial registers are wanting or deficient, gravestone inscriptions may prove invaluable. Though there are headstones dating from the early seventeenth century, a number of which have been transcribed and printed, most stem only from the eighteenth century or later. As the decennial federal censuses did not name everyone in each household until 1850, headstones identify the names of people whose existence and family relationships might otherwise remain elusive.

Immigrants were usually commemorated under the original spelling of their names, rather than ones later assumed by them or their offspring, and the headstones thus provide important clues to where they might have come from. The inscriptions often give details of date and place of birth, generally absent from the burial register.

In rural areas it was commonplace for families to have their own burial plots close to their farm or homestead. Some have been well tended and the gravestones remain in good condition, but many have been lost or destroyed, or their whereabouts are unknown. Most churches had attached graveyards, using new suburban sites when they were closed or full up. Public civic, county or local authority cemeteries permitted burials of people of all denominations, as do the more recently established commercial memorial parks. You can often determine place of interment from death certificates, wills and death announcements in local newspapers of the day.

Sextons' books, registering interments in public and municipal cemeteries and memorial parks, are augmented by cemetery deed books listing sales, transfers and bequests of plots. The sextons' records contain names, dates and causes of death, with the relationship and name of the next of kin, and sometimes birth details about the deceased, which may be missing from, or illegible on, the headstone. These are in the custody of the appropriate cemetery office, whose address can be obtained via a phone book, and online at **www.cyndislist.com**.

13

wills and other probate records

In this chapter you will learn:

- what wills are and contain
- what happened before and after 1858
- how to locate wills and administration grants, inventories and probate accounts
- how to use death duty registers

Strengths and limitations of wills

A will, expressing a person's final wishes for the distribution of his or her land and possessions after death, can be a telling summary of emotional preferences, prejudices, bonds of loyalty, duty and affection for family and friends. If you have located an ancestor's death certificate or date and place of burial, are curious about when and how certain property was acquired, his or her ultimate financial status and the eventual dispersal of your forebear's estate, or you want to establish approximately when and where a person died, then this may be your best source. As they pre-date parish registers, wills are your main springboard to the Middle Ages.

Although not everyone made a will (possibly as few as six per cent of the population), and seeking the formal sanction of an official probate grant was a matter of conscience on the part of the executors, nonetheless the existing body of wills can settle links of kinship and marriage, and demonstrate a family's geographic spread over time and place. However, from 1815 no deceased's estate was legally supposed to be distributed without a grant of probate or letters of administration if they had died intestate (without having made a will). As binding legal documents they are far more reliable than census returns or other sources where the person was the informant.

Where wills were taken to be proved before 1858

Until 9 January 1858, wills of people leaving property in England and Wales were proved in church courts. In ascending order, the archdeacon's court was utilized when the personal estate (personalty) was confined to a single archdeaconry; if scattered in more than one, both of which lay in the same diocese, then it was to the bishop's consistory court that the will was taken; the Prerogative Courts of York (PCY) and Canterbury (PCC) had jurisdiction over property (*bona notabilia*) in several dioceses within their own Provinces worth more than £5 (£10 in London). Dioceses covering the civil counties of Cheshire, Cumberland, Durham, Lancashire, Northumberland, Nottinghamshire, Westmorland and Yorkshire and the Isle of Man fell within the Province of York. The Prerogative Court of Canterbury was the highest church court, and exercised overall authority not only over estates left in the southern dioceses but over property owned in England

and Wales by overseas residents and by military and naval men on active service abroad. When people left estates in both Provinces you will find probate grants in PCY and PCC. The Prerogative Court of Canterbury was widely used after the outbreak of the Civil War in 1642, and when church courts were suspended between 1653 and 1660 it was converted into a Court of Civil Commission, and all wills were taken there to be proved. There were also a number of peculiar and secular courts outside the above framework, which were controlled by Royal patronage, boroughs and city corporations, lords of manors, the chancellors of the Universities of Cambridge and Oxford, by bishops with jurisdiction over places outside their own dioceses, deans and cathedral chapters, or by parishes.

Where to find them

Wills were drawn up in ancient times, but regular series of original or registered copies of those proved in the English and Welsh courts date only from 1384 for the Prerogative Court of Canterbury, and 1389 for York, though some diocesan court probates survive from a century earlier.

Original or registered office copies of wills proved locally before 1858 will be found in diocesan or county record offices, for Welsh dioceses in the National Library of Wales, Aberystwyth. Wills proved in the Prerogative Court of York are in the Borthwick Institute of Historical Research, York, whilst probate material of the Prerogative Court of Canterbury is in the National Archives, Kew. Digital images of the PCC registered copy wills back from 1858 are being scanned onto the Internet. You can search the online index at **www. documentsonline.pro.gov.uk** and then pay a flat fee using your credit card to view the will itself. This index can be used to find wills of people of the same occupation or inhabitants of the same place as your forebears. Otherwise, you can read microfilm copies both of the wills and administration grants (from 1559 to 9 January 1858) in both the National Archives and the Family Records Centre, in London, or hire them in for a small fee to consult in a family history centre.

Lists and indexes

There are personal name indexes or lists for each court of proved wills and grants of letters of administration of people dying intestate. The indexes and lists reveal at least the year when the grant was made, its reference number, and the place of abode of the deceased, which might differ from the place where the will was made if it was some years before probate. Many of the indexes and lists have been printed or microfilmed and are widely available in family history centres and local reference libraries. As well as the online database to 1858, there are printed indexes of PCC wills running up to 1800, and administration grants to 1660, and between 1701 and 1749. A copy of the index to PCC administration grants between 1750 and 1800 is held in the Family Records Centre. Published indexes of wills and administrations in the Prerogative Court of York extend as far as 1688 (with a gap between 1653 and 1660 as described above), though microfilm copies of the later grants are available for hire in family history centres, on payment of a small fee.

Finding the boundaries of each court

Indexes to wills proved in a number of local church courts are gradually being loaded onto the Internet. So far, they are confined to the diocese of Lichfield between 1524 and 1700 (at **www.wirksworth.org.uk/wills.htm**), the Archdeaconry Court of London from 1700–1807 (at **www.englishorigins.com/**) or a single county, such as Gloucestershire from 1541 to 1858 (at **www.gloscc.gov.uk/pubserv/gcc/corpserv/archives/genealogy.htm**), Derbyshire (running up to 1928) and Cheshire, 1492-1940 (at **www.cheshire.gov.uk/recoff/eshop/wills/home.htm**). Probate courts had a far broader jurisdiction than a county, because diocesan boundaries do not coincide with those of civil administration. If you look at the county maps in *The Phillimore Atlas and Index of Parish Registers*, you will see coloured boundaries demarcating the various probate courts with local authority. Executors could take wills to the most locally convenient court in the hierarchy, provided the estate was large enough, so you should always search the lists of each court with jurisdiction over where your ancestors lived. To discover the whereabouts of the records of all the probate courts, the periods covered, indexes and other finding aids, consult *Probate Jurisdictions: Where to Look for Wills*, by J. Gibson and E. Churchill.

Wills proved since 1858

On 12 January 1858, ecclesiastical authority over probate ceased. Thereafter wills were taken to be proved in civil district probate registries, or in the Principal Probate Registry in

London. This is still the case today. Until 1926, the local jurisdiction of district registries was rigidly applied, but since then any office may be used to suit the convenience of executors. You can search the indexed calendars of wills and administration grants over a year old in the public search room of the Principal Registry or in any of the district probate registries, and then pay a fee to inspect them, or alternatively have a copy posted to you. Their addresses and contact details can be found at **www.courtservice.gov.uk/using_courts/ wills_probate/probate_famhist.htm**, in Gibson and Churchill's book cited above, and in *The Family and Local History Handbook*. You may find it more convenient to search the annual National Probate Indexes of calendared wills and administration grants (which are indexed separately to 1870) on microfiche. These are widely available, though the end dates vary – generally you would expect them to run to 1943, as in the Family Records Centre in London, and in the National Archives, in Kew. The National Library of Wales has yearly calendars running up to 1972. If you prefer, you can make a prepaid postal application for a four-year search of the indexes and issue of a copy will or grant by writing to The Chief Clerk, the Postal Searches and Copies Department, The Probate Registry, Castle Chambers, Clifford Street, York YO1 9RG, quoting the person's name, address and date or approximate year of death. Registered copies of wills proved in the Welsh district probate registries are also held in the National Library of Wales, Aberystwyth.

Using the calendars

Besides recording the name, last address, status or occupation of the deceased, the date and place of death are given, and the calendars record to 1891 the current address, occupation and relationship to him or her of the named executors or administrators, plus the date and place of probate or grant of letters of administration. Before 3 August 1981 you can also discover the gross value of the estate from the calendars, and latterly the amount it was sworn under. After 1892, however, the addresses and relationships of the executors and administrators to the deceased were dropped. From 1968 you will only find the name and address of the deceased, the date of death, plus the date and place of probate or grant of letters of administration, and the estate value. A search of these yearly calendared indexes may well be quicker than looking for registered deaths in the quarterly indexes, until they are all computerized. However, not everyone left a will neither were letters of administration always applied for in such instances. The calendars may also help identify which of several candidates is the correct person before you buy a death certificate. You can also use the date of death to find out a person's age evinced in the registration indexes from 1866 onwards, and their date of birth from the death indexes after 1 April 1969. Don't forget that someone may already have extracted all the entries of your surname in the calendars for a one-name study. You can check on this from the registered members of the Guild of One-Name Studies at **www.one-name.org.**, or in the *International and National Genealogical Research Directory*.

Making a valid will

For a will to be a valid document, the person making it (the testator) must be aged at least 21, be of sound disposing mind (*compos mentis*), clearly declare it to be the last will and testament revoking all earlier wills, date and sign or mark it in the presence of at least two witnesses, who then themselves sign it in the presence of the testator and each other. If the document runs to more than one page the testator will need to initial each one at the foot before signing it. A will conveys the real estate (realty, comprising freehold, and between 1815 and 1925 when it was finally abolished, copyhold land held of the lord of a manor). A testament makes provision for the disposal of the personal estate (personalty). Until 1837, personalty could be bequeathed by boys at 14, and girls at 12, but afterwards only from the age of 21, as was always the case with real estate. Today, soldiers and sailors as young as 16, on active service, may will their personal effects.

Marriage and wills

Wills of single people become invalid on marriage, unless explicitly linked to a specific forthcoming union which actually materializes, just as they become void on the birth of subsequent children, if no specific provision is made for issue as yet unborn. The former rule does not apply to soldiers and sailors on active service.

Married women rarely left wills before 1882, unless with their husband's written consent, and from then until 1892 wills of women married after 1 January 1883 were re-executed on the husband's death. A means of circumventing this was for her to be given personalty or land by her own family for her sole use under a dated pre-nuptial settlement drawn up in anticipation of her marriage, to which her future husband was a party. This gave her a measure of independence, though the land was to be held by trustees for her benefit. If the agreement allowed her to dispose of this gift without restriction, she might devise it as she wished, but her will had to specifically refer to the settlement, name the various parties to it, give the date and clear details about the property or land involved. Her husband's will might also mention the deed to ensure the property remained untouched after his death, since a wife and her goods were treated in law as her husband's property. Even if the original settlement deed no longer survives, you should be able to glean sufficient information about it from the will to discover her maiden surname, her father's identity, residence and status, and perhaps those of other close relatives involved in the agreement, plus the terms and conditions of the settlement and the date around which the couple were married. Many settlements provided for the future destination of the estate after the woman's death, which was usually to one or all of her children.

Devising freehold land

Until 1540, freehold land in England held in fee simple was not entirely disposable by will, to protect its entire inheritance by the heir at law (the nearest blood relative, starting with the eldest son) and the revenue and services due to the feudal overlord. However, land which the testator had himself purchased, been granted or held for a term of years could be devised. A way round the prohibition was for the landholder to set up a kind of trust by deed of feoffment, whereby named trustees (feoffees) held the land as legal owners for the benefit of a specified person (usually the landholder), and after his death for individuals named in the deed or for uses as instructed in his will. The Statute of Wills, 1540, allowed for all but a third of fee simple land which was held by knight (military) service from a superior landlord or the Crown to be devised. When this ferdal revenue was abolished in 1660 this restriction also came to an end.

Freehold land held in fee tail passed on death in a way predetermined by the original deed of entailment, which might have been created many generations before. The entailment took a variety of forms. A deed of fee tail male meant the land went to the nearest male heir (the first son, or his son if he had predeceased his father, then the second son, and so on) with provision for what would happen if there were no male descendants; a deed of tail general meant the land was to go to the male descendants first, followed by the next female heir if the direct male line was extinguished; a deed of tail female might leave the land to be shared equally by heiresses of identical degree of kinship to the deceased; a deed of tail special followed a written set of instructions by the original settlor.

Any land excluded from a will was treated as passing on intestacy, so automatically went to the heir at law, unless in fee tail. If you find a deed of entailment, you can use it to trace the descent of the estate down the family over a long period, into collateral branches if a particular line became extinct. They may surface among family and estate papers, as subjects of family disputes or as exhibits in legal proceedings in the Courts of Chancery or Requests, whose records are both the in the National Archives, Kew.

Sometimes a will might set up a framework of alternate life estates and entailments, which were known as strict settlements. These were common from the second half of the seventeenth century, and it has been estimated that by the nineteenth century about half the land in England was protected in this way for future generations of landowning families. As it was a long time before heirs might become entitled, it was important to know exactly where in the family tree a particular individual was placed in order of precedence, in case a dispute should arise.

In Wales, until English law was introduced under the Acts of Union of 1536–43, the ancient custom of partible inheritance was applied, under which a landowner's estate was divided up equally among all his sons or grandsons at his death. Failing this, it next devolved among his male heirs in the male (agnate) line as far as the fourth degree (great-great-grandparents), after which it escheated to the lord. Sometimes daughters inherited. The land could however be disposed of with the consent of the heirs if the landowner wished to sell it. Partible inheritance lingered on in some parts of Wales until the seventeenth century.

Copyhold land and manorial records

An abstract of the relevant part of a will leaving copyhold land was enrolled in the minutes of the first meeting of the lord of the manor's court baron after the tenant's death so the will invariably named the manor. Surviving manorial records, disseminated in private or public custody, are not continuous or complete, but like wills, many date from the early Middle Ages. They were written in Latin until 1733, except during the Commonwealth period of 1653–60. You can find the known whereabouts of English and Welsh manorial court baron rolls or books, rentals and customals (setting out the way in which copyhold land was to pass on a tenant's death) by consulting the Manorial Documents Register, which is gradually being loaded onto the Internet at **www.hmc.gov.uk.mdr/mdr.htm** or by searching the indexes in the National Archives, at Kew. A local nineteenth- or twentieth-century trade directory of the county, or relevant *Victoria County History* volume will also name individual manors, for a parish might belong to several, or several parishes be part of a single manor.

Copyhold tenure was abolished in 1925, though after 1844 it had become possible to convert this to freehold by paying a lump sum in compensation to the lord of the manor for his loss of future rent and other dues.

The contents of a will

The name, abode, status or occupation of the testator come first in any will, followed by the date, though this might be deferred until the end. Reference might be made to sickness or old age, indicating that it was probably composed not long before death. A request for burial in a particular parish or graveyard may suggest where the person came from or had family connections, but such wishes did not always guarantee they were honoured. Medieval and early Tudor wills often contain instructions about elaborate funeral ceremonial, a sum of money being donated for the saying of masses and obits commemorating the deceased and certain named ancestors on special days or anniversaries by a priest. Funds might be donated to construct a chantry chapel. If you visit a church containing monumental brasses, tombs and memorial tablets, look at the inscriptions and the stylized effigies of the deceased and their family, and then read their wills to build up the picture of them as people. Such memorials make a statement about the family's wealth and prestige.

Distribution of the estate

After authorizing the payment of funeral expenses and all other debts, the remainder of the will concentrated on the distribution of the balance of the testator's possessions, and the appointment of executors and trustees to carry out his or her wishes.

The chosen fate of articles of special sentimental or intrinsic value might be intended to cement close emotional ties, though some heirlooms descended according to predestined family tradition.

You can discover the names of elderly or deceased kinsfolk and relatives by marriage, and learn the whereabouts of absent family members from wills. Sometimes beneficiaries were identified merely by their forename, with or without any family connection. These can occasionally be clarified from the contents of other family wills.

Changes in meaning

Unfortunately, the meaning of some terms of kinship has changed over time, so be wary of 'nephew' which might indicate a grandson, 'cousin' a nephew or niece, 'natural son' a lawful legitimate child, 'stepson' a son-in-law, 'son-in-law' a stepson or adopted son, 'son' a son-in-law, 'father' a father-in-law (but not necessarily the father of the testator's current wife). 'My now wife' signifies the testator had been married before, 'my wife's child' that it was a stepchild. 'Cousin' and 'kinsman' were loose terms applied alike to blood relations and people linked by marriage.

Changes of name

Sometimes a legacy or estate was left to a person on condition that he changed his surname to that of the testator, thus ensuring its continuity if the male line would otherwise become extinct. The usual method by which this was done was for the beneficiary to obtain a Royal Licence, which was registered after 1783 at the College of Arms, in London, as quite frequently the family was armigerous too, so its coat of arms was similarly assigned to him and his descendants. You can find out about name changes by Royal Licence, or by deed poll which were centrally enrolled by consulting the *London Gazette*, which has been published twice a week since 1665, and which from 1795 contains integral indexes. The deed poll enrolments are also included in *The Times,* to which there is a complete index available from 1790 to 1980 on CD-ROM in the National Archives and other places, and in *Index to Changes of Name, 1760–1901*, by W. P. W. Phillimore and

E. A. Fry, also available on CD-ROM, in the National Archives, the Family Records Centre and elsewhere.

Gifts to places or selected groups

Legacies entrusted or gifted to parishes or special groups of people may suggest an enduring personal, family or business link. References to land purchases, leases, or gifts of land will lead you to other sources such as title deeds and marriage settlements. When friends, neighbours and associates benefited you might find this generosity reciprocated, or that the testator was returning a favour, so it is a good idea to examine their wills too for references to your family. If you draw a blank looking for wills of your own family examine those of other local contemporaries for clues about them, especially those of the same occupation, and at those of families into which your own were married.

Wives and children

Although a wife might be named in a will, she might predecease her spouse, or die before the will was proved, which could be many years after it had been drawn up. Wives usually received land, the marital home and furniture, or part of it, for their lifetime or until remarriage. Sometimes, you may find that remarriage had taken place before probate was granted to her as one of the executors. She would then most likely have already lost the benefit and the estate would pass to the next in line according to the will's intentions. Usually the will would provide for the wife's portion on her death or remarriage to be sold and the proceeds divided in a prescribed way. When this was among the children in equal parts, it might be many years before such a contingency came about, so a *per stirpes* clause was normally inserted in the will, whereby any deceased's child's share was to be equally divided among his or her children. A will might make provision for children 'as yet unborn', to ensure that any posthumous child was not left out.

You may find known children excluded from the will. This might be because they had already been provided for. For instance, the eldest son might be the next in line for the landed estate, some sons and daughters might be in receipt of an annuity under a trust, had reached the age necessary to receive a portion (lump sum) paid out of estate income, or might have been significant beneficiaries of another relative's will, whereas the future financial security and support of dependent unmarried or under-age siblings remaining in the parental home was of paramount importance to the testator. A small token might therefore acknowledge continuing affection rather than disrespect, married daughters occasionally being left a gift or money exclusively for themselves, to avoid it passing to their husbands.

Appointment of executors

It was customary for the testator to appoint family or local friends as executors, who might be left a sum of money or the residue of the estate once all the debts and legacies had been paid. It is a good idea to note who they were, for the attached probate act will record who actually applied to the court for the grant, because an executor might have predeceased the testator, be under the minimum age of 17, be unavailable, or have changed surname on marriage (such as the widow, or a daughter). You may find that only one of the executors was granted probate, and when the absent person returned or under-age person reached majority another grant was made to enable them to share the responsibility. Sometimes the executor died before he or she was able to complete the distribution of the estate. When this happened, the deceased executor's executor would take over.

Codicils

If the testator died a long time after the will was made, children mentioned as infants might have grown up, married, died, left the family home or lost touch. Any later amendments or modifications might be added in the form of dated codicils. These were physically attached to the will, without the necessity of a completely new draft, but were required to clearly state the date of the will itself, and were signed and witnessed in the same manner as the will.

Oral wills

Wills were not always written. Up to 1837, in emergencies such as mortal illness, when no scrivener or writing materials were to hand, a dying person could declare his intention and dictate final instructions for the distribution of his or her personal estate as a nuncupative (oral) will before at least three witnesses, and appoint executors. The witnesses then repeated what they had been told in the appropriate probate court and the information was duly recorded as a memorandum.

The role of the executors

After the testator's death, the executors took the latest dated will to the relevant probate court to be examined for its validity. They swore on oath to faithfully and honestly carry out its directions and a dated endorsement of probate was appended to the will, authorizing them to act. When an executor declined to take the responsibility, was not available, had died or was under the minimum age, or the will had failed to make a nomination, the court intervened and usually appointed the residuary legatee as executor. The will was then listed as an administration with will annexed.

Original wills and office copies

Once the will was approved by the court, a copy was handed back to the executors, another was written up in the office register, and the original filed among the court's records after the will had been endorsed with the date and place of probate and the names of the executors. The probate acts were written in Latin until 1733, and then in English, as they were during the Commonwealth period of 1653–60. The dates were always written in full. A will could only take effect once the testator had died and probate had been granted. The date of probate is usually a surer guide to when that person died than the date the will was made, unless they came close together. Wills were generally proved within six months to two years after death, but might be delayed as long as 20 years.

Sometimes only registered office copies of wills survive, because the originals have been lost, destroyed, or are too fragile for production, the main difference being that the seal and authentic signatures of the testator and witnesses appear only on the originals, and clerical errors are less likely.

If the will was entirely written by the testator, it was known as a holograph, and did not require the presence of witnesses. People familiar with the handwriting attended the court, examined the script and swore an affidavit acknowledging it as belonging to the deceased. Their names, addresses, occupations and length and nature of their acquaintanceship with the dead person were recorded with the will.

If you are interested in collecting family autographs, or want to compare an ancestor's signature on a variety of documents over time, remember that he or she may have been *in extremis* when the will was signed, and the writing bear little relation to what it was like when the person was in full vigour or much younger.

Contested wills

If the will's validity or its interpretation was challenged, a caveat was lodged by the interested party (the plaintiff), and probate was suspended for up to three months by the court, pending its decision or judgment. The probate court index entry will be annotated with the words 'by sentence' after a hearing before a church court, or 'by decree' when the Court of Chancery was involved, as was the case with all matters affecting land or trusts. The eventual registered copy of the probated will was endorsed with the names of the litigants and a brief summary of the case outcome. The church court records are in Latin until 1733, but Court of Chancery proceedings are in English from their date of commencement in the late fourteenth century. Church court records are now mainly in county record offices, those for the Prerogative Court of Canterbury in the National Archives, and for the Prerogative Court of York in the Borthwick Institute of Historical Research, York. Chancery proceedings are held in the National Archives.

Family disharmony and conflicts over property spill out from the filed allegations, answers and the depositions of witnesses. The plaintiffs might want to show that undue pressure had been used when the will was made, or that the testator was then of unsound mind or not in possession of the property he or she claimed to own. The defendants would look at the allegations from a different standpoint, and even the evidence of witnesses might be skewed. Always look for the sentence or decree to see what the court made of it all.

Administration grants and *bona vacantia*

When a person died intestate, or no will was found, the distribution of the personal goods (personalty) could be formalized by the next of kin's or chief creditor's application to the probate court for a grant of letters of administration. On intestacy, a person's real estate automatically passed to the heir at law (nearest blood relation, starting with the children) until 1925, since when, like personalty, it has gone to the next of kin.

After the eldest son, birth seniority as next heir vested in his eldest son, followed by the second, third and so on, lineal male descendants first, then if there were no sons, any daughters of a dead heir at law shared equally as co-heiresses, the estate finally reverting to the descendants of the nearest direct ancestor of the deceased, if his own line of descendants was extinct.

Because next of kin are determined in strict order of precedence by the degree of proximity of their relationship to the deceased, you can learn from the administration grant who was the closest living relative and if he or she was willing to act as administrator. Here, the spouse comes first, then the children equally (any deceased child's children taking their parent's place), then the parents, followed by brothers and sisters jointly (their children or grandchildren stepping into their shoes if already dead), then half-brothers and half-sisters, then the grandparents, then uncles and aunts equally (their nearest descendants taking their place as before), then the chief creditor, and ultimately, for the want of any of these, the estate passes as *bona vacantia* to the Crown. Up to 30 years after an intestate's death, next of kin proving relationship may lay claim to *bona vacantia* held in England and Wales by the Treasury Solicitor, or by the Solicitors for the Duchy of Cornwall, or the Duchy of Lancaster, all of whom are based in London.

What the grant includes

The dated administration grant recorded, in Latin to 1733 (except for 1653–60, when it was written in English), the name, abode, occupation and marital status of the deceased, plus the name, residence and relationship to the intestate of the administrator, and the name and relationship of any nearer or equally entitled next of kin declining or too young to act. You may find recorded later administration grants made to next of kin on reaching 21. The original registered copy should note the dates of subsequent grants.

From the early nineteenth century until 2 August 1981, the gross value of the estate was inserted, thereafter only the amount it was sworn under. As the printed yearly indexed calendars of civil grants from 1858 virtually replicate the original documentation, you can freely extract their total contents, together with the intestate's date and place of death, without having to buy a copy.

If an administrator dies without distributing the whole estate,

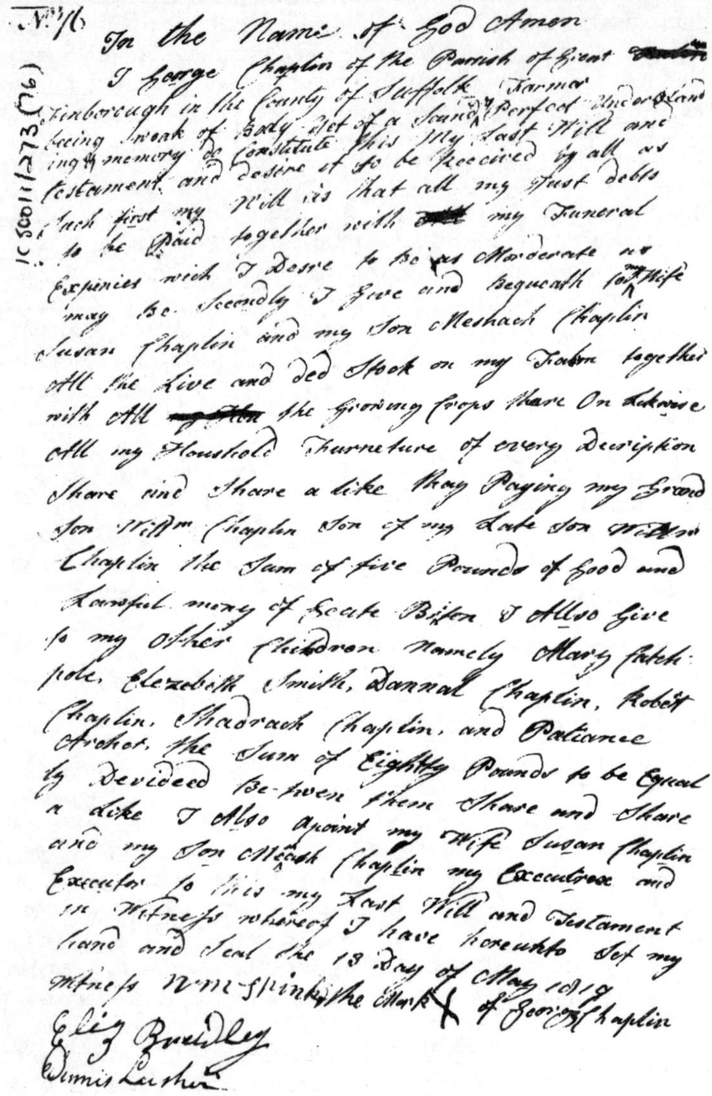
No 16

IC 500/1/273 (76)

In the Name of God Amen

I George Chaplin of the Parrish of Great Finborough in the County of Suffolk Farmer beeing weak of Body but of a Sound & Perfect Understanding memory do Constitute this My Last Will and Testament and desire it to be Received by all as such first my Will is that all my Just debts to be Paid together with my Funeral Expinces wich I desire to be as Moderate as may be. Secondly I Give and Bequeath to my Wife Susan Chaplin and my Son Meshach Chaplin All the Live and ded Stock on my Farm together with All the Growing Crops thare On Likewise All my Houshold Furneture of every Description Share and Share a like they Paying my Grand Son Willm Chaplin Son of my Late Son Willm Chaplin the Sum of five Pounds of Good and Lawful mony of Greate Briton I Allso Give to my Other Children namely Mary Fatch:pole, Elezebeth Smith, Dannal Chaplin, Robert Chaplin, Shadrach Chaplin, and Patiance Archer, the Sum of Eighty Pounds to be Equally Devided Be-twen them Share and Share a like I Also Apoint my Wife Susan Chaplin and my Son Meshach Chaplin my Executrex and Executor to this my Last Will and Testament in Witness whereof I have hereunto Set my hand and Seal the 13 Day of May 1819

Witness Wm Spink the Mark X of George Chaplin

Eliz Bradley

Dennis Luther

figure 12 George Chaplin's will, 1819

according to his gravestone inscription at Great Finborough, George died the day before he made his will!

he left his stock, crops and furniture on his farm to his wife Susan and son Meshech (reproduced by permission of Suffolk Record Office) the court appoints a replacement, granting an administration *de bonis non (d.b.n.)*.

Probate inventories

Between 1529 and 1732, mandatory 'true and perfect' probate inventories (valuations) were filed in the court with wills and administration grants, but subsequently only at the special request of the next of kin or legal representatives. Inventories are usually listed with the wills or grants to which they relate, and a number have been published. You can find out about surviving inventories and finding aids to them from Gibson and Churchill's *Probate jurisdictions: Where to Look for Wills*. They were appraised within a few days of the owner's death by at least three of his or her relatives, friends or neighbours, at the behest of the next of kin, to safeguard the interests of the executors and beneficiaries, and to prevent theft or fraud. Sometimes only the inventory survives and the will or administration grant to which they were originally linked have disappeared.

The dated inventory of the deceased's personal property was headed by the names, residences and occupations of that person and the appraisers. All the house contents were surveyed and given an estimated sale value, down to every stick of furniture, soft furnishings, books, pictures, kitchen utensils, domestic equipment, trade tools, debts and cash. This was usually done room by room, each being described by its prime function. Beds might be identified by their method of construction, whilst the words used for certain items may now be unrecognizable because they are obsolete, written in local dialect or phonetically. The contents of barns and outbuildings were listed and valued too, and some of the names given to farm implements may be unfamiliar to modern readers. You may be able to decipher them by referring to a dialect dictionary or *A Glossary of Household, Farming and Trade Terms from Probate Inventories*, by R. Milward. Quantities of growing and harvested crops, timber, animal carcasses and livestock were also evaluated, plus leasehold properties, and any money lent out on credit.

These documents reveal much about a person's lifestyle, status, contemporary taste and degree of refinement, local availability of certain commodities, as well as the degree of financial commitment. You can visualize house size and the way it might have looked inside, though empty rooms were missed out, as were certain items such as wearing apparel (paraphernalia) traditionally set aside for the widow. The work tools may indicate the scale and sophistication of a business enterprise, or suggest a secondary occupation. If you analyse probate inventories of other family members or local contemporaries, you can see whether his or her belongings and economic status were typical or atypical of the period or area.

Probate accounts

The total inventory assessment was usually less than the true market value of a person's assets and may have borne little relation to what was left once all the debts and liabilities had been settled, so the final probate accounts present a more accurate summary. From 1540, these were submitted to the probate court by executors or administrators when compelled to do so, or when requested after 1685, particularly if the estate was likely to be in debt or subject to dispute. Probate accounts were generally filed, like the inventories, with the relevant will or administration grant. Drawn up within a year of death, they note the deduction of administration costs, any medical, nursing and funeral expenses, taxes, rates, rent arrears, wages to employees, discharged debts and other disbursements, which were offset against estate receipts including the proceeds of any property sales directed in the will. The final total became the residuary estate once the various legacies had been distributed. If there were insufficient funds to pay these, the beneficiaries received an abatement (a part) of their gift, on a pro rata basis.

Probate accounts survive much less often than inventories, but *Probate Accounts of England and Wales,* edited by P. Spufford, lists about 30,000 known extant records in English church courts to 1857, This is also available on microfiche. It does not include accounts filed in the Prerogative Court of Canterbury.

Probate accounts are instructive because they name the deceased's wife and children (not always clearly identified in the will itself, or omitted because they had already been provided for), and sometimes their ages, places of residence and occupations are mentioned too. You will certainly learn the names of all the deceased's creditors and debtors. The purchase of clothing, schooling costs, apprenticeship premiums and payment of maintenance for infant children, minors or orphans in accordance with the deceased's wishes may be detected nowhere else. You can also find out how much was spent on the funeral entertainments, mourning rings and other gifts in compliance with the will, the names of their suppliers and of the recipients.

Tutors, curators and guardians

The probate court's approval was required for tutors and guardians nominated in wills or appointed as next of kin to look after the person and goods of infants under eight years of age, unmarried minors and orphans until 21, or of mentally or physically incapacitated family members. Its sanction was recorded in a special book. The dated and signed tuition bonds set out their names, abodes and kinship to their charges, with the names and places of domicile of sureties willing to be bound with them as guarantors of faithful performance of their duties. An inventory of the child's personal possessions was prepared and lodged by the appointed tutor with the court, and whilst these could be sold if necessary, any inherited land was unalienable and could not be.

Boys, on reaching 14, and girls at 12, were able to apply to the court via a proxy to overturn the arrangement and assign guardianship to a person of their own choice. The dated and signed deed of assignment gave the child's name, age and relationship to the new guardian, whose curation bond (similar to the tuition bond) was filed with the original documentation, and the court's consent recorded.

Between 1258 and 1724, the probate Court of Husting of the City of London supervised control over the personalty and person of unmarried orphan children of city freemen, appointing nominees when their wills failed to do so. Records about tutors and guardians are in the Corporation of London Records Office, and there is a printed calendar of freemen's wills up to 1688. At least two other cities, Bristol and Exeter, exercised similar powers.

Death duty registers

Less well-known records about wills and administrations are the indexed annual death duty registers, spanning the period 1796 to 1903, and available on microfilm in The National Archives and the Family Records Centre to 1857. The indexes to 1903 are similarly accessible, but later registers have to be ordered as documents in The National Archives, giving at least three days' notice, since many are held off-site. Copies of the microfilms can also be hired in for a small fee to search in family history centres. Originally administered by the Board of Stamps, administration of death duty came under the ambit of the Inland Revenue in 1849. The term 'death duties' applies to Legacy Duty, which was collected between 1796 and 1949, Succession Duty between 1853 and 1949, and Estate Duty from 1894 to 1975, which was succeeded by Capital Transfer Tax, the predecessor of Inheritance Tax. No records are known to have been preserved after 1903.

The yearly indexes and registers up to 1811 are organized in three series, for PCC wills, PCC administrations, and lastly for wills and administrations in all other country courts in England and Wales. It is planned to make indexed digital images of the country court wills from 1796 to 1811 available on the Internet at **www.documentsonline.pro.gov.uk**. From 1812, the will indexes are merged for all the courts, though the PCC administration grants and those of country courts continue to be indexed separately as far as 1857. There is a consolidated annual index to civil district and Principal Probate Registry wills from then onwards, and a separate series of administration grant indexes to 1863 (with a gap to 1881). From 1882 to 1903 there are annual union indexes to both wills and administrations. The indexes are initial-alphabetical by the first letter, first letter and vowel or the first three letters of each surname, and give the forename of the deceased, the names and addresses of executors or administrators, the relevant court and date of the probate or grant of administration, and the page or entry number in the register. From 1889, the indexes also disclose the date of death. Where the original will or registered copy no longer exists, as is the case with many West Country wills destroyed by enemy action in 1940, the death duty registers offer a ready substitute about estates over a certain value. They can be used in conjunction with the printed indexes of those courts' records compiled before the Second World War. You can examine the death duty indexes to see in which court your ancestor's will or administration grant was recorded. If you already know when and where a will was proved, you can go straight to the annual indexes to see if there is a register entry.

The scope of the various duties

Not every estate was caught by death duty, perhaps as few as a quarter before 1805, increasing threefold by 1815, so not all grants are registered. Duty was not always collected if the sum involved was considered insignificant (usually when the calculated duty was one per cent of £1,500) or the estate was valued over a million pounds. The index should indicate such instances by 'NE' ('no entry'). The registers only contain relevant extracts from wills which were appropriate to the duty then in force.

Where individual legacies were worth £20 (increased to £100 in 1853), or the residuary estate was valued at £100 (reduced to £20 in 1805) legacy duty was payable, the percentage depending on the degree of kinship of the beneficiary to the deceased. Until 1804, legacies and residual estates bequeathed to spouses, children, parents and grandparents were exempt. From 1805 to 1814, gifts to spouses and parents did not attract death duty, further limited from 1815 to spouses only.

Real estate was taken into consideration from 1796 until 1852 if the will directed that it should be sold to fund annuities, and from 1805 to pay legacies or form the residual estate. Thereafter, both personalty and realty were subject to duty on the owner's death, any other estate worth £100 or more passing under a trust or settlement, outside a will, attracting a new succession duty. From 1894, Estate Duty took precedence over legacy duty and succession duty and any part of the estate liable to these was excluded from the calculation for the new duty. The estates of soldiers, sailors and mariners dying in the service of the Crown were exempt.

What the registers tell you

The registered entries about liable estates are headed by the name of the deceased, his or her last address, occupation and date of death, the dates when the will was made and proved, in which probate court, the names, addresses and occupations of the executors, and the gross value the estate was sworn under before deduction of debts and expenses. However, land was not included until 1853. Underneath, in columns, are set out details of legacies, their stipulated purposes, names of the beneficiaries and their degree of kinship to the deceased, any contingency or succession of interest attaching to them, whether the gift was absolute, conditional, or an annuity. If there was an annuity, the age of each annuitant was recorded, since this determined the amount of duty, which was based on life expectancy. The value of the residuary estate and rates of duty payable on it and on each liable legacy were then recorded, and when and how much was paid. A typical contingency was when a spouse was left copyhold land and possessions for her lifetime or widowhood, whereupon what was left was to be sold and the proceeds divided according to the testator's instructions. Successions of interest arose when the next entitled person came into the property. Consequently the registers were kept open for many years to allow such events to happen, because although the first beneficiary might be exempt the next in line might be liable to pay duty, by which time the value of the gift might have increased or shrunk. The entries were accordingly annotated with the dates of death, marriage or remarriage of beneficiaries, absence overseas, and the births of posthumous children who were to benefit. As the rate of duty depended on the degree of kinship to the deceased, these were precisely recorded, so the registers provide a way of identifying illegitimate issue. If relationships are not clear in the will itself, the death duty registers should sort them out. They may also mention children unnamed in the will itself, and grandchildren who were to take their parent's share should the parent die.

Reversionary registers, compiled after 1853, contain details of trusts and settlement deeds drawn up outside wills, showing successive transfer dates and names of lineal heirs to property on which succession duty fell in due course. As this might happen over a long period, relevant marriages, deaths and changes of residence were recorded.

In the case of intestacy, the date of the administration grant, the court, administrator's name, address, occupation and relationship to the deceased are entered at the top, with the names of the next of kin entitled to a share in the personal estate, which may be lacking in the grant itself, and of course its gross value, the degree of liability and how much was paid.

BF	Brother of a father (uncle)
BM	Brother of a mother (uncle)
Child *or* Ch	Child of deceased
DB	Descendant of a brother (nephew, niece, etc.)
DS	Descendant of a sister (nephew, niece, etc.)
DBF	Descendant of a brother of a father (cousin)
DBM	Descendant of a brother of a mother (cousin)
DSF	Descendant of a sister of a father (cousin)
DSM	Descendant of a sister of a mother (cousin)
DBGF	Descendant of a brother of a grandfather
DBGM	Descendant of a brother of a grandmother
DSGF	Descendant of a sister of a grandfather
DSGM	Descendant of a sister of a grandmother
G child	Grandchild
GG child	Great-grandchild
G daughter	Granddaughter
G son	Grandson
SF	Sister of a father (aunt)
SM	Sister of a mother (aunt)
Str *or* Stra *or* Strag	Stranger in blood
Stra BL	Stranger, brother-in-law
Stra DL	Stranger, daughter-in-law
Stra NC	Stranger, natural child (illegitimate)
Stra ND	Stranger, natural daughter (illegitimate)
Stra NS	Stranger, natural son (illegitimate)
Stra NC (of a daughter)	Stranger, illegitimate child of a daughter
Stra NC (of a son)	Stranger, illegitimate child of a son
Stra (sent)	Stranger, servant of the deceased
Stra SL	Stranger, sister-in-law or son-in-law
Stra *or* 'daughter'	Stranger, natural daughter (illegitimate)
Stra *or* 'son'	Stranger, natural son (illegitimate)

what the various abbreviations mean in the Consanguinity column of the death duty registers

Government stockholders

Indexes to the ledgers of Bank of England will abstracts, relating to the transfer of ownership of Government stock between 1717 and 1845, can be searched at **www.englishorigins.com**, which offers a charged service. There is also a copy of the index from 1807 to 1845 available on microfiche and in print. The ledgers record names and addresses of people authorised to receive shares which were willed to them. Sometimes an accompanying baptism certificate was filed if the beneficiary was a minor, or a burial certificate if appropriate. From about 1810, the wills were invariably proved in the PCC, the only court recognized by the Bank.

Registries of deeds

Other places where you may expect to find extracts or copies of wills include the registers and enrolled memorials of devises of land between 1709 and 1938, and 1709 and 1837 respectively, in the Middlesex Registry of Deeds, in London Metropolitan Archives. The City of London was excluded, as was the City of York from similar Deeds Registries set up in Yorkshire. That for the East Riding was established in 1707 and abolished in 1976. The North Riding Deeds Registry was set up in 1735 and abolished in 1970, and the registry for the West Riding operated between 1704 and 1970. Records of the first are held by the East Riding of Yorkshire Council Archives and Records Service, Beverley, of the second by North Yorkshire County Record Office, Northallerton, and of the last by West Yorkshire Archive Service, Wakefield. A registry was also established for parts of the drained fens on the Bedford Level, whose records for the period 1649–1920 are in the County Record Office, Cambridge, though registration of conveyances and leases was often disregarded after 1860.

At each venue the contents of the registers are listed by year. The lists are arranged chronologically as an initial-index of surnames. The surnames relate to the testators or vendors of freehold land, lessors of property for 21 years or more, and mortgagees. The indexes include their forenames, the names of the new owners, lessees, and mortgagors (borrowers), then identify the parish, street or place where the property was situated, together with the registration reference. Some early registers have topographical indexes too, but there are no corresponding indexes of grantees. The actual registers briefly summarize details extracted from the will, conveyance, indenture of lease or mortgage deed, whereas the memorials are full transcripts of the original documents.

Dormant funds

The Court Funds Division of the Public Trust Office, in London, holds moneys to which no legal ownership has yet been determined, and where the accounts have lain dormant for five years. There is a printed nominal index of persons in whose names sums have been lodged, or their specific beneficiaries, available on the premises and in the National Archives, Kew. Documentary proof is required from anyone asserting a right to the money as the next of kin, but as most amounts are under £250 the cost of verifying entitlement may well exceed the sum claimed.

14

probate records elsewhere in the British Isles, Ireland and the United States of America

In this chapter you will learn:
- what courses were appropriate
- how to find the records
- how to find records about immigrants to the US

The Channel Islands

Nominally, the Channel Islands form part of the diocese of Winchester, but on Jersey, wills were proved locally in the Ecclesiastical Court of the Dean of Jersey until 25 May 1949, and thereafter in the Probate Registry, at the Royal Court of Jersey, St Helier. Real estate could not be willed before 1851, and it was common for subsequent wills of personalty and realty to be separately drawn up. Wills in which land was devised are filed and recorded in the Public Registry, also in the Royal Court of Jersey.

Original and enrolled copies of wills are indexed from 1660 up to 1964, at the Probate Registry, including later wills bequeathing both personalty and realty, with discrete calendars of administration grants made between 1848 and 1964. Neither Registry is open to the public, but searches can be undertaken for you, the fee depending on the time spent. There is an online index to Jersey wills at **http://jerseyheritagetrust.adlibsoft. com/publicaccess/** and you can search microfilm copies of both the indexes and wills in family history centres, on payment of a small hiring-in fee.

Indexed original and registered copy wills and administration grants of personal estate on Guernsey, Alderney, Sark, Herm and Jethou proved in the Ecclesiastical Court of the Bailiwick of Guernsey from 1660 to the present day, are held by the Bureau des Connetables, St Peter Port, Guernsey. Guernsey wills dating from 1841 onwards, in which only land was devised, are kept in the Royal Court of Guernsey, in St Peter Port. Land devised by will on Alderney since 1849 is registered at the island's Court House, together with a few earlier wills and intestacies relating to land, though none dating from earlier than 1946, as all previous records were destroyed during the Second World War. Land on Sark is not disposable by will, descending instead to the next heir as far as the fifth degree of kinship (the common ancestor being the great-great-great-grandparent), then to the Seigneur. A widow always has a right to dower on a third of it. No land can be disposed of by will on Herm or Jethou.

Estates held in England and Wales

In all cases where Channel Islanders held property in England or Wales before 1858, their wills were taken for probate to the Prerogative Court of Canterbury, later ones being lodged at the Principal Probate Registry in London.

Isle of Man

The two ecclesiastical courts alternately serving the Isle of Man for parts of each year up to 1873 were the Consistory Court of Sodor and Man, whose testamentary records commence in 1600, and the Archdeaconry Court of Man, with probate material from 1631. The Consistory Court then continued alone until 1884, being succeeded in 1885 by the High Court of Justice. Records up to 1910 are in the Manx National Heritage Library, the Manx Museum, in Douglas, after which you need to consult the Deeds and Probate Registry, at the Civil Registry, in Douglas. The indexes to wills, administration grants and inventories up to 1949, starting in 1659 and 1631 respectively, can also be seen on microfilm at the Society of Genealogists, in London, and in family history centres.

Estates held on the mainland

Until 1858, the Prerogative Court of York had superior jurisdiction over the Northern Province, including the diocese of Sodor and Man, the Prerogative Court of Canterbury having authority over any property which might be held in the Southern Province, so look at lists and indexes of wills proved in both these courts and in local church courts for property owned by Manx people on the mainland. From 1858 you can trace wills and administration grants of English and Welsh estates of Manx people in the annual National Probate Indexes, described earlier. Wills of property left in Scotland or Ireland were administered using their probate frameworks, which are set out below.

Scotland

Up to 1823, testaments relating to personalty were produced by executors for confirmation (*testament testamentar*) at the commissariot within whose boundaries a person died. Commissary court demarcations were identical to those of medieval dioceses, though bishops ceased to have any jurisdiction once the Crown took over in 1560. The chief commissariot, in Edinburgh, dealt with personal estates valued at £50 or more, and also received testaments of Scots dying overseas leaving property in Scotland. As in England and Wales, confirmation was a matter of conscience, so not every testament that was made was formally approved. A third of the personal estate passed automatically to the surviving widow, a third to the children, the remainder being freely disposable. If there was no widow, or no children, the estate was divided in half. If the deceased left neither, then all his personalty could be bequeathed as he wished. When a person died intestate, the commissariot appointed an administrator (*testament dative*), and the names of any surviving spouse and children were placed in the court records. The commissariot boundaries are shown on the regional maps in *The Phillimore Atlas and Index of Parish Registers*.

Records of the commissariots up to 1823

All confirmed testaments and extant inventories of goods, chattels, tools, cash and debts emanating from the commissariots have been deposited in the National Archives of Scotland, in Edinburgh. The Scottish Record Society has published indexes to the testaments confirmed in the Commissariot of Edinburgh between 1514 and 1800, and for the other commissariots from the sixteenth century or later up to the same year. Later confirmations are accessed by typescript indexes. A list of the various start dates of the commissariots are included in Gibson and Churchill's *Probate Jurisdictions: Where to Look for Wills*. The indexes may contain valuable details about family relationships, abodes and occupations.

The sheriff courts

In 1823, the commissariots were abolished and replaced by sheriff courts, the chief of which is in Edinburgh, and which confirms testaments of people dying 'furth of Scotland' leaving personal property there. The parameters of the sheriff court districts roughly correspond to those of counties, though some were later enlarged. A list of districts and constituent parishes can be gleaned from the current *Scottish Law Directory*. Most of the sheriff court registers and original confirmed testaments, testamentary deeds and inventories are filed in separate series in the National Archives of Scotland. Testaments from 1892 can be accessed by contacting the Commissary Department, Edinburgh Sheriff Court, 27 Chambers Street, Edinburgh EH1 1LB.

You can search indexes to all the above testaments confirmed between 1500 and 1875 at **www.scottishdocuments.com**, and then pay to view the digital images of them. It is planned to extend the period beyond 1875 soon.

There are three consolidated printed indexes to surviving inventories in *Personal Estates of Defuncts*, covering the sheriff courts of the Lothians, 1827–65, Argyll, Bute, Dumbarton, Lanark and Renfrew, 1845–65, and for the rest of Scotland between 1846 and 1867. Yearly indexed calendars of confirmations and inventories for the whole of Scotland since 1876 are available not only in the National Archives of Scotland, but up to 1935 in many local record offices and libraries. From 1960 to 1984 they are on microfilm and thereafter on computer. The Family History Library catalogue, at **www.familysearch.org** will tell you about copies which can be hired in to search in a family history centre near you.

Inventories are useful, though only prolific since the early nineteenth century, because they give date of death, and before civil registration of deaths began in 1855, where burial registers are defective they may be the sole source about a person's demise.

Disputed testaments and *bona vacantia*

Contested testaments were settled by the commissariots, passing on appeal to the Commissary Court of Edinburgh, and finally to the Court of Session. After 1830, the Commissary Court no longer exercised power of appeal. Full indexes to diocesan cases heard in the commissariots to 1800, and for the Commissariot of Edinburgh have been published. The papers themselves are in the National Archives of Scotland.

Enquiries about Scottish estates in the Crown's hands as *bona vacantia* for want of heirs, are dealt with by the Queen's and Lord Treasurer's Remembrancer, in Edinburgh.

Services of heirs (retours)

The testaments contain no reference to heritable land before 1868. In the National Archives of Scotland, however, are filed by county numerous services of heirs (or retours) relating to defined parcels of land inherited on the deaths of landholders, once the heirs' rights to them had been established, which might take several years. A brieve of succession was first sent out of Chancery to the county sheriff so that he could summon sworn jurors to enquire into what lands the owner had actually died possessed of within the county, and to obtain proof as to the next heir. Their verdict was then 'retoured' to Chancery and the heir issued with a certified copy of the 'retour' ratifying his entitlement. Personal name and topographical indexes of services of heirs from about 1544 to 1700 have been printed county by county in *Inquisitionum ad Capellum Domini Regis Retornatarum ... Abbreviatio*, with ten-yearly indexes running thereafter up to 1859, and then annual. The indexes prior to 1860 frequently contain abbreviated dated summaries of the original documentation, specify the heir's exact relationship to the previous owner, plus the latter's date of decease. Later indexes exclude the date of death.

In 1747, regality courts, exempt from the control of local sheriffdoms, also began to retour services of heirs, and most of their records are in the National Archives of Scotland.

Sasines

Registers of sasines from 1599 (excluding burghs before 1926) record an heir or grantee taking actual possession (seisin) of his land, once he had been served with his retour from Chancery. There are three series of registers, all of which are in the National Archives of Scotland: a secretary's register for every county or district, 1599–1609; a particular register for each; and a general register relating to sasines of lands held in more than one district or county, both the latter two registers covering the period 1617–1871. Some entries are duplicated. A general register is still kept today, and since 1926 has encompassed burgh sasines. Only inherited land was dealt with by retours and sasines until leases of 31 years or more became registrable after 1857.

The retours and sasines are in Latin to about 1680, except for the period 1653–60. The first two sets of registers of sasines are only partly indexed, though there is a complete nominal and topographical index to the general register in the National Archives of Scotland. There are printed county abridgements of registered entries from 1781, with corresponding personal and place-name indexes, although there is a gap in the latter series between 1830 and 1872. Similarly indexed annual minute books of abridgements from 1868 have been circulated to each county sheriff clerk. The registers may allude to previous dated land transactions within the family, stretching back several generations or into collateral branches, and name tenants and other kinsfolk besides the current heir.

Fifteenth- and sixteenth-century sasines were written in Latin in notarial protocol books, many of which were filed with burgh archives, and a number of have been published. Instruments of sasine from the same period may occasionally surface amongst family archives, the National Archives of Scotland being their main place of deposit.

Death duty register
There are some indexed records relating to various estate duties from 1804 and succession duty since 1853, which are held by the National Archives of Scotland.

Burgh sasines
Individual burgh protocol books to 1689, and later burgh registers of sasines to 1925 have been lodged in the National Archives of Scotland, and are partially indexed. These enshrine other registered deeds too.

Registries of deeds

Besides the notarial protocol books, and a sixteenth-century register of acts and decreets of the Court of Session to 1581, another place where you might find testaments, marriage contracts, trust deeds and settlements recorded for permanent preservation or for execution is the Register of Deeds, instituted by the Court of Session in Edinburgh in 1554. The first series of registers covers the period 1554–1657, the second (in three sections) 1661–1811, and the third extends from 1812 to the present day. You can inspect these in the National Archives of Scotland, using the printed indexes up to 1694, then the manuscript indexes for 1750 and 1751, which become continuous from 1770. Minute books for the gaps between 1695 and 1749 and 1752 and 1760 contain brief chronological entries of registrations.

From the seventeenth century to 1809, local commissariots, and regality courts to 1747, maintained their own registries of deeds, as do their successor sheriff courts today. The records of the first two have been deposited in the National Archives of Scotland, and are indexed. Those of the sheriff courts are held locally by sheriff clerks.

Tutors, curators and guardians

Brieves of tutory and brieves of idiotry or furiosity concern appointments made by Chancery of tutors-at-law (and curators after 1696) for minors under 21, or after 1585 for mentally incapacitated people, when the deceased father had failed to nominate anyone. The nearest kinsman on the paternal line, aged 25 or more, acted as guardian of the estate, the mother becoming the child's physical guardian. From 1672, an inventory of the child's personal possessions was required from the tutor-at-law on taking up his responsibility. At 14 a male minor (a female minor at 12) could apply to Chancery to administer the property himself or appoint a curator of his choosing, as in England and Wales, but from 1696 curators were appointed in the same way as tutors-at-law. Indexed services *de tutela* to 1699 have been published with the retours described above. There is a general index to later tutorships and curations between 1700 and 1897, in the National Archives of Scotland.

Estates in England

Scots leaving property over the border in England had their wills proved in the appropriate church court before 1858, and afterwards you can trace their wills and administration grants in the annual National Probate Indexes. Until 1876 these are listed at the end of the index, later entries being indexed alongside all the others.

Dormant funds

Unclaimed funds are retained for seven years by the Accountant of the Court of Session before being transferred to the Queen's and Lord Treasurer's Remembrancer in Edinburgh, to whom any enquiries should be sent.

Ireland

Up to 1858, wills of Irish people were proved in diocesan consistory courts. As diocesan and county boundaries were invariably not coincident, a person might own possessions in several dioceses. When personalty exceeding £5 in more than one diocese was involved, the superior Prerogative Court of Armagh was utilized, but where property in the other diocese totalled less then probate was granted in the consistory court serving the diocese where the bulk of the estate lay. There were also a few peculiar courts outside this two-tier hierarchy.

How to find out what exists

In 1922 all centrally housed original local probates and administration grants before 1858, and most office copies, were destroyed by fire, as well as the records of the civil Principal

Probate Registry, established in Dublin 1858, and original local wills up to 1903 which had been transferred there from district probate registries. A list of surviving material is included in Gibson and Churchill's *Probate Jurisdictions: Where to Look for Wills*.

Indexes to wills and administrations before 1858

In the National Archives of Ireland, in Dublin, surviving indexes to wills and administration bonds in each pre-1858 court give an indication of what was lost. Some have been published, including indexes to wills proved in the Prerogative Court between 1536 and 1810, and Dublin diocesan grants from 1270 to 1858. There are gaps for most courts before the mid-eighteenth century, and many probates stem only from the preceding century. The alphabetical list of wills, and yearly surname initial-indexed administration bonds usually disclose the testator or intestate's full name, address, year of probate or administration bond, and often his occupation. You can also search the indexes from 1484 to 1858 on CD-ROM.

Betham's pedigrees and abstracts

In the early nineteenth century, Sir William Betham compiled sketch pedigrees from his notebooks of genealogical abstracts of almost all the wills proved in the Prerogative Court of Armagh up to 1800, administration grants up to 1802, and wills proved in the Kildare Consistory Court before 1827. His Prerogative Court notebooks of will abstracts can be accessed in the National Archives of Ireland via the published index of Armagh wills, whilst the alphabetically listed administration grants and alphabetical sketch pedigrees are held in The Genealogical Office, in Dublin, to which later amendments and additions were made. Indexed photostats of the notebooks and pedigrees are held by the College of Arms, in London, and they can be searched on microfilm in the Society of Genealogists. Consult the Family History Library catalogue at **www.familysearch.org** for references to copies you may hire to study in a family history centre near you.

These abstracts, and an ever-increasing collection of other card-indexed extant will and grant book copies, transcripts, and abstracts of wills and administrations before 1858 which have been accumulated by the National Archives of Ireland, can be seen on microfilm in the Public Record Office of Northern Ireland, which also holds an unannotated copy of Betham's sketch pedigrees. Other concentrations of will abstracts may be found in the National Library, and in the libraries of the Representative Church Body, Royal Irish Academy, and Trinity College, all in Dublin.

Complete printed alphabetical annual union calendars of wills and administrations from 1858 onwards can be found at both the National Archives of Ireland, in Dublin, and Public Record Office of Northern Ireland, in Belfast, to which there is a consolidated index for the period 1858–77. Until 1917, the calendars extend over all Ireland, thenceforward they are in Dublin for the 26 southern counties and in Belfast for the six northern counties. They contain references to will and grant book copies, which are complete from 1922. Because the calendars divulge the deceased's name, address, occupation, date and place of death, and date and place of probate or administration grant, plus the name, address and relationship to him or her of the executors or administrators, and the value under which the effects were sworn, they reveal a modicum of genealogical information, although the original material before 1904 has now largely disappeared. In the case of administration grants, the names of all entitled next of kin are recorded in the calendars.

You can examine will copies transcribed in locally kept district registry books and administration grant books from 1858 in the National Archives of Ireland. Surviving incomplete copies in will books of the Principal Probate Registry for 1874, 1876, 1891 and 1896, and copy administration grant books for 1878, 1883, 1891 and 1893, are available in the National Archives of Ireland, and complete will books for the districts of Armagh, Belfast and Londonderry from 1858 onwards are available on microfilm to 1900 in the Public Record Office of Northern Ireland. These are indexed.

Original and registered copy wills and administrations since 1904 are held by the National Archives of Ireland, though those filed or registered in Belfast, Londonderry and many in Armagh since 1900 are in the custody of the Public Record Office of Northern Ireland. The annual calendars are similar to those for England and Wales. Wills proved more recently than 20 years ago are retained by district registries before transfer to the National Archives of Ireland, whilst those for the northern counties are kept for ten years by the Royal Courts of Justice in Belfast.

Estates in England, Wales and Scotland

Wills of Irish people leaving property in England or Wales before 1858 were proved in the Prerogative Court of Canterbury, Prerogative Court of York, or local diocesan court having jurisdiction over their personal goods. The indexes to London and North Country courts are particularly worth scanning, because of the heavy influx and two-way traffic of Irish people through northern ports, or long-term Anglo-Irish family associations with the mainland. Where property was held in both Ireland and England, double probates were granted.

Incomplete copies of abstracts of PCC and some other local wills of estates liable to death duty which were filed in London between 1821 and 1857 have been transferred to the Public Record Office of Northern Ireland, together with indexes covering 1812–57. The full contents of the original or registered copies of these wills can be searched with other records of the PCC, or relevant diocesan material. From 1858 onwards, you can elicit information about London-filed Irish probates and administration grants to 1876 at the end of the yearly alphabetical National Probate Indexes, and thereafter absorbed into the main index. Some of these duplicate Irish registrations. Where original wills and administrations were destroyed by the fire in Dublin in 1922, this source may serve as an effective substitute.

Testaments of Irish people leaving personalty in Scotland were confirmed in the commissary or sheriff court where it lay.

Death duty registers

Inland Revenue registers of Irish will abstracts and administrations in all its courts concerning estates subject to death and other duties between 1828 and 1839 are deposited in the National Archives of Ireland. The information embedded in them is similar to that in the English and Welsh death duty registers. The indexes, originally compiled in London, run on to 1879, and yield the names and addresses of the deceased, the executors or administrators, the date and place of probate or grant of letters of administration, and when the original wills and majority of the death duty registers themselves no longer exist, these entries at least convey some idea of when a person died, his or her last whereabouts and who were the legal representatives. Extant registers will of course give precise date of death, detail legacies, names and kinships of recipient beneficiaries or next of kin.

The *Registry of Deeds*

You can read in the National Archives of Ireland and in the National Library, in Dublin, published *Abstracts of Wills at the Registry of Deeds*, edited by P. B. Phair and E. Ellis, which relate to enrolments in the Registry of Deeds in Dublin between 1708 and 1832. This mechanism was to protect devises of land against any future dispute. The volumes name and index each testator, beneficiary and witness, whilst the indexed books of office copies and original witnessed memorials (transcripts of the original deeds), at the Registry, contain full details of relevant will clauses, sales, rent charges, pre-nuptial marriage settlements, leases for three or more years or for specified lives, and mortgages.

There is an alphabetical grantors' index from 1708, but although the surname of the first grantee or lessee, register volume, page or memorial number are recorded, no property locations are mentioned until counties were included from 1834. The lands index, running from 1708 to 1947, is arranged under counties, corporate towns and cities, and then by initial letter of townland until 1828, when the counties were sub-divided into baronies, and then into townlands. As with the English registries, there is no index to grantees. Microfilm copies of both indexes are in the National Library, in Dublin, and in the Public Record Office of Northern Ireland, where the microfilmed memorial books can also be inspected. If you find the task of searching these indexes too outfacing, you may be able to locate the whereabouts and descent of a family's land during the nineteenth century from the tithe applotment books, Primary Valuation and Valuation Office Books, described in Chapter 08, all of which have surname indexes.

The actual transcripts and memorials of leases for lives supply the names and ages of people nominated by the lessee at the time the agreement was signed, and because they were often his children or close relatives, they are a valuable indicator of family composition and survival at a specific date. Leases of 900 years or for lives renewable in perpetuity were common in Ireland, making the land virtually freehold.

From about the mid-nineteenth century, their genealogical worth decreases as more comprehensive sources become available, and as registration was never compulsory, the registers contain only a selection of actual conveyances registered to furnish evidence of legal title should any challenge arise.

Land Commission records

Nineteenth-century and some earlier wills deposited with the Irish Land Commission as proof of ownership of smallholdings by vendors intending to sell to occupying tenants with the help of public subsidies, are kept by the National Archives of Ireland, to which there is a card index of testators in the National Library.

Dormant funds

Unclaimed funds in all Ireland before 1921 and subsequently in the southern counties, are held by the Accountant of the Courts of Justice in Dublin, those for the six northern counties by the Accountant General, in Belfast, to whom any enquiries should be addressed.

United States of America

In many ways, the probate procedure adopted by British colonial America imitated that of England and Wales. It has been estimated that between 25 and 40 per cent of the American male populace and less than 10 per cent of females left wills which were proved. Wills of personalty can still be made by young men on reaching 14, and by girls at 12 (though 18 is the minimum legal age in Connecticut, Massachusetts and Virginia, 18 for males and 16 for females in the State of New York, and 21 for Vermont residents). Land can only be devised by will at 21. Similar age limits of 14 and 12 qualify a person to act as executor, though in Massachusetts, Missouri and Rhode Island the minimum age is 17, and 18 in Mississippi.

What happens when no will is found

On intestacy, in most States a widow becomes entitled to a third of her husband's estate as her dower, and the balance is distributed evenly among their children, any dead child's share going *pari passu* to his or her offspring. In some states, the eldest son has double the share allotted to each of his siblings. If the deceased was unmarried, then the parents are deemed the next of kin. By 1811, realty descended on intestacy to the legal next of kin, on the universal repeal of the colonial laws of inheritance by primogeniture under which freehold land automatically devolved on the eldest son. Entailed land continued to descend as provided for under the terms of the original settlement, as in England. In certain States, on intestacy property owned independently by a couple when they married and any subsequently inherited by either party belongs solely to that person, whilst any they purchased or owned jointly vests entirely on the survivor. In others, a widow's right of dower contrasts with her husband's claim to all property in her ownership on their marriage and any she later inherited so long as they have a surviving child who will ultimately be the heir. If not, then he too is entitled only to a third. Thus the laws of probate and intestacy varied according to when and where a person resided, especially in relation to realty.

Probate records

Probate packets and case files are lodged in county courthouses set up in every State from early colonial times, where they remain today, alongside will books into which probated wills were copied, and invalid unregistered, unindexed wills which were separately stored. The original probate papers and will books are indexed. Abstracts and incomplete transcripts of many colonial wills and administrations have been published, but these are of varying quality and reliability, so you should not totally depend on them to distil or accurately reproduce every genealogical detail in the original, or on the will books alone, as transcription errors may be found in these as well.

What can you expect to find

The files and packets are stuffed with original signed and attested wills, the executors' petitions for letters testamentary for probate or those of administrators seeking letters of administration of an intestate's estate, administrators' bonds, probate inventories, preserved copies of newspaper and other public notifications of pending probate, guardians' bonds, petitions to the court for changes of guardianship initiated by minors, interim annual estate accounts filed by executors and administrators, final financial statements, division documents listing all the beneficiaries and their addresses, and their dated, signed receipts for specific gifts or estate portions thereby discharging the executors or administrators from further liability. Because a sequence of dated and autographed documents was generated by and kept together for each probate or administration grant, where one batch of papers is missing, unclear or deficient, the content of the rest may overlap or be more instructive.

Tracing a death

Dates of death may be elicited from the probate papers' or indexed will books. They may otherwise be deduced from the date when probate was applied for, since it was in most states obligatory between 30 and 90 days after demise. The document itself was then produced to the court to be validated, the witnesses appearing in person to certify its authenticity before the executor was authorized to act on its instructions. Occasionally however, the verification stage occurred whilst the testator was still alive, or probate was granted to him so that he could control transfer of part of his estate during his lifetime. The will book copy was invariably written up between 30 and 90 days after death.

Procedure leading to probate

Petitions for letters testamentary were often presented orally at the county court, and written up in a probate minute book. Some courts insisted on full dated documentary particulars from the executors, incorporating the names and addresses of the petitioner and deceased, the latter's date of death and the estimated values of his realty and personalty, plus the names and addresses of the witnesses who had attested his signature on the will, the names, ages, domiciles and exact relationship to him of all devisees and legatees.

If the defunct was intestate, the nearest kinsman petitioned for a grant of letters of administration, and provided similar information about the heirs. Because the spouse ranks first in order of precedence as next of kin, followed by the children, the parents, grandparents, siblings, uncles and aunts, nephews and nieces, great-uncles and great-aunts, first cousins, then the chief creditor, you can determine who was the closest living relative. There may be regional variations in the order of seniority.

The executor or administrator, once formally approved by the court, lodged a dated and signed bond as a guarantee of proper performance of his duties, a relative or friend serving as surety in a sum equal to the estate's value, to safeguard the interests of the heirs against misconduct. The bond was redeemed once the final distribution had taken place, and their liability ceased.

Inventorying personal property

The court assigned three independent appraisers to inventory the deceased's personal possessions (including, up to the nineteenth century, number, names and values of any slaves), for return within 90 days, so as to protect the estate from excessive claims, and the heirs from fraud or theft.

Maintenance allowances were set aside during the probate process for named dependants, such as the wife's dower and towards the children's annual upkeep and education, which might be defrayed by sales of certain articles with the court's sanction. Periodic estate accounts were lodged from time to time to show the purpose of administrative expenditure and sums received.

Looking after minors or incapacitated heirs

A nominated guardian (tutor, curator, conservator or receiver, depending on where the person lived) was formally charged by the will or county court with management of the estate of minor orphaned males under 21, and females under 18, or mentally or physically incompetent persons. An 'orphan' might actually still have one living parent, who was usually appointed. The guardian signed a bond undertaking faithful execution of his or her responsibility, backed up by a surety in a sum equal to the child's quantified share in the estate. Boys on attaining 14, and girls at 12 could petition the court for its consent to their nomination of a guardian, and a further similar bond was sworn by the new nominee and a guarantor. The dated applications divulge the names and current ages of the minors, the names of their appointee and deceased parent.

Advertising probate and filing estate accounts

At this stage, notices of pending probate were posted before final probate accounts were submitted to the court, enumerating the total estate administration charges, disbursements, expenses and income, and expressing the balance left to be apportioned according to the deceased's instructions or under the law of intestacy. Embodied in them are names of indebted or creditor relatives, friends and associates.

Distribution of the assets

The division documents are useful in that they give an intimation of death dates or new married names of beneficiaries since the will was drawn up, and any remarriage of the widow. Their signed receipts record their comparative legacies, and indicate their standard of literacy.

Sharing out the land, and original land grants

You may come across consequent property partitions among estate heirs enrolled in land entry books in local land offices of the appropriate State and county. These, original and copy wills, bills of sale of slaves, deeds, gifts, leases and releases, patents and grants of land in state-land States (of which there were 20, including all 13 original states), marriage settlements, quitclaims of future rights, and mortgages, are kept with other land office papers and deeds in State archives or libraries, town or county courthouses. Where the original material has been lost, these are a worthy substitute.

Manorial copyhold tenure was virtually unknown in the American colonies. Records of federal land grants after about 1800 in the 30 public-land States, private land claims and military bounty land applications are held by the National Archives in Washington, DC, and in the 16 National Archives Regional Archives. Leases were not usually recorded. Sometimes these books contain wills found nowhere else.

Using the indexes

The means of reference to the land entry books is generally by alpha-, initial- or first three letter-index of the surname of the first seller, grantor or testator, running chronologically by date of registration, frequently with a companion set of indexes organized under the name of the first buyer, grantee, devisee or heir. Sometimes there is a tract index, arranged under the nomenclature of the land involved.

Each index enshrines both first-named contracting parties, the land's identity, and the date of registration of the conveyance, which might be some years after the agreement was carried out. If your ancestor was a joint vendor or purchaser, his or her name may thus be absent from the indexes. The indexes are not a complete directory either. Because there was no union system of inheritance among the colonies or over time, you may also find it difficult to sort out a person's precise kinship to the decease without recourse to other documents. As some neighbouring county and State boundaries were adjusted or extended, you may need to consult the indexes and books of several, depending on the period and area involved, but they can prove rewarding in tracking down people's movements within a county or State, or across country.

Deed books

From many deed books up to at least the Civil War, 1861–5, State, county and city land deeds have been microfilmed and made available through the Family History Library catalogue at **www.familysearch.org** for hire in family history centres. The cumulative indexes have not been filmed.

The book enrolments specify a named property's exact location, bounded by natural features such as rocks and creeks, trees and man-made artefacts, giving compass bearings and measured distances, which are often sketched or demarcated on an accompanying survey map or town plan. Names of current tenants, previous proprietors, and of neighbouring occupiers of plots on which the property abutted, may also be set out. If the new owner was an immigrant or the tract was being granted for the first time, the name given to the property might signal where the settler originally came from.

Estates held in England and Wales and a bridge over the Atlantic

Many early settlers, armed military and naval personnel in the colonies or dying elsewhere overseas left possessions in England or Wales. Wills or grants of letters of administration of their estates and probate inventories listing their possessions were most frequently filed in the Prerogative Court of Canterbury and listed under 'Parts' rather than by individual county or country. Details of wills and administrations, taken from the act books, are arranged alphabetically by testator's or intestate's surname and forename in *American Wills and Administrations in the Prerogative Court of Canterbury, 1610–1857*, by P. W. Coldham. The entries disclose the last place of residence, details of death, name of the executor or administrator, and cite the whereabouts of any known printed abstract or transcript of the dated will or grant. There is an index of ships and of place-names, which is helpful if you want to trace compatriots or other contemporary settlers leaving property at the same place of provenance.

Sometimes colonial wills were proved not only in the colonial county court, but in the prerogative court too for reasons of security or in expectation of future litigation, and if the county records have subsequently been lost, this may be mitigated somewhat. The English grant might however come some years after the colonist's death.

Filed PCC warrants for probate and administration grants, surviving from 1660, may be trawled for precise dates and places of death. A limited probate or administration grant restricted it to time or place, for example the final distribution of assets within 12 months, or within England only.

Dated probate inventories, though indexed under the surname and forename of the deceased, exist only in any quantity in the Prerogative Court of Canterbury after 1660, but they demonstrate the widespread practice of borrowing and lending among overseas merchants and traders, naming kinsfolk, agents and associates in England and abroad, the whereabouts of migrants' houses and warehousing of trade stock, plus the approximate market value of their goods.

Indexes to Scottish confirmations of testaments and Irish probates of wills should also be searched for references to property left there by emigrants or travellers overseas.

Settlers with London connections

American Wills proved in London, 1611–1775, also compiled by P. W. Coldham, concentrates on probates in the Bishop of London's Consistory Court relating to local estates of people dying in the colonies, which were nominally part of his diocese. Organized under year, the date of probate or administration grant, names of the deceased, his or her principal legatees, executor or administrator, and a short summary of the document are recorded, to which there is a comprehensive personal name index, plus indexes to ships and places mentioned.

Freemen of the City

If the status of the deceased was that of a citizen and merchant, tradesman or craftsman, it is likely that a record of his admission as a city and livery company freeman can be traced. Extant freedom registers of the City of London date from 1681, those of some livery companies from the fifteenth century, records of the former up to 1940 being held in the Corporation of London Records Office, and of the latter for the most part being on deposit in the Guildhall Library nearby.

In order to be a freeman of the City, the candidate had first to become a freeman of one of the livery companies. If such freedom was by virtue of servitude, the apprenticeship bindings registers of the relevant company will disclose the person's paternity or guardianship and place of residence at the time of binding-out. Binding-out was usually for seven or eight years, commencing between the ages of 12 and 14. The place of residence may be the key to birthplace, and thus the church of baptism of the apprentice that number of years before. If freedom was conferred by patrimony, then the father would himself have been a freeman of the company at the time that person was born. You might be able to track a family's association with a company over several generations. Colonial merchants maintained similar links with other cities and ports such as Southampton and Bristol. Wills of contemporary city, company or guild freemen, or burgesses may refer to kinsfolk, friends, business partners or agents abroad, from which you may be able to fix where they came from and when, and where they were at a particular date.

If your family had a coat of arms

A forebear described as a gentleman or 'armiger' may have been granted or inherited a coat of arms or have his lineage recorded in one of the thousands of pedigrees compiled during the periodic county by county heraldic visitations of England and Wales between 1530 and 1689. The heralds or their deputies enquired into, and regulated, the display and entitlement to coats of arms, a by-product of which were the numerous registers of narrative and tabular family trees based on the information and family muniments furnished by the gentry. Many allude to relatives overseas, especially in Virginia, so it is worth looking for published (though not always authentic) copies of these, or you may prefer to pay an officer of the College of Arms for a search of the more reliable official records of the visitations.

Tracking people with unusual surnames

If your surname is unusual, probate lists and indexes of the Prerogative and other local courts of the era, county marriage and census indexes, the *International Genealogical Index*, and *British Isles Vital Records Index*, one-name society websites, databases, or bulletin boards on the Internet may help show where it was prevalent, and by patient examination of wills of people of the same surname, or finding out what became of the wedded couples and their issue, you may succeed in picking up an otherwise elusive transatlantic link.

American Loyalists to the British Crown

Abstracts of wills submitted as evidence by petitioners for compensation, allowances or pensions from the British Crown for their loyalty or practical support which resulted in their loss of possessions during, and after, the Revolutionary War, 1775–83, bear testimony to what they surrendered or left behind. Two series of indexed files of these, between 1776 and 1835, are in the National Archives, Kew, but microfilmed copies of them are widely available. Extracts from the original memorials and papers have been published in *American Loyalist Claims*, by P. W. Coldham.

By their nature retrospective, the memorials, evidence and depositions of witnesses for the claimants comprise not only wills, but marriage settlements and land deeds from previous generations in support of the applications, which relate to people and places much earlier in the eighteenth century. They almost invariably contain a meticulous inventory valuing the claimants' lands, houses and their contents, listing crops, fruit trees, timber, livestock and slaves at the time they fled or were driven out, and compared this with their pre-War values, so that compensation could be calculated accordingly. Names, relationships and ages of dependants were also given. Such claim papers help recreate a vivid portrait of colonial life, and where wills and deeds no longer exist, at least you have a partial summary of them, and can learn what became of the family, whether returning to England, escaping into Canada or elsewhere.

Some other sources for tracing origins of immigrants

Once you have found wills of immigrants you might be able to trace their origins from customs or immigration passenger lists, records of land border crossings and naturalization papers.

There are a number of websites devoted to databases of American immigrants. You can access these at **www. cyndislist.com**. Many of these overlap, or are not official sites, and the information may be incomplete or inaccurate. Try **www.ellisislandrecords.org** for details of new arrivals at the Port of New York between 1892 and 1924, and at the CD-ROM of Mormon immigrants between 1840 and 1890, since these databases may provide the answer as to where they came from, who they travelled in company with, and their ages. Both of these allow you to find the names of other passengers on board the same ship, and provide a picture and history of the ship itself.

Try searching *Passenger and Immigration Lists Index, 1538–1900*, edited by P. W. Filby with various co-editors. These volumes consist of an alphabetical string of personal names, with the dates and places or ships in which they are mentioned, together with a number linking it to the publication from which this information was taken. The author's name and full title of each book is found in the endpapers of each annual supplement. This index is available on CD-ROM, as is another database, *Immigrants to the New World 1600s–1800s*, which also draws on published work. Names of certain individuals recur again and again, because their personal details were extracted from a variety of sources. Always check the publication, because this will set the person's name in its context, and with those of other people. Search the Family History Library catalogue at **www.familysearch.org** to see if you can hire a copy in a family history centre near you. If you can, seek out the original source itself to ensure nothing was missed out and there were no copying errors.

Because of their arrangement and bulk, you will need to know the persons name at the time of immigration, date of birth, ethnic group, date of arrival and port to access the passenger lists with ease.

Regular runs of customs' passenger lists start only in 1820, and are arranged by month, year and port of arrival, to which there are indexes. The musters give the name, age, occupation, port of embarkation, countries of origin and ultimate destination of every passenger, and details of deaths during the voyage. The lists end in 1902.

Indexed immigration passenger lists, 1883–1957, also include birthplace and the last place of residence, after 1893, marital status, nationality, whether in the US before and if some when and where, if going to join a relative and that relative's name, address and relationship to the passenger, and from 1907 the name and address of a relative in the country of origin. These may be inspected on microfilm in the National Archives, in Washington, DC, and in its regional branches. The New York entries to 1924 are included at **www.ellisislandrecords.org** described earlier. *The Morton Allan Directory of European Passenger Steamship Arrivals* lists by year, the steamship company, name and date of arrival of each vessel in the ports of New York, 1890–1930, and Baltimore, Boston and Philadelphia, 1904–26.

Records concerning Canadian and Mexican bordercrossings into the US begin in 1895 and about 1903 respectively. There is a card for each person giving name, age, sex, point of arrival and final destination.

Naturalization papers contain dates and places of birth of petitioners, their current nationality, and indicate whether the dated applications were successful. The original records are kept by the appropriate National Archives Regional Archives from about 1790 onwards up to 1950. Prior to 1906, naturalization could be conferred by the States themselves, so some applications will be filed in State rather than federal archives. Duplicates of naturalizations not held in the National Archives from 26 September 1906 to date are held by the Immigration and Naturalization Service (INS), 425 Eye Stree, NW, Washington DC 20536, to whom written requests for information may be sent. Colonial grants have been published in *Naturalizations in the American Colonies, 1740–1772*, edited by M. S. Giuseppi.

15

Fred Karno and two of his army: case studies

In this chapter you will learn:
- how the sources described in this book were used to trace three people's ancestries
- the limitations and frustration of records
- how personal name indexes can be invaluable

Fred Karno

Fred Karno began his working life in Nottingham, as Frederick John Westcott, plumber. He had moved there with his parents, John and Emma, and his younger brother Frank around 1871. The 1881 census shows that the family lived at Careys Place. Frederick was then 15, and his father gave his son's birthplace as Exeter, in Devon, but by the time Frank was born, in about 1870, they were in Salisbury, in Wiltshire, and the two youngest sons, John and Mark, were both born in Nottingham, in about 1871 and 1879. By 1881 Emma was 34, so she was 19 when her first son arrived. Like her husband, her senior by four years, Emma originally came from Exeter. Emma called herself Emily Westcott (formerly Barden) when she registered Frederick's birth on 26 March at the registrar's office in Exeter on 23 April 1866. Like many women of the period, she gave birth at home, in Paul Street. Her husband was described as a cabinet maker, but by 1881 he was a French polisher.

Young Fred goes on the stage

Within a year after the 1881 census, Frederick had made his performing debut, appearing as Leanaro, the lady acrobat, at the Crown and Cushion free and easy, in Nottingham. He quickly proved his versatility on the trapeze, miming short comic sketches and clowning, before joining a circus troupe for a tour of Germany and the Low Countries. By 1889, when he married, he was a seasoned traveller, appearing in music halls up and down the country, using London as his base. His wedding took place on 15 January, in the register office, Lambeth, south of the River Thames, and he gave his employment as a gymnast, living at 14 Little Canterbury Place, within a short walking distance of his bride's home at 118 Kennington Road. Edith Cuthbert, his new wife, professed her age as 21, and her father, John Cuthbert, was described as a journeyman rope manufacturer.

Soon after his marriage, Fred and two other acrobats were asked to stand in for 'The Three Carnos' at the Metropolitan, Edgware Road, and were so well received that they continued to perform there for a month before securing a season's booking at the Westminster Royal Aquarium, billed under the dangerously similar title of 'The Three Karnos'. In the mid-1890s the Three Karnos were but a part of his 'Fred Karno Fun Factory', an operation conducted from premises in Camberwell, which he crammed full of scenery, props and costumes for the various companies of speechless comedians he sent out on engagements to perform his comic pieces, pantomimes and sketches. One of the locals, Charlie Chaplin, recalled first seeing and being deeply impressed by 'Early Birds', which he watched from a gallery seat as a teenager in 1903, while waiting for his half-brother Sydney's return from sea, and his mother languished in the local lunatic asylum. Before long, both Charlie and Sydney were on Karno's payroll.

Fred forms his army and meets his Waterloo

Quite when Fred assumed the name of Karno is unknown, though it has been claimed that he changed his name by deed poll in 1914 (J. P. Gallagher, *Fred Karno, Master of Mirth and Tears*). If so, it was not enrolled in the Supreme Court of Judicature in London. By then he had traversed America, establishing an international reputation as a showman and theatre manager for his companies of slapstick comedians.

Charlie Chaplin's and Stan Laurel's first trip to America in September 1910 was as part of Karno's troupe. Their names appear with other members of the troupe on the ship's passenger list for the *Cairnrona*, which left Southampton for Quebec and Montreal. The passenger list is in The National Archives, Kew. Charlie was the star of the company with Stan as his understudy. When Charlie was taken ill, Stan took over, and thus began his long career in comedy. In 1913, to provide more scope for his sense of the burlesque, Karno leased Tagg's Island, situated in the Thames near Hampton Court. He sank £70,000 of his own money into the construction of 'Karsino', a fun palace which served dinners and other entertainments to paying guests, who first had to bear the cost of being ferried across the river. His troupe came to be known during the Great War of 1914–18 as 'Fred Karno's Army', a military byword for anything farcical, ridiculous or inept. But for him the War brought financial catastrophe, as few people came to his island, and before long he was embroiled in protracted and costly litigation over the lease. In May 1928 the hotel, its fixtures and fittings, the dancing pavilion and the river craft were estimated as being worth no more than £1,850, and he was declared a bankrupt. An immensely long list of his assets and an even longer one of his liabilities is in the National Archives, Kew.

Two women in Fred Karno's life

Fred Karno died at Parkstone, in Dorset, on 17 September 1941, aged 75. His widow, Marie Theresa Karno, was granted probate of his will on 29 October, as his sole beneficiary and executrix. His total effects amounted merely to £42 7s 4d. When the will was drawn up on 15 January 1934, he was living in a flat in Charing Cross Road, London, and he referred to his former name of Westcott. This date would have been his 45th wedding anniversary, but exactly three weeks after Edith's death on 27 May 1927 he had married Marie Moore, on 16 June.

The index of deaths for the June quarter of 1927 gave Edith Blanche Westcott's age as 56, placing her birth about 1871, which was confirmed by the index entry in the March quarter of 1870. To assert that she was 21 when she married in 1889 thus stretched the truth somewhat, suggesting that her parents had not approved of her wedding, and would not have given their consent as required for a minor. Edith's own will, though composed on 10 December 1926, was not proved until 8 September 1927, several months after her widower's remarriage. The probate registrar appointed her son and her sister as administrators because she had nominated the two witnesses as executors, which was disallowed. Her total effects were £353 18s 3d, none of which went in Fred's direction. It is clear that it was a holograph will, being an artless, misspelt and poignant summary of her worldly possessions, and who she wanted to have them. It hints at a once-luxurious lifestyle. Her sister Florence Entwistle was left her black fur coat, all her feather cushions, curtains, draperies and household linen and two pictures. She was to share the table plate and cutlery with Edith's son, Leslie Karno Westcott. Leslie was bequeathed her large photograph in the drawing room, on condition that an exact copy was made and presented to her niece, Dora McCreesh. Dora, in turn, was to have the Sheffield silver tray. Another sister, Mary Mosley, was given a brown trimmed fur coat and any other clothing Florence might choose for her. Six sheets, two large blankets, six pillow cases, a bedspread, two large towels, six tea towels, four pairs of lace curtains, three table cloths, two large feather pillows, a pair of heavy curtains, all her underclothing and any dresses found to be useful were destined for Louise Karno Westcott. These items would have gone a long way to furnishing a first home. Edith failed to mention Louise's relationship to her though. Various pieces of jewellery, rugs, pictures, a Spode soup tureen and eight plates, a tea service, fruit servers and fish servers, fur articles and a gold brocaded eiderdown were bestowed on various friends. Half the sale proceeds of the furniture and remaining effects were to pass to Leslie, the other half being equally divided between her sister Florence and grandchildren Edith Patricia Karno Westcott, Frederick Karno Westcott and Kenneth Douglas Westcott, the granddaughter receiving the piano. Mrs Queenie Karno Westcott was left Edith's pearls and brilliants, and the will concluded with the significantly cryptic and meaningful bequest 'To my husband Fred Karno my wedding ring'. And who can be surprised? It was not for nothing that he was renowned for his love of the absurd, and it is a relief to know that he would not have received this gift in time for his second wedding.

An early Karno recruit: Charlie Chaplin

Charlie Chaplin's published autobiography opens with his birth on 16 April 1889, at 8 o'clock in the evening, at East Lane (East Street), in Walworth, South London. Alas, it would seem that his birth was not registered by either parent, though *The Magnet*, issued on 11 May, announced the birth of 'a beautiful boy' on 15 April to the wife of Mr Charles Chaplin (nee Miss Lily Harley). Neither the boy's name nor birthplace was mentioned, and not even his mother's real name.

Charles Chaplin, Charlie's father, who was a professional singer, had married Hannah Harriet Hill at St Paul's Church, Walworth, on 22 June 1885, as from 57 Brandon Street, where the 19-year-old bride had previously been delivered of an illegitimate son, Sydney John Hill, on 16 March the same year. Charles and his new wife parted company about 1891, soon after his return from New York; she then bore another son, to another successful music hall singer, 'Leo Dryden' (otherwise George Dryden Wheeler), on 31 August 1892. Charles stayed in the vicinity, close to his brother Spencer, who was a publican, and maintained a tenuous link with his spouse, not always at his own choosing.

Family misfortunes

Hannah was a vaudeville actress, performing under the name of Lily Harley, but the strain of trying to earn enough money to support herself and her young family from her dwindling stage bookings and any extra income she could bring in from nursing and dressmaking soon took its toll on her health, culminating in periodic bouts in the local workhouse or infirmary from 1895. In 1894, aged five, Charlie had stood in for her when her voice gave way on stage at Aldershot, in Hampshire. By the time of her first admission to St Saviour's Union Workhouse, her youngest child (by 'Leo Dryden') had been spirited away by his father. On 19 June 1896, the clerk to the Board of Guardians wrote to the Local Government Board in Whitehall to report the admission to the workhouse of her two eldest sons, owing to the father's absence and the destitution and illness of the mother. It was decided the boys should stay together and that their father be ordered to contribute 12 shillings a week for their upkeep. He was described in the correspondence, in the National Archives at Kew, and in London Metropolitan Archives, as 'a Music Hall Singer, able-bodied and … in a position to earn sufficient to maintain his children.' It was proposed to send the boys to Hanwell School, and by 1 July the father had acquiesced.

Admissions and discharges of pupils recorded in the religious creed and general register of the school at Hanwell, in Central London School District, on deposit in London Metropolitan Archives, reveal that they had already been taken there on 18 June on the instructions of the same clerk. Sydney was discharged on 18 November to join the *Exmouth,* a naval training ship moored at Grays, in Essex, where workhouse boys of his age could opt to be sent. The particulars about Charlie show he was discharged from the school and handed over to his mother on 18 January 1898. The register recorded her address by 26 October 1897 as in Oakden Street, Kennington Road.

His father, meanwhile, frequently passed his days with his brother Spencer, who ran several public houses in the Lambeth area. It was Spencer who prevented his arrest for maintenance arrears of £44 8s in 1897. Charles absconded that December and a warrant was issued for his arrest to enforce a Board decision that he should take the two boys into his care. When apprehended, he settled the fine and requested that Hannah should have responsibility for them.

Charlie's autobiography paints a graphic picture of the grim conditions he and his brother experienced at the school while all this was going on. Throughout his childhood he was shunted in and out of a variety of local schools depending on the Union where the family happened to be lodged. He spent three months with his father from September 1898 when his mother was an

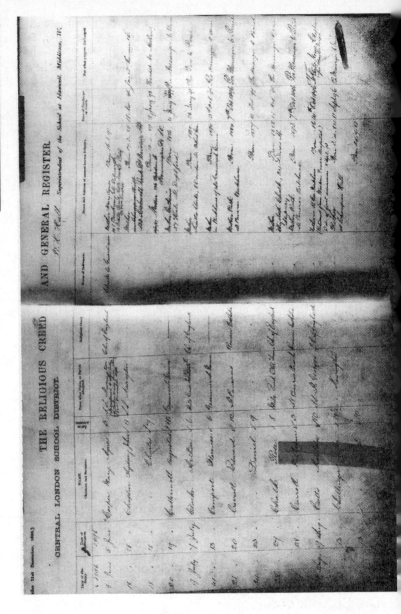

figure 13 the Religious Creed and General Register of Hanwell School, London, 1896, showing admisson and discharge of Sydney and Charles (Charlie) Chaplin as pupils their birth dates are included (reproduced by permission of the London Metropolitan Archives)

inmate of Cane Hill Lunatic Asylum, sharing two rooms with his four-year-old half-brother and Louise, the boy's mother, as well as his elder half-brother Sydney. Charles and Louise were apparently quarrelsome and Charles sought refuge in alcohol, an occupational hazard, since many music halls had evolved from drinking establishments.

Men at the bar

Charles and Spencer Chaplin's father was also named Spencer, and he traded as a butcher at least until Charles married in 1885, but when he died on 29 May 1897, at 63, he too was a licensee, managing the Devonport Arms, in Devonport Mews, Radnor Place, Paddington, Middlesex. His short will, made 11 days before he expired, directed that his son Charles should carry on the business for 12 months during which he was 'to find a home for Mrs Machell' (a person mentioned without any further comment. A Lucy Mackhill and her husband lived with Spencer Chaplin in 1881). He was then to sell up and share the proceeds with his siblings unless an amicable agreement could be reached among them. As the effects totalled £1,259 when probate was granted on 2 September, this must have eased Charles Chaplin's fiscal status somewhat, although this did not prevent his disappearing act three months later. He himself succumbed within four years, a victim of his predilection for the bottle. The death certificate shows that when he died, in St Thomas's Hospital on 9 May 1901, it was his widow, H. Chaplin, of 16 Golden Place, Chester Street, Lambeth, who was the informant next day, rather than his regular companion, Louise. His occupation was described as 'comedian of Lambeth'. He was only 37, and was buried in a pauper's grave in Tooting Public Cemetery.

One of the hostelries Charles patronized was the Queen's Head, at 46 and 48 Broad Street, about half a mile away from his rooms at 289 Kennington Road. The 1891 census returns record that it was occupied by nine people that night, his brother Spencer W. Chaplin at its head. Spencer was then 35 and gave his birthplace as Ipswich, in Suffolk.

The Suffolk connection

Seven years Spencer's junior, Charles Chaplin was born on 18 March 1863, at 22 Orcus Street, Marylebone, Middlesex, to Spencer Chaplin and his wife Ellen Elizabeth (formerly Smith), and they were married by licence on 30 October 1854, in the Church of St Margaret, Ipswich. The parish register recorded them both as minors, and Spencer's father as Shadrach Chaplin, an innkeeper. Spencer applied to the Archdeaconry Court of Suffolk for the licence on 27 October, gave his parish of residence as St Margaret and his age as 19, the same as his bride, and asserted that parental consent had been given by both sets of parents.

The 1851 census returns of Ipswich have been indexed, so that Spencer and his father were quickly found, at Carr Street, in the parish of St Margaret. Shadrack (*sic*) Chaplin was by then a master brewer aged 40, supporting his wife Sophia, 43, and five children, the eldest of whom was 16-year-old Spencer. Shadrack himself was born at Finborough, in Suffolk, his offspring at Ipswich, and his wife at Tunstall, in Staffordshire. Perhaps they had met through a connection with the brewing industry, since Staffordshire people seem to have regularly travelled down to Suffolk to help with the brewing process. By the time he died in Ipswich on 2 April 1893, aged 79, Shadrach had become a bootmaker, leaving a widow, Susannah, 14 years his junior, who survived him but one day. Susannah Eyres was widowed when they married at Crown Street Congregational Chapel, Ipswich, on 25 August 1872, when Shadrach was 58. Shadrach volunteered his occupation then as a commercial traveller, and that of his deceased father, also called Shadrach, as a farmer. Possibly Shadrach added a few years on to his age in 1851 to close the six-year age gap with his first wife; why a few years were not knocked off her age instead seems slightly unchivalrous on his part.

The marriage of Shadrach Chaplin and Sophia Hancock is included in the *International Genealogical Index*. They married on 29 April 1834, at St Margaret, Ipswich, but none of their children was baptized there between 1836 and 1856, and the *Index* contains no references to them either.

The Great Finborough Chaplins

As Shadrach Chaplin was evidently born about 1811 or 1814, at Finborough, the parish registers were gleaned for his baptism. The entries begin in 1558, and can be searched on microfiche in Suffolk Record Office. According to his baptism entry on 8 April 1814, Shadrach was born on 15 January, the second of six children of Shadrach Chaplin, a shoemaker, and his wife Elizabeth. Shadrach had two younger brothers named Meshech

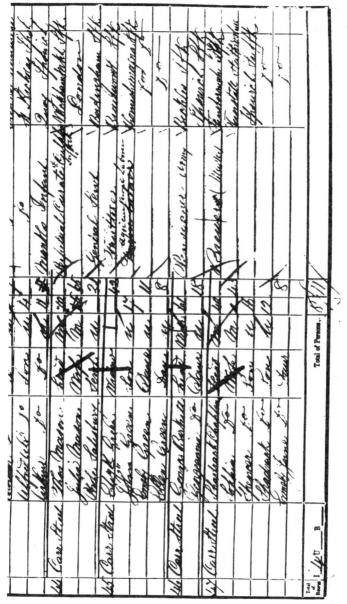

figure 14 census return, Ipswich, Suffolk, 1851, showing Shadrack (sic) Chaplin, his first wife and children.
his son Spencer was Charlie Chaplin's grandfather (reproduced by permission of the National Archives, Kew)

and Abednego. The 1851 census index of Ipswich tracked down Abednego to his home in Butter Market, in the parish of St Lawrence, where he worked as an ironmonger. His young wife Jane, and his parents, Shadrach and Elizabeth Chaplin, were also in the house. Like his son, 65-year-old Shadrach, a retired farmer, was a native of Great Finborough, his wife coming from the next parish, Buxhall. (Incidentally, the census index wrongly ascribed Shadrach's age as 68.)

Shadrake (*sic*) Chaplin and Elizabeth Wilden were married in Buxhall Church on 29 August 1809, after banns, and their daughter Philippa's baptism took place at Great Finborough four months later, on Christmas Day, when the mother's maiden name was spelt as Wilding.

Extracting all the Great Finborough Chaplin and variant baptisms to 1883, marriages to 1840 and burials before 1900, it was possible to construct a family tree spanning two further generations back before any break. Daniel, Shadrach's older brother, born in 1779, was succeeded as a thatcher by his own son Daniel, and grandson Charles, who was still carrying on this craft in 1878 when his last known child was baptized there, some 64 years later. Daniel and Shadrach's youngest brother was baptized Meshech in 1788, and they were all the progeny of George and Susanna Chaplin (nee Bacon).

Unfortunately there are gaps in the registers in the seventeenth century (no baptisms survive for 1634–40, 1643, 1645, 1648, 1650–1, 1654–69, 1671, 1680, 1682–5, and 1687–8, and there are no marriage entries for 1634–43, 1645–90, or 1695), which may explain why I have been unable to extend the pedigree beyond the marriage of John Chaplin and Elizabeth Burman in 1728, though Caleb and Elizabeth Chaplin had three daughters baptized there, the first in 1695. John and his wife Elizabeth did not name any of their known sons Caleb. Whilst there is continuity of surname in these registers, there is so far no evidence to connect the two Chaplin families, or any proven link with a Thomas Chaplin who married there in 1609.

When Great Finborough church was rebuilt in 1875, many of the gravestones in the churchyard were uprooted to create a pavement around it. About 1892, Charles Partridge, of Stowmarket, in Suffolk, copied down 152 surviving inscriptions, and although six of the headstones commemorated nineteenth-century Chaplins, none was dated any earlier.

Stuck with the Chaplins

Percival Boyd's Marriage Index, covering 489 out of 504 Suffolk parishes, drawing on printed copies rather than original parish registers, failed to yield up the wedding of a Caleb Chaplin between 1676 and 1750, but this may be because many other registers were defective during this crucial period. The marriage between Jn Chaplin and Mary Jourdaine was noted in 1680 at Buxhall, so the parish registers were then examined for baptisms of any children, without success. A John Chaplin and his wife Bridget had six offspring baptized at Buxhall between 1697 and 1706, including Daniel, and a Thomas Chaplyn and his wife Elizabeth's two daughters and son Thomas were baptized there between 1676 and 1683/4. No trace has been found of either of these two marriages in the registers, the above index, or in the *IGI*.

Indexes to wills proved in the local probate courts serving this part of Suffolk contained various references to the surname from 1660 until 1857, but not to Caleb or any Chaplin at Great Finborough, Buxhall or proximal parishes, before George Chaplin's will was proved in the Archdeaconry Court of Sudbury on 30 September 1819. Caleb Chaplin's will was not proved in the superior Prerogative Court of Canterbury between his year of death in 1741 and 1755.

The Chaplins take up community service

The contents of the Great Finborough parish chest have been deposited in Suffolk Record Office, Ipswich. The inventory lists vestry minute books from 1684 until 1915, a book containing details of collections of poor rates and disbursements of the overseers of the poor between 1742 and 1800, summary churchwardens' accounts, 1755–76, summary highway surveyors' accounts, 1754–67, and three volumes of overseers' accounts from 1800 until 1835.

The first book of vestry minutes records the annual appointments of parish officers; the Chaplin family's first chronicled call to duty was the election of John Chapling (*sic*) as constable on 27 March 1744, three years after Caleb's death. A long catalogue of the Chaplins' more or less continuous service to the parish can be traced down five generations to the signature in the vestry minute book of Charles Chaplin as churchwarden in April 1912. Charles was obviously a valued member of the community, for on 11 May 1887 he was elected

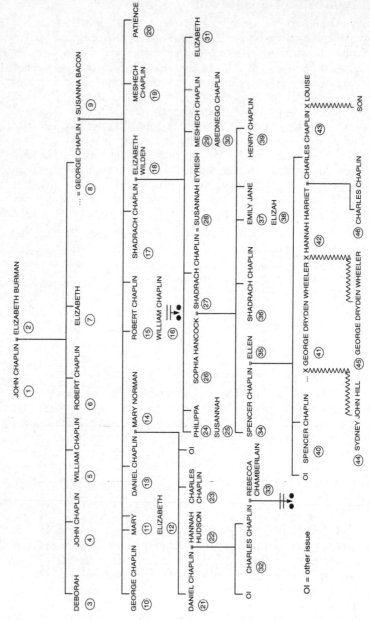

figure 15 the Chaplin family tree

Key:

(1) of Great Finborough, co. Suffolk, 1728, parish constable, 1744, 1746, overseer of the poor, 1768, 1773, churchwarden, 1774, bur 12 Oct 1787, Great Finborough.

(2) marr 11 July 1728, Great Finborough afsd, after Banns.

(3) bap 15 Dec 1728, Great Finborough, afsd.

(4) bap 22 Nov 1730, Great Finborough, afsd.

(5) bap 25 Dec 1732, Great Finborough, afsd.

(6) bap 15 June 1734, Great Finborough, afsd.

(7) bap 6 June 1737, Great Finborough, afsd.

(8) of Great Finborough, afsd, farmer, 1771–1819, bap there 24 May 1741, parish constable, 1781–1809, overseer of the poor, 1809, died 12, bur 19 May 1819 Great Finborough, aged 78, M.I., will dd 13 May, pr 30 Sept 1819.

(9) marr 8 May 1771, Great Finborough afsd, after Banns, named executrix in husband's will, 1819, died 6, bur 10 April 1827, Great Finborough, aged 78 or 80, M.I.

(10) bap 20 June 1773, Great Finborough, afsd.

(11) bap 10 Sept 1775, Great Finborough, afsd, named in father's will, 1819.

(12) bn 25 Apr, bap 17 May 1777, Great Finborough, afsd, received into the church 14 Sept 1783.

(13) of Great Finborough, afsd, thatcher, 1802–50, there bn 8 Jly, bap 10 Aug 1779, and received into the church 14 Sept 1783, aged c60 in 1841, died 22, bur 28 Feb 1850, Great Finborough, aged 70, M.I.

(14) of Ipswich, co. Suffolk, 1852, marr 9 Dec 1802, Great Finborough, afsd, after Banns, aged c60 in 1841, died 7, bur 12 May 1852, Great Finborough, aged 71, M.I.

(15) bn 15 Mch, bap 29 Aug 1781, Great Finborough, afsd, received into the church 14 Sept 1783.

(16) bn 2 Aug, bap 14 Sept 1783, Great Finborough, afsd, named in father's will as deceased, 1819.

(17) of Great Finborough, afsd, 1809–19, Butter Market, Ipswich, afsd, 1851, shoemaker, 1814–22, retired farmer,1851, bap 21 May 1786, Great Finborough, named in father's will, 1819, aged 65 in 1851, dead by 1872.

(18) (WILDING) of Buxhall, co. Suffolk, there marr 29 Aug 1809, after Banns, aged 67 in 1851.

(19) of Hadleigh Road, Great Finborough, afsd, farmer, 1841, bap 3 Aug 1788, Great Finborough, overseer of the poor, 1828, 1840, 1847, aged c50 in 1841, exectr of father's will, 1819, died 20, bur 25 Aug 1849, Great Finborough, aged 61, M.I.

(20) bap 21 Jly 1793, Great Finborough, afsd, named in father's will, 1819.

(21) of Village Green, Great Finborough, afsd, thatcher, 1841, bap 2 Jne 1803, Great Finborough, parish constable, 1851, 1855–61, aged c35 in 1841.

(22) Banns read at Great Finborough, afsd, 8,15 Dec 183-, aged c30 in 1841, died 8, bur 13 Dec 1878, Great Finborough, aged 69, M.I.

(23) bap 22 Apr 1821, Great Finborough, afsd, parish constable, 1850, 1854, 1862-64, 1868, nominated but not chosen as overseer of the poor, 1869, parish clerk 1872, Rate Collector and Assistant Surveyor, 1875, Surveyor, 1876, aged c20 in 1841.

(24) bap 25 Dec 1809, Great Finborough, afsd.

(25) bap 5 Jne 1812, Great Finborough, afsd.

(26) bn c1808, Tunstall, co. Stafford, marr 29 Apr 1834, St. Margaret Ipswich, afsd, after Banns, aged 43 in 1851.

(27) of Carr Street, Ipswich, afsd, 1851, and Old Cattle Market, Ipswich, 1881, master brewer, 1851, innkeeper, 1854, commercial traveller, 1872, boot-maker. 1881–87, bn 15 Jan, bap 8 Apr 1814, Great Finborough, afsd, aged 67 in 1881, died 2 Apr 1893, at Ipswich, aged 79, will dd 19 Feb 1887, Admon 12 May 1893.

(28) dau of the late SAMUEL ROBIN-SON, labourer, deceased, marr 2nd, 25 Aug 1872, Crown Street Congregational Chapel of the Independents, Ipswich, afsd 3 Apr 1893, aged 65, Admon 5 May 1893.

(29) bap 20 Apr 1817, Great Finborough, afsd.

(30) of Butter Market, Ipswich, afsd, ironmonger, 1851, bap 6 Feb 1819, Great Finborough, afsd, aged 31 in 1851.

(31) bap 12 May 1822, Great Finborough, afsd.

(32) of Great Finborough, afsd, thatcher, 1873, bap 14 Jne 1846. Great Finborough.

(33) Banns read at Great Finborough, afsd, 3, 10, 17 Dec 1871.

(34) of St. Margaret, Ipswich, afsd, 1854, Orcus Street, Marylebone, co. Middx, 1863, Fillington Place, co. Middx, bap 1 Dec 1849, received into the church in Devonport Mews, Radnor Place, co. Middx, 1897, butcher, 1854-63, unemployed, 1881, public house manager, 1897, bn c1835, Ipswich, aged 16 in 1851, died 29 May 1897, aged 63, will dd 18 May 1897, 2 Sept 1897.

(35) dau of WILLIAM SMITH, dealer, marr 30 Oct 1854, St Margaret, Ipswich, afsd, by Licence, dead by 30 Mch 1851.

(36) bn c1839, Ipswich, afsd, aged 12 in 1851.

(37) bn c1843, Ipswich, afsd, aged 8 in 1851.

(38) bn c1845, Ipswich, afsd, aged 6 in 1851.

(39) bn c1849, Ipswich, afsd, aged 2 in 1851.

(40) of Northcote Hotel, Battersea Rise, London, 1881, Queens Head, Lambeth, co. Surrey, 1891, manager to a publican, 1881, licensed victualler, 1891, bn c1856, Ipswich, afsd, aged 25 in 1881.

(41) (LEO DRYDEN), music hall singer.

(42) (LILY HARLEY) of Southwark, 1881, Brandon Street, Walworth, 1885, Oakden Street, Kennington Road, 1898, all co. Surrey, Golden Place, Chester Street, Lambeth, afsd, 1901, mantle machinist, 1881, dau of CHARLES HILL, bootmaker, marr 22 Jne 1885, St. John Walworth, after Banns.

(43) of Northcote Hotel, Battersea Rise, afsd,1881, Brandon Street afsd, 1885, Albert Street, Newington, co Surrey, 1891, Lambeth, afsd, 1901, barman, 1881, professional singer, 1885, music hall singer, 1891, comedian, 1901, bn 18 Mch 1863, Orcus Street, Marylebone, afsd, died 9 May 1901, St Thomas's Hospital, Lambeth.

(44) bn 16/17 Mch 1885, Brandon Street, afsd.

(45) (WHEELER DRYDEN), bn 31 Aug 1892.

(46) (CHARLIE CHAPLIN) bn 12/15/16 Apr 1889.

one of the parish committee with Robert Chaplin to help plan a festival including a roast beef dinner with plum pudding, and a tea, to celebrate Queen Victoria's Golden Jubilee.

As an overseer of the poor in 1768 and 1773, John Chaplin recovered all his necessary outgoings from the poor rates, which he helped fix each half-year with the vestry's approval. The amounts varied, and from 17 April until 4 October 1742, it was set at elevenpence-halfpenny in the pound, assessed on each householder's rent. He himself had a property worth £9 then and another valued at £5. The fluctuating scale of half-yearly payments can be tracked through the overseers' rate books, his son George being first listed as a contributor on a rent of £5 in October 1769.

The overseers' outgoings show that at Easter 1751, John Chaplain (*sic*) was paid 3s 6d for clothing 'for ye girl Whittum', and a further £1 4s for Sarah Boor's board for 24 weeks. His third account, for unspecified services, came to 15 shillings, making his total receipts £2 2s 6d for the half-year, while he contributed seven shillings in poor rates. A later overseers' book records that a boy was boarded out with his son George Chaplin for a year on 2 September 1807 at the expense of the parish, and in 1827 George's youngest son, Meshech, had a girl balloted to him, having been taken from the Hundred House (workhouse) into the homes of other parishioners during the previous two years.

It seems bizarre that at one end of the nineteenth century and even as late as 1890, rural Suffolk Chaplins should be involved in dispensing poor relief, whilst in the depths of teeming Lambeth their distant urban cousins were dependent upon it.

Trouper Stan Laurel

When Fred Karno's company of comedians set sail for Canada en route to America in September 1910, young Stanley Jefferson was there as Charlie Chaplin's understudy. His father, a notable theatre manager, had engineered his passage, but the contract did not last long, as Stan found it impossible to survive on his pay of 20 dollars a week, which Karno refused to increase, so he left the troupe in Colorado Springs and made his own way back to England. After an unsuccessful interval trying out different acts, he took up typing, but then Karno's manager offered him a higher salary to rejoin the tour. Chaplin announced his withdrawal, and Stan took over his role to great acclaim. Chaplin watched the show several times and decided he would take part after all, so Stan was put back in the chorus. Nonetheless he was one of the troupe when it went to America again, and this time he stayed behind, joined forces with other former members of the company, and exacted a brand of revenge by impersonating Charlie Chaplin. In 1918 he became one of a duo called 'Stan and Mae Laurel', before eventually going into films, and teaming up with Oliver Hardy in 1926.

Stanley Jefferson becomes Stan Laurel

Arthur Stanley Jefferson, later known as Stan Laurel, was born on 16 June 1890, at Foundry Cottages, Ulverston, in Lancashire. His parents were Arthur Jefferson, a comedian, and Margaret (formerly Metcalfe), who already had another son, George Gordon Jefferson. When the 1891 census was taken, neither the baby nor his parents were in Ulverston, but George Metcalfe, a master shoemaker, aged 54, was living at 3 Foundry Street with his wife Sarah, 59, and their grandson, George G. Jefferson, a schoolboy of six. Arthur and Madge Jefferson were then lodging with Sarah Barker, in High Tenters Street, Bishop Auckland, Co. Durham. Arthur was a theatrical manager, aged 28, and a native of Birmingham, Warwickshire, like the other lodger, John Price, a 60-year-old comedian. Next door were the Thorns, another theatrical family, the father, Thomas, being Arthur's partner in the lease on the Old Theatre Royal from 1889, though he bought himself out in 1891.

Arthur Jefferson's mysterious past

Arthur and Margaret were married on 19 March 1884, at Holy Trinity Church, Ulverston. Arthur described himself as an unmarried man of 21, a comedian, and a resident of Manchester, in Lancashire, the son of Frank Jefferson, a solicitor. The 1881 census showed up only one likely Arthur Jefferson, who, at 17, was boarding with Mrs Julia Kair, a merchant's wife, at 6 Jassall Street, Chorlton-upon-Medlock, Manchester. He was working as a coal canvasser, and gave his birthplace as Birmingham. If this is the same person, then he would have been only 20 when he married, so may have lied about his age and parentage, because he was marrying without their permission. There is no trace of any Frank Jefferson in the printed *Law Lists* between 1855 and 1884, suggesting that this might have been a fictional name. No Jefferson witnessed his wedding.

According to J. Owen-Pawson and B. Mouland, *Laurel before Hardy*, Margaret (also called Madge) was a singer, and had first encountered Arthur when he worked in a theatre known as Spencer's Gaff, in Ulverston. They performed together all over the North of England, generally leaving their young brood behind in Ulverston with the Metcalfes or with Madge's married sister, Sarah Shaw. Beatrice Olga was born in December 1894, at Bishop Auckland, Sydney Everitt on 30 April 1899, in North Shields, Northumberland, who died as an infant, and Edward Everitt completed the family in April 1901. There is a spectacular entry for the Jefferson household in the 1901 census, taken on the night of Sunday 31 March. It appears from this that young Edward was born at 3.45 a.m. on 1 April, and although his name was entered in the household schedule, it was crossed out as being too late to qualify him for inclusion. His older brothers Gordon and Stanley were in the house at 8 Dockwray Square, North Shields, as was their grandmother, Sarah Metcalfe, the monthly nurse (presumably the midwife), and two domestic servants. In this census Arthur Jefferson gave his birthplace 38 years before as Lichfield, Warwickshire (*sic*), which was corrected by the Registrar General's clerk to Staffordshire.

By 1905, the family had moved North of the border to Rutherglen, Glasgow, in Scotland, Arthur having got the post of manager of The Metropole Theatre. Madge died in Glasgow in December 1908, and on 14 November 1912 Arthur took a second wife, Venetia Matilda Robinson, a widow of 40, in a ceremony held in St George's Hanover Square, Middlesex. Arthur gave out his age as 50 and his current profession as a theatrical proprietor. Two of the witnesses were George Gordon Jefferson and Henry H. Robinson, her son. The register entry this time identified Arthur's father as the late Christopher Jefferson, gentleman (deceased). By 1922 he was back in Bishop Auckland running the theatre he had first left in 1895. This time he faced severe competition from the cinema, so he migrated to London in 1925 to improve his luck, living out his final years in the Lincolnshire public house run by his married daughter.

Arthur Jefferson died on 15 January 1949, at the Plough Inn, Barkston, Lincolnshire, apparently aged 93, having made his will on 7 October 1947, the same year that Laurel and Hardy paid him a visit. Beatrice was left everything, unless she were to predecease him, whereupon his son Stanley Jefferson (professionally known as Stan Laurel) was to be the sole beneficiary. His total assets were £203 3s 11d when the will was proved on 11 February 1949. The *Grantham Journal,* published on 21 January 1949, reported his age as 94, whereas the gravestone inscription in Barkston Cemetery gave his birth year as 1862. Clearly there is a discrepancy between this and the given age on his death certificate, which would have placed his birth in 1855 or 1856, and there is the small matter of the identity of his father as Frank or Christopher.

The quest for Arthur

A search of the birth registrations between 1853 and 1867 failed to produce any relevant entry for Arthur Jefferson, born in the Birmingham or Lichfield area, or for any male Jefferson child registered there with different given names whose father's name tallied with either of the above.

Quite out of the blue, I was contacted by someone who was tracing his own ancestry and had come across Arthur Jefferson as the beneficiary of Alexander Clement Foster Gough, a Wolverhampton solicitor, who died unmarried in 1892. Intriguingly, Arthur was described as the brother of Clara, wife of J. Mitchell Riley, of Greenhays, Manchester, who was to receive a similar sum of money. A look at the relevant death duty register entry showed them as strangers of the blood to Mr Gough. This was the first time I had any positive information about other members of Arthur's family.

Clara was married as Clara Wilson Jefferson to Joseph Mitchell Riley on 14 February 1884, in the register office, at Chorlton-upon-Medlock, Lancashire, when she was aged 30. He father's name was given as Christopher Jefferson, then deceased. This was also the name given by Arthur Jefferson for his father, when he married for the second time, in 1912. Clara's husband was a widower of 50, a yarn agent. The 1881 census database was searched for Clara, and she was found to be living in Portsmouth Street, Chorlton-upon-Medlock, where she was described as the head of household, and as a housekeeper. Her age was then apparently 23, so in the space of three years to her marriage in 1884 she seems to have aged by seven years, possibly to make the age gap with her husband less significant. Her birthplace was Manchester, like that of her younger brother, William Jefferson, a clerk, aged 16, and her nephew, William Jefferson, eight. Young William's birth certificate indicated that far from being Clara's nephew, he was actually her illegitimate son, born on 16 January 1873, at 54 Upper Moss Square,

Hulme, Lancashire. His mother was employed as a milliner, and was the informant of the birth a month later. An Arthur Jefferson, aged 17, had already been located at an address in Chorlton-upon-Medlock in the 1881 census, making it all the more likely that he was her brother, though he was not one of the witnesses of her marriage, nor she of his a month after her own.

A search for the registered births of Clara and her brother William failed to yield any entry at all, just as the search for Arthur's birth had proved of no avail. Since Arthur had professed to being born in Birmingham, a search of the 1851 census database for the whole of Warwickshire was made, and a Christopher Jefferson was found to be living in the parish of St Peter's, at 92 Moor Street, with his wife Harriet, and baby daughter, Mary, aged three days. They were lodging in the household of James and Mary Hunt, his parents-in-law. James was then aged 47, a lathe maker from Smethwick, in Staffordshire (*sic*), whilst Christopher himself was described as a grocer, aged 22 or 23 (the second digit is unclear), and a native of Scotland. Harriet was 21 and born in Birmingham, like her younger brother, George Wilson, aged 18. The appearance of the surname Wilson suggested that James Hunt was perhaps not her father, although Harriet and George were both described by him as his daughter and son. Christopher Jefferson was married to Harriet Wilson on 28 March 1850, when he gave his age as 21, and Harriet as a minor. Her father's name was identified as William Wilson, a builder, and Christopher's as Thomas Jefferson, gentleman. Christopher was then living in the parish of St Mary's Lichfield. Alas, no trace was found of their daughter Mary's birth in 1851, and another look at the civil registration indexes failed to yield any Jefferson infant registered in Lichfield to 1875.

The next step was to examine the 1871 census returns of Chorlton-upon-Medlock and Hulme for the Jefferson family when Clara and Arthur might have been there with their parents. This was a lengthy task, because the returns are not indexed by personal name. The parish of St Peter's Birmingham, and St Mary's Lichfield were similarly examined for 1861 in case Clara could be found, but again without success. No trace could be found of a Christopher or Harriet Jefferson in the 1881 census database, whose details matched what was known already about them, nor could any death registration be traced with any certainty for Christopher. The *International*

Genealogical Index, British Isles Vital Records Index and the index to the Old Parochial Registers for Scotland, similarly failed to yield an entry of his baptism, so like his son, he remains a man of mystery for the time being, probably until county personal name indexes become available for Lancashire, Warwickshire and Staffordshire for 1871. I can hardly wait, and much appreciate the difference such indexes have made when researching people on the move or living in large cities and towns.

A self-made man

It seems that Arthur Jefferson was not only a comedian, but reinvented his past as well. It is fitting that he should claim Birmingham as a birthplace, for it was then the manufacturing centre of the British Empire. Not every family tree has firm roots. If it had not been for a purely serendipitous e-mail from that one person, I would not have got as far as I have, and to him I am immensely grateful for making what further progress I have.

16

writing it all up

In this chapter you will learn:
- how to tell your family's story
- what questions you need to ask yourself
- what to do with the finished product

When I was ten years old I wrote my autobiography, and reading through it now I can vividly relive how it felt to be growing up in a Lakeland village of the 1950s. It stirs memories of the long forgotten goings-on which punctuated my short existence. Some day I hope others in my family will also read that fresh and innocent account, when most of my life lay uncharted ahead of me, and my personal values and perceptions of the world were still being moulded.

When and where do you begin?

One of the obvious and most pleasurable ways of bringing the past alive in a personal context is to write up your family's history. When should you start? It is never too soon, for the longer you delay it, the more material you will have to negotiate, and the less inclined you will be to tackle and unravel it all. Writing up your story concentrates the mind wonderfully, and draws your attention to points of uncertainty or spurious family connections which need resolving before you proceed further. Older relatives may still be around to help sort out some of these conundrums, pepper your story with anecdotes and photographs, and lend encouragement.

Who is it for?

Decide first for whom your text is intended. Is it for your own delectation, for your descendants, all your known kinsfolk, or a wider audience? Is it for private circulation only, or publication? You will have to be careful about the amount of detail and disclosure you indulge in if you want a wide readership. You want to avoid your story becoming bogged down in minutiae, and offending the very people who have assisted you.

Have a look at other people's writings, to see which ones grip you and analyse why. By adopting a similar approach, scribbling an unvarnished and flowing narrative, you will soon warm to your task, and your script will move at a cracking pace, which you can edit later. Two evocative and most enjoyable books are *The Simple Annals*, by P. Sanders, an account of how his family moved from Stansted Mountfitchet in the seventeenth century into London by the nineteenth, and *Hannah, The Complete Story*, by H. Hauxwell with B. Cockroft, recounting a farmer's life in the Yorkshire Dales, and describing the family networks and histories house by house. You may have your own favourites you want to emulate.

From present to past or fast forward?

You could begin by explaining the possible etymology and distribution of your surname and its variants over time, with a map plotting out its incidence. This could be followed by a potted proven history of your own family from earliest times. You may prefer to act as the family's storyteller, working back from the present day. This has the advantage of carrying your readers with you on your quest, sharing in your discoveries and disappointments, and you can continue to add to the narrative without detriment to the earlier sections. Try not to let your script get out of hand, by running on forever, so fix a structure and stick to it.

The essentials

Do you want the work to contain personality profiles of individual members, confine it to your direct ancestors, or widen the story to say something about their life and times in the community, perhaps relying on other people's published research? In any event, bear in mind the following points:

- Always date your text and identify yourself as the author. Do not overlook your own story, and do draw on the reminiscences of living relations, taking care to obtain their consent for their inclusion first. If in any doubt about the truth you can always preface a statement by 'it is alleged', 'according to', 'supposedly', or 'it is said', because you do not want to alienate family goodwill or risk being sued for libel.

- Reveal what happened when, how and why, rather than cataloguing what and where. Stick to the facts and don't make false assumptions that cannot be supported by any documentation. Tell enough to make the story succinct, and places identifiable, perhaps enlivened with some old photographs to illustrate and break up the text.

- Resist the temptation to express personal opinions and judgments about people's actions and attitudes, remembering that you exist in a different cultural environment or era to that of your ancestors.

- Pad out your writing with accounts of locals contemporary with your forebears. Always acknowledge your sources and be careful not to use huge chunks of someone's else's work so that you contravene their copyright. If in doubt check with the publisher.

- If you do use someone else's text, give the full title, author's name, publisher and date of publication, so that the reader can follow up your quote by reading the original book in full.
- Numbered explanatory footnotes at the bottom of each page, end of the chapter, or at the conclusion of your story, enable the reader to understand certain statements or words, and if you cite your original sources these can be checked, or suggest material for the reader's own researches. Some authors have a new set of numbers for each chapter, particularly if they are listed at the end of the book. Be sparing with footnotes, though, as it can be a maddening experience ploughing through pages dotted with countless footnote references, or going backwards and forwards to the end of the chapter or book hunting for a particular numbered note.

Adding pictures

- Include regular, accurate, clear and simple family trees, pictures, and diagrams to break up the narrative and keep the reader abreast of your story. Always ensure they are relevant to their place in the text, sufficiently sharp or legible, and that they enhance rather than conflict with or detract from their context. Acknowledge their derivation, dating and identifying any people in photographs. If the material comes from a record office, or publication, make sure you have the appropriate permissions to use it. Most repositories will have a standard form of words for you to use in reproducing copies of documents. Include these in the caption, as well as the full document reference. The captions should explain what the picture is all about.
- A map of the area covered in the story is another important feature, especially for a reader who might be unfamiliar with it. You can shade in the places mentioned in your text. Do not neglect to give compass bearings and the scale used.

Editing your script

- Consider the length, final layout and presentation of your text. It is helpful to have an independent and sympathetic outsider read a copy of your typewritten or word-processed script, which should be double-spaced until finalized. Any constructive suggestions about strengths and weaknesses of the narrative will prove invaluable at this stage, before it reaches a wider audience. You may need to prune it or rewrite parts to make it clearer or more punchy. This is particularly the case with the introduction, which is what most people will read first, before deciding whether they like your style of writing and are enticed into reading more.

- Never pass original drawings or photographs to anyone else before they go to a printer, in case of loss or damage; use photocopies of them if necessary.
- When you are happy with your script type it up or put it onto computer disk, leave it a week or two, and come back to it anew. It is amazing what you will find once made sense, no longer does, or fails to make a point strongly enough. You may even discover you have missed out important parts of the story. You can now edit the text, and move it around if it is on computer.

How are you going to publish?

- You may want to restrict circulation to a few bound photocopies or printouts, or produce a regular newsletter to subscribing family members, which could be created online at a special website. This does mean that you will have to keep your promise of updates, find sufficient interesting items to capture and hold the reader's attention and maintain its quality, which can prove a time-consuming commitment.
- If you intend to publish or present your story in a polished and professional style, have adequate computer software, and a high-quality printer, a desktop publishing course will instil confidence and teach you technical expertise in deciding page size, number of lines per page, text layout and alignment, fonts and typesizes. You can practise your design skills in scanning in pictures and enhancing their quality if necessary. You will also find out what to look for when investing in appropriate software.
- Study other published family histories to see what makes them attractive or otherwise.
- If you go for the professional printing option discuss with the printer the different paper qualities and weights, to avoid bleed-through. The cover paper weight is also important; should it be card or paper? Should it be matt or gloss? What about colour compatibilities? How can your illustrations best be reproduced? You may have to reduce their number, or opt for black and white only, to cut the cost. What type of

binding would be strongest and best for the approximate number of pages? Mistakes on such technical points can be costly if you are inexperienced.

Using a professional printer

You can submit camera-ready text, with crop-marks as a guide to page size, which will keep down the cost of professional printing. If you have no inclination or aptitude for home publishing, you might select a local printer to undertake the design and layout for you. You can produce your text on disk from which the printer will prepare artwork for you to inspect, check and approve before printing. It is surprising how many page inconsistencies, spelling errors, missing lines or words, or artificially broken words at the end of lines can creep in at this stage. Page lengths and overall layout should be closely scrutinized, and photographs and illustrations studied to make certain they appear in the right place, the right way up and right way round, are correctly numbered and captioned.

Check that your software is compatible with the printer's, as otherwise a charge may be made to convert the disk. A printout of your text will show any coding such as italics, in case these are lost during the conversion. Always keep an updated back-up disk in case of gremlins.

And the cost

The cost of publishing will be governed by text length, number and type of illustrations, paper quality, number of jacket colours and print-run. The more copies you have printed the more cost-effective it becomes, but be realistic and balance definite and likely demand with what you can afford and may be expected to keep in store.

By casting around for prepaid subscriptions you can estimate how many copies you will need to sell yourself to recoup your initial outlay, and offset at least part of the cost if not all of it before you have to settle up with the printer. Are you going to charge each person a calculated proportion of the printing cost plus postage and packing? If so, you will need to know the actual weight and postal charge. Relatives might be enticed by a special pre-publication discount, but you will have to convince them that their investment will be worthwhile, in other words, that there is something in it for them. It is no good selling your story to members of the family who are not mentioned in it, or will learn nothing new. You will also need to make sure you acknowledge at the front of the book everyone who has helped you, in however small a way.

Obtain several quotations from different printers for the cost of a print-run 100, 250, 500 and 1,000. These will vary, as some specialise in print-runs lower than 2,000 and will offer a better price than printers used to producing bulk runs. You then need to calculate the unit cost per copy, dividing the total amount by the number of copies to be printed, multiplying this between three to five to reach a competitive selling price, thus taking into account permission fees, any free, presentation copies on which you will make nothing, the cost of advertising and any hidden unforeseen extras, to make sure you have a profit and not a nasty loss.

Marketing, promotion and delivering the goods

Decide how you wish to market your story, as harbouring spare copies indefinitely will not only turn out to be inconvenient, and take up space, but will result in their gradual deterioration before you can recover your expenditure. Before committing yourself financially approach likely outlets in the area with which your family was associated or where members were prominent to see if they will sell some stock, but be sure you agree on written trade terms in advance. Bookshops are in business to make money, and not all authors are good at self-promotion. You could draft a flyer for local distribution and display, compose a short item for the local press, publicize your book via the local family history society at its events or in its magazine, and of course resort to publicizing it over the Internet on a message board at sites like **www.rootsweb.com**, **www.genealogy.com** or **www.ancestry.com**. In this way you will reach a global audience.

Once customers have paid their dues they will expect the book to be delivered promptly. Printers usually hold their quotations firm for a month or so, and when you know your print-run (trying to avoid the need for a small reprint, which can be expensive), you can submit the text in the agreed format. Printing may be turned round in as little as ten days, but may take up to a month, depending on the input you expect from the printer, his current workload, speed of proof-reading, and time taken over corrections, so do not make promises you cannot keep. Always agree a timescale with the printer to avoid any misunderstandings, and add an extra fortnight for any unknown eventualities. Planning publication to coincide with a special family event or Christmas is more likely to kindle demand, provided you give sufficient notice, and can meet the deadline.

Ensuring permanent preservation and publicity

Lodge a copy of your work with the relevant county record office, local studies library, family history society, and the library of the Society of Genealogists in London, and put your name and dated address inside if you would welcome feedback. You can request reviews by sending copies to relevant journals with a large circulation, but remember that a free copy is lost money. However, that free copy may generate sales of a few more thus reducing your surplus stock. The local newspaper is another good sales outlet, if prepared to run a small feature article about your story, particularly if it contains something sensational (which is true and not reflecting badly on living or recent family members).

And finally ...

The more sound and accurate printed and circulated family histories there are the more family historians and others interested in the past can utilize them to compare individual and community experiences in time and place, and thereby add to our knowledge about our shared cultural heritage.

You can build on what you have learned by pursuing clues in the records tapped so far about occupations, places of abode, migration, social and economic status into the rich assortment of other archives. Your family's history may then broaden into biographical studies of individual members, and into the history of a whole community.

Tracing your ancestry is a constant learning process, for a family's history is never complete. It is much more fun reconstructing it for yourself. Now go to it.

appendix 1

A checklist of questions to ask your family

Always write names in capital letters so they can be easily picked out. The why and how questions should provide fuller answers than the what, when or where type, as they often explain the motives propelling certain actions.

1 Full name. Are any of these nicknames? How was the nickname acquired? Are the names in the correct order?
2 Relationship of that person to you.
3 Name of his/her father.
4 How long ago or when and where did the father die and where was he buried? Include the county/country (place-names are frequently duplicated so make sure you know which one is relevant).
5 Name of his/her mother.
6 How long ago or when and where did the mother die and where was she buried?
7 Date and place of the subject's birth, including the county/country.
8 Place in the family (eldest child, younger child).
9 Full names of any brothers and sisters. Are any of these nicknames? Why? How much older/younger was each of them and the date and place of birth if known? Which was the subject's and parents' favourite, and why?
10 Are they still alive? If not, how long ago or when and where did they die, and where are they buried? If still alive, where are they now, or last known to be and when?

11 Religious denomination: where did the subject worship?

12 Where did the subject go to school? How old was he/she when schooling started/ended? Did he/she go to university or other place of further education? When, where and what qualifications were obtained?

13 Where does the subject live? Where has he/she lived before and when? Why did he/she move?

14 Occupation now and name and address of employer. How big is the place of employment? When did this employment begin and how did he/she get the job?

15 What other jobs has he/she done? Dates of the various jobs and names and addresses of previous employments. Why did he/she change jobs?

16 Which job was most enjoyable? Why?

17 What clubs and associations does he/she belong to? Does he/she serve on any committees? What are his/her hobbies? Why?

18 Who did he/she marry? At what age? Was this the only marriage? If not, when and where did he/she marry again? Is the first partner still alive? When and how did the first marriage end? (You will need to tread carefully with this one.) Were there any children by each marriage? Who are they and when and where were they born? Are they still alive?

19 Does he/she own any property? Where? Was it inherited or purchased? When and from whom?

20 Has he/she a family Bible? If not, does he/she know of someone in the family who has? Who did it originally belong to?

21 Did he/she serve in the armed forces? When and where? What rank, regiment, ship or squadron? Has he/she any campaign or gallantry medals? Where are they and what do they commemorate? Was he/she wounded or taken prisoner, and if so when and where?

22 Did he/she ever work or live overseas? Why, when and where? When and why did he/she return?

23 Has anyone researched the family's history before?

About deceased family

24 How long ago or when and where did the person die? Where is he/she buried?

25 Did he/she leave a will?

appendix 2

Some abbreviations used in pedigree charts

bn	born	wid	widow
bap, bp	baptized	dd	dated
co.	county	cod.	codicil
afsd.	aforesaid	pr	(will) proved
m, marr	married	Admon	(letters of) administration
o.t.p.	of this parish	Inv.	inventory
b.o.t.p.	both of this parish	o.i.	other issue
by Lic.	by licence	.↓.	unnamed issue
ML	marriage licence	dau	daughter
coelebs, unm	unmarried	s and h	son and heir
fl.	flourished (alive)	coh.	co-heiress
temp.	in the time of	M.I.	monumental inscription
c.	about		
d	died		
b' bur	buried		
ob.	died		
ob.s.p., d.s.p.	died without issue		
d.s.p.m.	died without male issue		
d.s.p.legit	died without legitimate children		
ob.v.p., d.v.p.	died during father's lifetime		

Before visiting any of the repositories, first visit their website or telephone to check on current whereabouts, opening times, fees and search regulations.

United Kingdom and Ireland

The Accountant General
Royal Courts of Justice
Chichester Street
Belfast

Accountant of the Courts of Justice
The High Court
Dublin

Ad.O.P.T.
V.S.B.
The Peskett Centre
2/2a Windsor Road
Lisburn Road
Belfast BT9 7FQ
Tel: 01232 382353
http://freespace.virgin.net/adopt.ni/

Adoption Counselling Centre and Adoption Contact Service
Family Care / Birth Link
21 Castle Street
Edinburgh EH2 3DN
Tel: 0131 225 6441

Army Personnel Centre
Historic Disclosures
Mailpoint 400
Kentigern House
65 Brown Street
Glasgow G2 8EX

Bedford Level Deeds Registry
Cambridgeshire County Record Office
Shire Hall
Castle Hill
Cambridge CB3 0AP
Tel: 01223 717281
www.camcnty.gov.uk/

The Bodleian Library
Department of Western Manuscripts
Broad Street
Oxford OX1 3BG
Tel: 01865 277152
www.bodley.ox.ac.uk/guides/wmss

The Borthwick Institute of Historical Research
St Anthony's Hall
Peasholme Green
York YO1 7PW
Tel: 01904 642315
www.york.ac.uk/inst/bihr

British Association for Cemeteries in South Asia
76 1/2 Chartfield Avenue
Putney
London SW15 6HQ
[excludes war graves]

The British Library
96 Euston Road
London NW1 2DB
Reader admissions: 020 7412 7677
Department of Manuscripts
Tel: 020 7412 7513
www.molcat.bl.uk

National Sound Archive
Tel: 020 7412 7440
www.bl.uk/collections/sound-archive/nsa.html
Oriental and India Office Collections
Tel: 020 7412 7873
www.bl.uk/collections/orientalandindian.html

Newspaper Library, British Library
Colindale Avenue
London NW9 5HE
Tel: 020 7412 7353
www.bl.uk/collection/newspaper

British Record Society
The Secretary
College of Arms
Queen Victoria Street
London EC4V 4BT

Bureau des Connetables
St Peter Port
Guernsey
Tel: 01481 721732

Cambridge University Library
Department of Manuscripts and University Archives
West Road
Cambridge CB3 9DR
Tel: 01223 333000 ext. 33143 (Manuscripts)
www.lib.cam.ac.uk/

Catholic Central Library
Lancing Street
London NW1 1ND
Tel: 020 7383 4333
www.catholic-library.demon.co.uk

Catholic Record Society
The Secretary
12 Melbourne Place
Wolsingham
Co. Durham DL13 3EH
Tel: 01388 527747
www.catholic-history.org.uk/crs

Channel Islands Family History Society
PO Box 507
St Helier
Jersey JE4 5TN
www.user.itl.net/~glen/

Church of Jesus Christ of Latter-day Saints
British Isles Family History Service Centre
185 Penns Lane
Sutton Coldfield
West Midlands B76 1JU
Tel: 0121 384 2028
www.familysearch.org

Distribution Centre
399 Garretts Lane
Sheldon
Birmingham B33 0UH
Tel: 08700 102051

Civil Registry
Registries Building
Deemster's Walk
Bucks Road
Douglas
Isle of Man IM1 3AR
Tel: 01624 687038
www.gov.im/deptindex/

College of Arms
Queen Victoria Street
London EC4V 4BT
Tel: 020 7248 2762
www.college-of-arms.gov.uk

Commonwealth War Graves Commission
2 Marlow Road
Maidenhead
Berkshire SL6 7DX
Tel: 01628 634221
www.cwgc.org

Corporation of London Guildhall Library
Manuscripts Section
Aldermanbury
London EC2P 2EJ
Tel: 020 7332 1862
http://ihr.sas.ac.uk/gh

Corporation of London Records Office
PO Box 270
Guildhall

London EC2P 2EJ
Tel: 020 7332 1251
www.citylondon.gov.uk

The Court Funds Division
Public Trust Office
25 Kingsway
Stewart House
London WC2B 6LE
Tel: 020 7269 7000
www.courtservice.gov.uk/notices/cfo/dormant.htm

Dr Williams's Library
14 Gordon Square
London WC1H 0AG
Tel: 020 7387 3727

Duchy of Cornwall
The Solicitor
10 Buckingham Gate
London SW1E 6LA
Tel: 020 7834 7346

Duchy of Lancaster
The Solicitor
Lancaster Place
Strand
London WC2E 7ED

East Riding Registry of Deeds
East Riding of Yorkshire Council Archives and Records Service
County Hall
Champney Road
Beverley
East Yorkshire HU17 9BA
Tel: 01482 392790
www.eastriding.gov.uk/learning

The Family Records Centre
1 Myddelton Street
London EC1R 1UW
Tel: 020 8392 5300
www.familyrecords.gov.uk/frc

Federation of Family History Societies
PO Box 2425
Coventry
West Midlands CV5 6YX
Tel: 070 41 492032
www.ffhs.org.uk

The Genealogical Society of Utah
(see Church of Jesus Christ of Latter-day Saints)

General Register Office for England and Wales
PO Box 2
Southport
Merseyside PR8 2JD
Tel: 0870 243 7788
www.statistics.gov.uk/registration

Adoptions Section
General Register Office
Smedley Hydro
Southport
Merseyside PR8 2HH
Tel: 0151 471 4830

Overseas Section
General Register Office
PO Box 2
Southport
Merseyside PR8 2JD
Tel: 0151 471 4801

General Register Office (Northern Ireland)
Oxford House
49–55 Chichester Street
Belfast BT1 4HL
Tel: 028 9025 2000
www.groni.gov.uk

General Register Office of Ireland
8–11 Lombard Street
Dublin 2
Tel: 003531 6354000
www.groireland.ie

General Register Office for Scotland
New Register House
Edinburgh EH1 3YT
Tel: 0131 334 0380
www.gro-scotland.gov.uk

Glamorgan Record Office
Glamorgan Building
King Edward VII Avenue
Cathays Park
Cardiff CF10 3NE
Tel: 029 2078 0284
www.llgc.org.uk/cac/

The Greffier
The Royal Court House
St Peter Port
Guernsey GY1 2PB
Tel: 01481 725277

The Greffier
Registry for Births, Deaths, Companies, Land and Marriages
St Anne
Alderney GY9 3AA

Guernsey Island Archives Service
29 Victoria Road
St Peter Port
Guernsey GY1 1HU
Tel: 01481 724512

Guildhall Library
(see Corporation of London Guildhall Library)

Guild of One-Name Studies
The Secretary
Box G
14 Charterhouse Buildings
Goswell Road
London EC1M 7BA
www.one-name.org

Historical Manuscripts Commission
(see The National Archives)
www.hmc.gov.uk

The Huguenot Society of Great Britain
Huguenot Society Library
University College London
Gower Street
London WC1E 6BT
Tel: 020 7679 7094
www.ucl.ac.uk/library/huguenot.htm

Irish Adoption Contact Register
26 Templeview Green
27 Clare Hall
Dublin 13
Tel: 3531 867 4033
www.adoptionireland.com

Jersey Archives Service
Clarence Road
St Helier
Jersey JE2 4JY
Tel: 01534 833300
www.jerseyheritagetrust.org

Lambeth Palace Library
London SE1 7JU
Tel: 020 7928 1400
www.lambethpalacelibrary.org

Laurel and Hardy Museum
4c Upper Brook Street
Ulverston
Cumbria LA12 7LA
Tel: 01229 582292

Linenhall Library
17 Donegall Square North
Belfast BT1 5GD
Tel: 028 9032 1707
www.linenhall.com

London Metropolitan Archives
40 Northampton Road
London EC1R 0HB
Tel: 020 7332 3820
www.cityoflondon.gov.uk

Manorial Documents Register
(see The National Archives)
www.hmc.gov.uk.mdr/mdr.htm

Manx National Heritage Library
Douglas
Isle of Man IM1 3LY
Tel: 01624 64800

Ministry of Defence
Navy Records Centre
DR2a (Navy Search)
Room 3
Bourne Avenue
Hayes
Middlesex UB3 1RF
Tel: 020 8573 3831

The National Archives
Ruskin Avenue
Kew
Richmond
Surrey TW9 4DU
Tel: 020 8876 3444
www.nationalarchives.gov.uk

The National Archives of Ireland
Bishop Street
Dublin 8
Tel: 003531 4072300
www.nationalarchives.ie

The National Archives of Scotland
HM General Register House
Edinburgh EH1 3YY
Tel: 0131 535 1314
www.nas.gov.uk

The National Library of Ireland
Kildare Street
Dublin 2
Tel: 003531 6030200
www.nli.ie

The National Library of Wales
Department of Manuscripts and Records
Aberystwyth SY23 3BU
Tel: 01970 632800
www.llgc.org.uk

The National Organisation for the Counselling of Adoptees
    and Parents (NORCAP)
112 Church Road
Wheatley
Oxford OX33 1LU
Tel: 01865 875000

National Register of Archives
(see The National Archives)
www.hmc.gov.uk/nra

North Riding Deeds Registry
North Yorkshire County Record Office
County Hall
Northallerton
North Yorkshire DL7 8AF
Tel: 01609 777585

Office for National Statistics
(see General Register Office for England and Wales)

Priaulx Library
Candie Road
St Peter Port
Guernsey GY1 1UG
Tel: 01481 721998
www.gov.gg/priaulx

Principal Registry of the Family Division
First Avenue House
42–9 High Holborn
London WC1V 6NP
Probate Search Room, Tel: 020 7947 7022
**www.courtservice.gov.uk/using_courts/wills_probate/probate_
    famhist.htm**

Decree Absolute Search Section
Tel: 020 7947 7017
(postal probate applications)
The Postal Searches and Copies Department
The Probate Registry
Castle Chambers
Clifford Street
York YO1 7RG
Tel: 01904 666 777

Public Record Office of Northern Ireland
66 Balmoral Avenue
Belfast BT9 6NY
Tel: 028 9025 5905
www.proni.gov.uk

Queen's and Lord Treasurer's Remembrancer
Crown Office
5/7 Regent Road
Edinburgh EH7 5BL

RAF Personnel Management Agency
PMA (CS) 2a (2)a (for officers)
PMA (CS) 2a (2)b (for airmen)
RAF Innsworth
Gloucester GL3 1EZ

Registry of Deeds
Kings Inns
Herrietta Street
Dublin 7
Tel: 003531 6707500
www.imgor.ie/landreg

The Religious Society of Friends
The Library
Friends House
Euston Road
London NW1 2BJ
Tel: 020 7663 1135
www.quaker.org.uk

Representative Church Body Library
Braemor Park
Churchtown
Dublin 14
Tel: 003531 4923979
www.ireland.anglican.org

Royal Courts of Justice
Chichester Street
Belfast BT1 3JF
Tel for probates after 1993 and divorces: 028 9023 5111

Royal Marines, Historical Record Office
HMS Centurion
Grange Road
Gosport
Hampshire PO13 9XA
Tel: 023 9282 2351

La Société Guernesiaise (Family History Section)
PO Box 314
Candie
St Peter Port
Guernsey GY1 3TG

La Société Jersiaise
Lord Coutanche Library
7 Pier Road
St Helier
Jersey JE2 4XW
Tel: 01534 730538
www.societe-jersiaise.org

Society of Antiquaries of London
Burlington House
Piccadilly
London W1J 0BE
Tel: 020 7479 7084
www.sal.org.uk

Society of Genealogists
14 Charterhouse Buildings
Goswell Road
London EC1M 7BA
Tel: 020 7251 8799
www.sog.org.uk

Superintendent Registrar
10 Royal Square
St Helier
Jersey JE2 4WA
Tel: 01534 502335
www.jersey.gov.uk

Traceline
PO Box 106
Southport
Merseyside PR8 2HH
Tel: 0151 471 4811
www.statistics.gov.uk/registration/traceline/default.asp

The Treasury Solicitor
Treasury Solicitor's Department
Queen Anne's Chambers
28 Broadway
London SW1H 9JS
Tel: 020 7210 3046

West Riding Deeds Registry
West Yorkshire Archive Service
Wakefield HQ
Newstead Road
Wakefield
West Yorkshire WF1 2DE
Tel: 01924 305982
www.archives.wyjs.org.uk

United States of America

Daughters of the American Revolution Library
1776 D Street, NW
Washington
DC 20006-5303
Te: 202 628 1776
www.dar.org

Family History Library of the Church of Jesus Christ of
 Latter-day Saints
35 North West Temple Street
Salt Lake City
UT 84150-3400
Tel: 801 240 2331
www.familysearch.org

Library of Congress
101 Independence Avenue, SE
Washington
DC 20540
Tel: 202 707 5000
http://catalog.loc.gov

National Archives and Records Administration
700 Pennsylvania Avenue, NW
Washington
DC 20408-0001
Tel: 202 501 5400

National Archives and Records Administration (for mail)
8601 Adelphi Road
College Park
MD 20740-6001
Tel: 1 866 272 6272
www.archives.gov

Newberry Library
60 West Walton Street
Chicago
IL 60610-7324
Tel: 312 943 9090
www.newberry.org/nl/genealogy

New England Historic Genealogical Society
101 Newbury Street
Boston
MA-02116-3007
Tel: 617 536 5740
www.newenglandancestors.org

New York Genealogical and Biographical Society
122 East 58th Street
New York
NY 10022-1939
Tel: 212 755 8532
www.nygbs.org

select bibliography

The following list includes books mentioned in the text.

Atkins, P. J., *The Directories of London, 1677–1977* (London, 1990)

Atterbury, T. (ed), *Trade Associations and Professional Bodies of the United Kingdom and Eire* (London, 16th edn, 2001)

Bardsley, C. W., *A Dictionary of English and Welsh Surnames, with Special American Instances* (London, 1901, rev. reprint 1981)

Barrow, G. B., *The Genealogist's Guide: an index to printed British pedigrees and family histories, 1950–1975* (London, 1977)

Bentley, E. P., *The County Courthouse Book* (Baltimore, 2nd edn 1995, reprinted 1996)

Bevan, A., *Tracing Your Ancestors in the Public Record Office* (PRO Publications, 6th edn, 2002)

Blatchford, R., *Family and Local History Handbook* (York, 7th edn, 2003)

Bigwood, R., *Tracing Scottish Ancestors: a practical guide to Scottish genealogy* (Glasgow, 1999)

CBD Research Ltd, *Directory of British Associations and Associations in Ireland* (Beckenham, 16th edn, 2002)

Chaplin, C., *My Autobiography* (London 1964, reprinted 1979)

Cheffins, R. H. A., *Parliamentary Constituencies and their Registers since 1832* (British Library, 1998)

Cheney, C. R, rev. by M. Jones, *A Handbook of Dates for Students of English History* (Cambridge, 1945, 2000)

Christian, P., *The Genealogist's Internet* (PRO Publications, 2001, corrected edn, 2002)

Coldham, P. W., *The Lives, Times, and Families of Colonial Americans, who remained Loyal to the British Crown* (Baltimore, 2000)

Coldham, P. W., *American Wills and Administrations in the Prerogative Court of Canterbury, 1610-1857* (Baltimore, 1989)

Coldham, P. W., *American Wills proved in London, 1611–1775* (Baltimore, 1992)

Cole, J. and Church, R., *In and Around Record Repositories in Great Britain and Ireland* (Ramsey, Huntingdon, 4th edn, 1998)

Collins, A., *Basic Facts About…Using Wills After 1858 and First*

Avenue House (Federation of Family History Societies, 1998)

Colwell, S., *The Family Records Centre, a User's Guide* (PRO. Publications, 2nd edn, 2002)

Craig, F. W. S., *Boundaries of Parliamentary Constituencies, 1885–1972* (Chichester, 1972)

De Breffny, B., *Bibliography of Irish Family History and Genealogy* (Cork, 1974)

Eales, A. B. and Kvasnicka, R. M. (eds) *Guide to Genealogical Research in the National Archives of the United States* (Washington DC, 3rd ed, 2000)

Eichholz, A. (ed), *Ancestry's Red Book, American State, County and Town Sources* (Salt Lake City, 3rd edn, 2003)

Ellis, M., *Using Manorial Records* (PRO Publications in association with The Royal Commission on Historical Manuscripts, 1994)

Estcourt, E. E. and Payne, J. O. (eds), *The English Catholic Non-Jurors of 1715...* ([London, 1885], facsimile edn, 1969)

Falley, M. D., *Irish and Scotch–Irish Ancestral Research* (Baltimore, reprint 1998)

Ferguson, J. P. S., *Scottish Family Histories* (Edinburgh, 2nd edn, 1986)

Filby, P. W. (with various co-editors), *Passenger and Immigration Lists Index, 1538–1905* (Michigan, 1981, with annual supplements)

Foot, W., *Maps for Family History* (PRO Publications, 1994)

Foster, J. and Sheppard, J., *British Archives, a Guide to Archive Resources in the United Kingdom* (Basingstoke, 4th edn, 2002)

Franklin, L. and York, J. (comp), *Libraries and Information Services in the United Kingdom and the Republic of Ireland* (London, 29th edn, 2003)

Gandy, M. (ed), *Catholic Missions and Registers, 1700–1880* (London, 6 vols, 1993)

Gandy, M. (ed), *Catholic Parishes in England, Wales and Scotland, an Atlas* (London, 1993)

Gibson, J., *Bishops' Transcripts and Marriage Licences, Bonds and Allegations: A Guide to their Location and Indexes* (FFHS, 4th edn, 1997)

Gibson, J., *The Hearth Tax, other later Stuart Tax Lists and the Association Oath Rolls* (FFHS, 2nd edn, 1996)

Gibson, J., *Quarter Sessions Records for Family Historians: A Select List* (FFHS, 4th edn, 1995)

Gibson, J. and Churchill, E., *Probate Jurisdictions: Where to Look for Wills* (FFHS, 5th edn, 2002)

Gibson, J. and Hampson, E, *Census Returns 1841–1891 in Microform* (FFHS, 6th edn, 1997)

Gibson, J. and Hampson, E., *Marriage and Census Indexes for Family Historians* (FFHS, 8th edn, 2000)

Gibson, J. and Hampson, E., *Specialist Indexes for Family Historians* (FFHS, 2nd edn, 2000)

Gibson, J. and Medlycott, M., *Local Census Listings, 1522–1930:*

Holdings in the British Isles (FFHS, 2nd edn, 1994)

Gibson, J. and Peskett, P., *Record Offices: How to Find Them* (FFHS, 9th edn, 2002)

Gibson, J. and Rogers, C., *Electoral Registers since 1832; and Burgess Rolls* (FFHS, 1989)

Gibson, J. and Rogers, C., *Poll Books c.1696-1872: a directory to holdings in Great Britain* (FFHS, 3rd edn, 1994)

Gibson, J., Rogers, C. and Webb, C., *Poor Law Union Records (in England and Wales)*, 4 parts, the last of which is *Gazetteer of England and Wales* with F. A Youngs, Jr (FFHS, 1993–2000)

Giuseppi, M. S. (ed), *Naturalizations in the American Colonies, 1740–1772* (Huguenot Society, London, 1921, vol xxiv)

Grannum, K. and Taylor, N., *Prerogative Court of Canterbury, Wills and Other Probate Records* (PRO Publications, 2nd edn, 2003)

Grenham, J., *Tracing Your Irish Ancestors: the Complete Guide* (Dublin, 2nd edn, 1999)

Grieve, H. E. P., *Examples of English Handwriting 1150–1750* (Essex Record Office, 1954, 5th impression 1981)

Groome, F., *Gazetteer of Scotland*, 6 vols (Edinburgh, 1882–85)

Guildhall Library Research Guide 2: *The British Overseas, Guide to Births, Marriages and Deaths of British Persons Overseas before 1945* (3rd rev. edn, 1995)

Hauxwell, H., with Cockroft, B., *Hannah, The Complete Story* (London, 1991)

Herber, M. *Clandestine Marriages in the Chapel and Rules of the Fleet Prison 1680–1754*, 2 vols (London, 1998, 1999)

Higgs, E., *A Clearer Sense of the Census* (HMSO, 1996)

Houston, J., *Index of Cases in the Records of the Court of Arches at Lambeth Palace Library 1660–1913* (London, 1972)

Humphery-Smith, C. R. (ed), *The Phillimore Atlas and Index of Parish Registers* (Chichester, 3rd edn, 2003)

Ifans, D. (ed), *Nonconformist Registers of Wales* (National Library of Wales and Welsh County Archivists Group, 1994)

Johnson, K. A. and Sainty, M. R. (eds), *Genealogical Research Directory, National and International* (Sydney, annual 1981–)

Kain, R. J. P. and Oliver, R. R., *The Tithe Maps of England and Wales, Cartographic Analysis and County by County Catalogue* (Cambridge, 1995)

Kaminkow, M. J., *Genealogies in the Library of Congress* (1972, with Supplements 1977, 1987, 1992)

Kelly's Handbook to the Titled, Landed and Official Classes (London, 1874–)

Kemp, T. J., *The American Census Handbook* (Scholarly Resources Inc., 2001)

Kemp, T. J., *International Vital Records Handbook* (Baltimore, 4th edn, 2000)

Kershaw, R., *Emigrants and Expats, Guide to Sources on UK Emigration and Residents Overseas* (PRO Publications, 2002)

Kershaw, R. and Pearsall, M., *Immigrants and Aliens, Guide to*

Sources on UK Immigration and Citizenship (PRO Publications, 2000)

Lainhart, A. S. (ed) *State Census Records* (Baltimore, 1992, reprinted 2000)

Lewis, S., *Topographical Dictionary of Ireland* (London, 1837)

MacLysaght, E., *Bibliography of Irish Family History* (Dublin, 1982)

Marshall, G. W., *The Genealogist's Guide* (London, 1903, reprinted 1980)

Martin, C. T., *The Record Interpreter, a Collection of Abbreviations, Latin Words and Names used in English Historical Manuscripts and records* (London, 1910, reprinted 1994)

Maxwell, I., *Tracing your Ancestors in Northern Ireland* (HMSO, 1997)

Meller, H., *London Cemeteries, an Illustrated Guide and Gazetteer* (Brookfield, Vermont, 3rd edn, 1994)

Milward, R., *A Glossary of Household, Farming and Trade Terms from Probate Inventories* (Derbyshire Record Society, 3rd edn, 1986, reprinted 1993)

The Morton Allan Directory of European Passenger Steamship Arrivals (Baltimore, 1931, reprinted 2001)

Mullins, E. L. C. (ed), *Texts and Calendars: an analytical guide to serial publications* (Royal Historical Society, 1958, reprinted with corrections 1978)

Mullins, E. L. C. (ed), *Texts and Calendars II: an analytical guide to serial publications 1957–82* (Royal Historical Society, 1983)

Munby, L. M., *How Much is That Worth?* (Chichester, 2nd edn, 1996)

Neagles, J. C., *The Library of Congress, a Guide to Genealogical and Historical Research* (Salt Lake City, 1990)

Newington-Irving, N. J. N. (ed), *Directories and Poll Books, including Almanacs and Electoral Rolls, in the Library of the Society of Genealogists* (Society of Genealogists, 6th edn, 1995)

Newington-Irving, N. J. N. (ed), *Will Indexes and Other Probate Material in the Library of the Society of Genealogists* (SoG, 1996)

Nissel, M., *People Count, A History of the General Register Office* (HMSO, 1987)

Norton, J. E., *Guide to National and Provincial Directories of England and Wales, excluding London, published before 1856* (London, 1950)

O'Duill, E. M., and ffeary-Smyrl, S. C., *Exploring Irish Genealogy no 2: Irish Civil Registration – where do I start?* (Council of Irish Organisations, 2000)

Phillimore, W. P. W., and Fry, E. A., *Index to Changes of Name, 1760–1901* (London, 1905, reprinted 1986)

Raymond, S. A, *Births, Marriages and Deaths on the Web*, 2 parts (FFHS, 2002)

Raymond, S. A., *Family History on the Web, an Internet Directory for England and Wales* (FFHS, 2002/3)

Raymond, S. A., *Irish Family History on the Web* (FFHS, 2001)

Raymond, S. A., *Monumental Inscriptions on the Web* (FFHS, 2002)

Raymond, S. A., *Occupational Sources for Genealogists* (FFHS, 2nd edn, 1996)

Raymond, S. A., *Scottish Family History on the Web* (FFHS, 2002)

Return of Owners of Land of One Acre and Upwards in England (excluding the Metropolis), and Wales 1873, 2 vols (London, 1875)

Return of Owners of Land of One Acre and Upwards in Ireland (London, 1876)

Return of Owners of Land of One Acre and Upwards in Scotland, 1872–3 (London, 1874)

Reynard, K. W. (ed), *The ASLIB Directory of Information Sources in the United Kingdom* (London, 11th edn, 2000)

Richards, M, *Welsh Administrative and Territorial Units* (Cardiff, 1969)

Royal Commission on Historical Manuscripts, *Record Repositories in Great Britain: a geographical directory* (PRO, 11th edn, 1999)

Ryan, J., *Irish Records: sources for family and local history* (Salt Lake City, rev. edn, 1997)

Sanders, P., *The Simple Annals, the History of an Essex and East End Family* (Gloucester, 1989)

Shaw, G. and Tipper, A., *British Directories: a bibliography and guide to directories published in England and Wales (1850–1950) and Scotland (1773–1950)* (London, 2nd edn, 1997)

Shorney, D., *Protestant Nonconformity and Roman Catholicism, Guide to Sources in the Public Record Office* (PRO Publications, 1996)

Sinclair, C., *Tracing your Scottish Ancestors, Guide to Ancestry Research in the Scottish Record Office* (HMSO, rev. edn, 1997)

Society of Genealogists, *A List of Parishes in Boyd's Marriage Index* (SoG, 6th edn, corrected reprint 1994)

Society of Genealogists, *Marriage Licences: abstracts and indexes in the Library of the Society of Genealogists* (SoG, 4th edn, 1991)

Society of Genealogists, *Monumental Inscriptions in the Library of the Society of Genealogists*, 2 parts (SoG, 1984, 1989)

Society of Genealogists, *Parish Register Copies in the Library of the Society of Genealogists* (SoG, 11th edn, 1995)

Spufford, P. (ed), *Index to the Probate Accounts of England and Wales*, 2 vols (British Record Society, 1999)

Stafford, G. (comp), *Where to Find Adoption Records, a Guide for Counsellors, Adopted People and Birth Parents* (British Agencies for Adoption and Fostering, London, 3rd edn, 2001)

Stevenson, D. and W. B. (eds), *Scottish Texts and Calendars: an analytical guide to serial publications* (Edinburgh, 1987)

Stuart, D., *Latin for Local and Family Historians* (Chichester, 1995)

Stuart, M., *Scottish Family History, Guide to Works of Reference on the History and Genealogy of Scottish families... To which is prefixed an essay on 'How to write the history of a family, by Sir James Balfour Paul'* (Edinburgh, 1930)

Szucs, L. D. and Luebking, S. H. (eds), *The Source: a guidebook of American genealogy* (Salt Lake City, rev. edn, 1997)

Szucs, L. D. and Wright, M., *Finding Answers in U.S. Census Records* (Salt Lake City, 2002)

Tate, W. E., *A Domesday of English Enclosure Acts and Awards* (Reading, 1978)

The Times Tercentenary Handlist ... of English and Welsh Newspapers, Magazines and Reviews 1620–1920 (*The Times*, 1920)

Thomson, T. R., *Catalogue of British Family Histories* (London, 3rd edn, 1980 with Addenda)

Titford, J., *Succeeding in Family History, Helpful Hints and Time-saving Tips* (Newbury, 2001)

Turner, G. Lyon, *Original Records of Nonconformity under Persecution and Indulgence,* 3 vols (London, 1911–14)

Wagner, A. R. *English Genealogy* (Chichester, 3rd edn, 1983)

Waters, C., *A Dictionary of Old Trades, Titles and Occupations* (Newbury, 1999)

Whitaker's Almanack, annual 1869–(London)

Whitmore, J. B., *A Genealogical Guide. An Index to British Pedigrees in Continuation of Marshall's Genealogist's Guide* (London, 1953)

Williams, C. J. and Watts-Williams, S. J. (comps), *National Index of Parish Registers* vol 13: *Parish Registers of Wales* (National Library of Wales and Welsh County Archivists Group, 1986)

Willing's Press Guide, 3 parts (Chesham, 2003)

Winterbotham, D. and Crosby, A., *The Local Studies Library, a Handbook for Local Historians* (Salisbury, 1998)

Wolfston, P. S. rev. by C. Webb, *Greater London Cemeteries and Crematoria* (SoG, 6th edn, 1999)

Wood, T., *Basic Facts about... Using Record Offices for Family Historians* (FFHS, 1996)

index